Integration in Action

Integration in Action
Case Studies in the Intergration of Pupils with Special Needs

Seamus Hegarty and Keith Pocklington
with Dorothy Lucas

NFER-Nelson

Published by The NFER-Nelson Publishing Company Ltd,
Darville House 2 Oxford Road East
Windsor, Berks SL4 1DF

First published 1982
© NFER 1982
ISBN 0-85633-238-0
Code 8087 021

All rights reserved. No part of this publication may be reproduced
or transmitted, in any form or by any means, without permission.

Photoset by Butler & Tanner Ltd, Frome and London
Printed in Great Britain

Distributed in the USA by Humanities Press Inc.,
Atlantic Highlands, New Jersey 07716, USA

Contents

Introduction vii

Part One: Provision for Pupils with Learning Difficulties   **1**
1. A special department for pupils with learning difficulties   3
2. Primary provision for pupils with learning difficulties   27
3. Secondary department for pupils with learning difficulties   46
4. Special provision for children with severe learning difficulties   65

Part Two: Provision for pupils with Physical Handicaps   **89**
5. Individual integration of physically handicapped pupils   91
5. A special department for the physically handicapped   115
7. Links between a special school and an ordinary school   132

Part Three: Provision for pupils with Impaired Hearing   **155**
8. Special centres for the hearing impaired   157
9. Individual integration of hearing impaired pupils   181

Part Four: Provision for Pupils with Impaired Vision   **201**
10. Resource area for the visually impaired   203

Part Five: Provision for Pupils with Speech and Language Disorders   **221**
11. Special class provision for pupils with communication disorders (1)   223
12. Special class provision for pupils with communication disorders (2)   241

v

Part Six: Links between Special Schools and Ordinary Schools 259
13 Supporting the ordinary school 261
14 Transferring pupils from special schooling 282

Bibliography 293

Introduction

The integration programmes described here derive from a research project – Education of Handicapped Pupils in Ordinary Schools – sponsored by the Department of Education and Science at the National Foundation for Educational Research. This project is reported in a sister publication, Hegarty and Pocklington (1981), which considers the process of educating pupils with special needs in ordinary schools and discusses the wide range of factors that bear on it. The project was based on the detailed study of a number of integration programmes. In order to give an account of integration in action, fourteen of these have been selected for detailed description and analysis. The general pattern followed is: historical résumé; organisation and aims; pupils; staffing; accommodation and resources; curriculum; (preparation for adult life); monitoring progress; academic integration; social development; parents; and summary.

A few preliminary points need to be made. First, the programmes are grouped in terms of the statutory categories of handicap that prevailed when they were selected in 1977. Most saw themselves in fact as providing for a particular category. In any case, it would have been extremely difficult to choose a sample that was representative of a different categorisation of special needs.

Secondly, our accounts refer to a particular stage of development in the programmes being described, broadly speaking 1977-79. Many of them were starting off and trying to evolve ways of working with little precedent to go on. There was a great deal of change and development and 'learning by doing'. Many of the weaknesses identified have since been remedied, and indeed most of the programmes are more effective now than when our study started. This is to be expected as needs emerge more clearly and ways of dealing with them are evolved. We have not refrained from discussing difficulties and weaknesses just because they no longer obtain. By common consent, difficult passages in early development are most instructive and it is valuable to document these and how staff dealt with them.

Thirdly, the descriptions were compiled in consultation with the practitioners involved. Each description was circulated in draft form among school and other staff. Following on this, the project team met with staff to receive their feedback. These meetings usually entailed lively discussions! Most staff accepted the broad thrust of our accounts but had numerous points to make: amplifying and putting in different contexts information given to us earlier; updating on recent developments; correcting errors on our part; drawing attention to potentially unfortunate consequences or embarrassment for individuals; and on occasion seeking to rewrite history. Some of these points came via written submissions after the meetings. We incorporated many of these points into the final drafts, though always maintaining editorial control. It is our firm understanding that the great majority of staff in the integration programmes concerned would agree that the account pertaining to them was a fair and accurate description of their work. Staff in a majority of locations affirmed that the document and the fieldwork which preceded it had been instrumental in bringing about major improvements in practice.

Fourthly, we would want to stress that most of these programmes constitute good practice and in some cases very good practice. This may not be evident at first glance since we have not refrained from discussing problematic areas. If our accounts were compared with the glowing descriptions of practice which more usually find their way into print, it might seem that these programmes are poor and the staff in them lacking in competence. Nothing could be further from the truth. Staff impressed us by their commitment to meeting pupils' needs and their lively awareness of the problems facing them. If the problems and difficulties are more visible in our accounts than in other descriptions, that is because of staff's clearsightedness and determination to improve provision.

The project is described in detail in the sister publication. We have acknowledged there the help and support from many people that made the project possible. We would recall here one convention that applies throughout this text also, viz single quotation marks signify extracts from written material, double quotation marks extracts from spoken material.

Part One
Provision for Pupils with Learning Difficulties

The size of this group quite dwarfs the other groups subsumed under the statutory categories of handicap. Over 60 per cent of pupils ascertained as needing special educational treatment fall into this category. This does not include those with mild learning difficulties, those styled as slow learners and many pupils grouped under other categories who also have learning difficulties.

While many point to a continuum of disability ranging from those with severe learning difficulties to slow learners, there are considerable differences in the educational needs of different groups along the continuum. This is reflected in the historical development of educational provision. Those at the severe end of the continuum were excluded from education until the passage of the Education (Handicapped Children) Act 1970. (In many countries they are still the responsibility of health or welfare agencies rather than educational ones.) Since 1971 education has been provided for them, for the most part in special schools or hospital schools. In a very small number of cases they are educated in special classes or centres set up within ordinary schools.

Most other pupils with learning difficulties will at least start their educational careers in the mainstream of education. Those experiencing moderate learning difficulties are often recommended for placement in a special school at the end of infant stage. Increasingly, however, special classes and centres are being set up in both primary and secondary schools to provide for pupils with moderate learning difficulties. These can be quite self-contained within their schools catering only for those pupils formally allocated to them or they can become integral parts of their schools and provide assistance for other pupils as well.

We present here four examples of special classes or centres in ordinary schools for pupils with learning difficulties. The first is a large secondary department for pupils with moderate learning difficulties that also serves as the school's remedial department. The second comprises two special centres in a junior school catering for pupils with moderate and severe learning difficulties respectively. The third is a large secondary department catering, like the first example, for pupils with mild and moderate learning difficulties but also for pupils with severe learning difficulties. The final example comprises a set of special classes attached to four infant or primary schools and catering for infants with severe learning difficulties.

1
A special department for pupils with learning difficulties

This special department in a newly opened comprehensive school caters for pupils with mild and moderate learning difficulties. It is a mixed school, covering the age range 11–16. The department – known as the Basic Studies department – has primary responsibility for about 80 pupils but provides help for a large number of others in a less intensive way.

Historical résumé

This provision must be seen in the context of a policy decision by the authority in question to provide resource centres in its secondary schools. Part of the intention behind this is that all schools should be responsible for educating the vast majority of pupils in their catchment areas. Considerable importance is attached to schools developing a facility for dealing with pupils who display special educational needs. A reflection of the importance accorded this is the fact that the teachers in charge (heads of department) are appointed at a senior level.

The Basic Studies department (BSD) is housed at Brightwell comprehensive school which opened in 1973 and is still expanding. Its eventual complement will be over 1200 pupils aged 11–16. The school is located on the fringe of an ancient market town which has recently seen considerable development in connection with its large metropolitan overspill population. Although planned from the outset, the special department did not open until 1976 and even then only in makeshift accommodation. The first intake, of 20 pupils who began in autumn 1976, was housed in a former language laboratory while building work continued. It was hoped to have the department ready by the end of term, but in the event it was not finished until the following February. The head of department had been in post for two terms before the building was completed, and a term before the first pupils arrived. This was intentional – it was perceived as a valuable opportunity to make himself, and the thinking behind the proposed department, known to staff of the school as a whole.

The initial batch of pupils were the responsibility of two full-time teachers, one of whom was the head of department. Two early concerns – to involve pupils in main school lessons, and to meet the special needs of a much broader group of pupils – were instrumental in determining the early working practice. As regards the first of these, individual time-tables for partial integration were drawn up, in consultation both with the pupils themselves and the teachers whose classes they would be joining. As a general rule, no more than two special pupils were placed in any one class. With pupils attending mixed ability classes in main school, staff of the department could begin to provide remedial assistance to main school pupils. This was urgently required as the school was, at the time, suffering badly from the first round of cuts forced upon local authorities. There was considerable pressure upon main school staff's time, and the teaching carried out in main school by staff from the department served to ease this pressure.

With the completion of building work in February 1977, both pupils and resources were transferred into the new purpose-built premises, though not all facilities were available initially. It was only as further equipment arrived (eg-benches, lathes) that the department was able to begin offering supplementary work in woodwork, craft and cooking.

By the close of the first year of operating staff had established a withdrawal system for pupils with moderate learning difficulties based upon classes within the department. Nearly all pupils were registered in main school and took some lessons in main school.

Throughout this initial period the head of department sought to publicise the work of the department and the needs of its primary clients (those with moderate learning difficulties). This was done in a low profile way, in the belief that teachers would otherwise automatically reject any pupil facing difficulty, whether it be academic or behavioural: "We don't want to label the kids too much." With regard to communicating information on a given pupil or providing specific guidance, he considered this was best done informally through personal contact. He sought to establish good personal relations with members of staff throughout the school, capitalising upon interest or curiosity as the opportunity arose.

A cause for concern in those early days was the limited number of staff available in relation to the increasing number of pupils being served. The department began its second year with 35 pupils. It now had its own ancillary, but there were still only two full-time teachers, both of whom were committed to some teaching time in main school. As members of staff took on an increasingly diverse role, various teachers from the main school taught lessons within the department. During the year the financial situation eased somewhat and the department was able to take on its third member of staff, initially on a temporary basis. By the following September (1978) a fourth appointment was made. (It should be noted that subsequently the authority has always sought to staff all newly established departments and resource centres such as this with a full complement of teachers from the outset (even before pupil numbers have built up) in line with DES circular 4/73.)

Organisation and aims

The primary aim of the department is to meet the educational needs of a large number of pupils who exhibit a wide range of learning difficulties. A second focus that has developed gradually since the department opened is a concern for pupils' social and emotional wellbeing, though this has been a subsidiary matter: "We're not set up to deal with kiddies' emotional problems... We are very much learning based... *not* therapeutic" (head of department). In practice, of course, there is not a sharp division between the two goals. There is great emphasis upon teaching basic skills – though not to the exclusion of wider aspects of the curriculum, eg craftwork and home economics, nor to the neglect of pupils' social development. The head of department summarised their aims overall as follows: "To teach the basic skills, hopefully so that pupils can get by at work and socially, to offer them a much wider curriculum... [and to] try to make them feel worthwhile, wanted, important..." He was concerned that they should get away from the attitudes of over-protectiveness and under-stimulation still considered to prevail in many special schools.

Meeting pupils' special educational needs may or may not involve their taking lessons in main school. In point of fact, the majority of pupils with moderate learning difficulties will spend a high proportion of their school time (70–80 per cent) within the department. However, all except four or five pupils of low ability who have displayed disturbed behaviour spend some time in ordinary classes. This exchange with the main school was not the intention of officers of the authority when the plans were originally drawn up: the department was planned as a self-contained entity – as evidenced by the self-contained facilities for craftwork and home economics. However, the head teacher was anxious that this specialist resource should be assimilated into the school. His views coincided with those of the head of department, who regarded active working links between school and resource as imperative. The latter explained to subject specialists what the purpose behind this department was, the most common difficulties that his pupils were faced with and so forth, and persuaded certain main school staff to accept individual pupils on a trial basis.

The first batch of pupils were registered in the department. Specialist staff soon identified pupils who seemed quite capable of joining main school registration groups. At the close of the first year, this practice was appraised and considered sufficiently successful to warrant being extended. The head teacher formalised the procedure for the intake as a whole, and the existing 'withdrawal' principle enshrined in current practice was born. All new entrants now register with a mainstream form, whereupon specialist teachers commence the process of determining their need of specialised attention and how this may best be met.

This exchange is not confined to pupils – there is an interchange of staff which occurs as a matter of course. In the past, when the staffing resources of the department were severely stretched, six subject specialists – mainly from the English department – came and taught in the department at different times. Most staff from the department for their part have been timetabled to teach mixed ability classes in main school for an average of two and half hours a week each. More recently this practice has suffered on account of the greater emphasis on preventative work. Whereas in the past the focus had been very largely on those with marked learning difficulties and pupils with less severe problems were fitted in around the edges as it were, now a higher proportion of each new intake receives specialist attention from the outset. Following this intensive intervention some pupils will then join main school classes for most if not all of their time. A consequence of working in this way is that staff have less time available for teaching in main school. This is particularly regretted by the head teacher, who would like all Basic Studies staff, as a matter of policy, to teach a mixed ability or higher ability group from main school at least every two years.

The extent of the integration attained is not restricted to academic matters. It is recognised that mixing with main school pupils – both within and outside the classroom – contributes to 'normal' standards of achievement and behaviour. From a social standpoint, as well as the various curriculum components which have a social and/or emotional emphasis, the department serves as a focal point for social interactions. This is facilitated by the wide range of social facilities (eg bar billiards, table tennis) that exist on the premises.

An important factor behind the level of assimilation achieved – perhaps best exemplified in the fact that the head of Basic Studies is also the elected staff representative on the Board of Governors – is the care taken in setting it up. Mention has already been made of the low-key stance adopted initially by the head of department. In the four years subsequently, more formalised measures have been taken. In spring 1978 the head of department organised a series of five evening meetings for teachers in primary and secondary schools in the vicinity who were interested in knowing more about the special educational needs of pupils with learning difficulties. A range of speakers addressed a variety of theoretical and practical matters concerning the education of such pupils. Probationer teachers at the school are assigned to a professional tutor who is responsible for organising a course of induction. This includes an introduction to Basic Studies when the head of department addresses them, and where they have the opportunity to visit and see its work.

The effort to service pupils from main school depends, in part, on Basic Studies staff being familiar faces about school, since it is hoped that pupils experiencing difficulty would want to seek out assistance. Here again, a more formal procedure has followed from the initial very informal attempts to inform and influence attitudes. Some two years after the department opened the teacher in charge was urged by staff from main school to explain its work and role to the first year intake. Subject specialists "felt they couldn't explain", and were uneasy at handling pupils' questions; some felt that pupils in main school "needed reassuring", more especially those who came from a particular feeder school which housed a junior provision that operated as a segregated unit. The head of department agreed. He outlined what he and his staff sought to achieve, relating pupils' specific difficulties to more general handicaps: 'People have all sorts of difficulties – some can't ride a bicycle very well, others can't read or write very well ... Our job is to help those who need it.' This approach was subsequently modified. Now each first year group visit the department along with their form tutor. The workings of the department are explained and they can look around, talking perhaps with pupils who are receiving assistance. The visit concludes with the offer of support and attention for any of them should they experience difficulty with their schoolwork. It is emphasised that it is *their* decision to come across and ask for guidance or help.

The way the department is organised in academic terms is worth noting. There are five teaching members of staff. Each teaches across the department as a whole, rather than providing all basic subjects for a particular group of pupils. Each has a commitment to the English or number curriculum team. In addition, it is deliberate policy to encourage staff to develop their own particular area of expertise. Thus, one member of staff is responsible for English and reading; a second has developed a programme of preparation for post-school life, as well as assuming responsibility for woodwork, art and craft; another is responsible for maths, and the biology component of a social studies course; a fourth, for home-management and art; a fifth, for the history and geography components of the social studies course. The head of department has general responsibility for the provision.

A recent innovation has been the allocation of members of staff to one of two specialist teams – basic English or basic number. Staff of the department as a whole meet briefly every week before splitting into these respective groups for the purpose of discussing curriculum matters and preparing resources. This development also has an important in-servicing function, more particularly in regard of the latest appointments to the staff.

The head of department maintains that if their department is to be fully part of the school then their internal organisation should mirror that of the parent school. This organisational basis is further justified on the grounds that it maximises the efficient use of resources. There is also the belief that a system which encourages teacher initiative and promotes specialist skills will lead to staff becoming better teachers. This in turn makes for a more balanced and absorbing curriculum for the pupil.

Staff of the department all carry out pastoral responsibilities for a particular year group. In an effort to ensure continuity, members of staff move up with their respective year group until the end of the third year. Thereafter, pupils are the responsibility of the teacher in charge of preparation for post-school living.

Pupils

The primary responsibility of the Basic Studies department is to provide an appropriate education for those pupils with moderate learning difficulties who, in all probability, would have entered special schooling had there been a suitable special school within the area. Over time the department has come to cater for all pupils within the catchment of Brightwell school who have either a specific learning difficulty or who experience problems in learning across the curriculum. Pupils with severe learning difficulties are not regarded as suitable clients, partly because the education as currently provided would be inappropriate, partly because it is felt that the self-perception of pupils with less severe difficulties would suffer in consequence. Equally inappropriate is the individual who manifests severe behavioural disturbance – though a number of pupils with severely disturbed behaviour were accepted in the past.

Three main groups of pupil can be identified as the department's clients:

i) Pupils with considerable learning difficulties requiring specialist individual attention over a period of time. These are its main clients and they numbered about 60 in the course of our study. All are registered with a main school form. They receive a modified curriculum on a withdrawal basis for between 30 and 70 per cent of their time, according to individual need; otherwise they follow selected aspects of the main school curriculum, with some support from the department.

ii) Slow learners. These follow the full curriculum of the main school. They are withdrawn for short periods (two to four lessons a week) of intensive remedial work in the special centre. These numbered about 100.

iii) Pupils who function at normal level in most areas but have specific learning difficulties in one or more of reading, writing and spelling. Totally individual programmes are devised and implemented for the small number (10–15) of these pupils.

The above figures should be seen as giving a rough indication since staff are reluctant to assign pupils to rigidly defined categories. Furthermore numbers can fluctuate quite considerably over a given period. In addition, a small number of pupils (five in all), described as "rather special cases", were in attendance throughout much of our fieldwork. These pupils exhibited a variety of special needs, having markedly disturbed behaviour in common. Most came into the school in their third or fourth year of secondary schooling, their school careers having been severely disrupted (in some instances Brightwell was the third secondary school that they had attended). They were the only pupils to register in the department, and were retained within it. Four have since left or been transferred elsewhere.

Pupils are drawn from four particular primary schools as well as a number of village schools. In the past they have reached Brightwell either with an accompanying report from an educational psychologist recording moderate learning difficulty, or by teachers' more subjective reports that they are of very low ability. Apart from the amount and usefulness of the information which sometimes has accompanied pupils, staff of the department expressed reservations about the appropriateness of some of the candidates that were fed through. There was a feeling that sometimes primary school authorities placed too much reliance upon IQ scores and paid too little attention to what a pupil was actually capable of or to particular strengths and weaknesses. Some pupils had transferred with low IQ ratings and yet had been able to spend considerable time in ordinary classes at Brightwell.

In an effort to improve matters the head of department visited the feeder primary schools with a view to seeing for himself pupils in the transfer pipeline and, in particular, the kind of information that was available on these pupils. It was also an opportunity to publicise the department: what it was seeking to achieve, which kind of information they would like to receive from primary schools, and so forth. He also worked with the area educational psychologist to develop more precise selection criteria for admission based upon educational needs rather than simply test scores. A variety of tests are used to provide details of pupils' methods of learning and actual attainments. Additional information is collected on home background, medical history and school attendance.

Under the revised system the class teacher is responsible for collating much of this information. A case conference comprising the class teacher, educational psychologist and head of department is then convened at which likely candidates for admission are discussed.

The main advantage claimed for this new approach, which is supplemented by a screening of all first year pupils – a standardised reading comprehension test and a spelling test – is that it will identify more readily those pupils of average intelligence who are nevertheless underachieving. Current thinking is to regard the first year of secondary schooling as a screening year, an extended opportunity for differentiating between pupils with long and short term special needs. Thus, for example, up to 30 pupils from each new intake may be withdrawn from main school to take English in the department. After one term those who have made most progress may well return to main school lessons if staff feel they are now able to cope. Other pupils will of course continue to require specialist attention from the department.

Staffing

The department has five teaching members of staff (including the head of department) and a classroom ancillary. The official staffing ratio is 1:12, but in a situation where the department is operating in such a diverse way this figure has only relative meaning. An interesting dispensation that applies here is that where the 1:12 ratio is exceeded then the department will receive an additional teacher. Thus, if it is providing for 24 pupils it is eligible for two teachers; should the number increase to 26 then a further teacher is made available. Account must be taken of the complexity of the department's operations, however, in assessing the relatively generous approach to its staffing.

The present staff possess a variety of qualifications and experience. The head of department has a basic teachers' certificate and has worked in residential schools for the educationally subnormal. He also has a Diploma in the Education of Handicapped Children, and has taken a variety of in-service courses (eg the teaching of reading, pastoral guidance, school management). He had no prior experience of teaching in a secondary school before coming to Brightwell. With regard to his staff, one holds the Art Teachers Diploma and the postgraduate Certificate in Education. She has taught across the ability range in a variety of secondary schools as well as lecturing in further and higher education. A second undertook a course of teacher training which included a component on special education. He then taught for four years in a school for pupils with moderate learning difficulties before coming to Brightwell. A fourth member of the department trained as a nursery/infant teacher. She has experience of teaching in both an ordinary junior school and a special school for the severely subnormal.

This is yet another centre where the deployment of an ancillary has much to commend it. Although the only official 'educational' training of the person in question has been a part-time course for ancillaries run by the authority covering, among other things, specialist art and craft and an introduction to reading development, she has of her own accord attended courses intended for teachers. This has relevance in the light of the fact that she is, in effect, carrying out a teaching role. She spends time each week with all five teachers from the department, working to their instructions and assuming responsibility for a number of pupils within the particular teaching group. She also assumes sole responsibility on occasions, (eg four periods of home economics weekly with four girls) accompanying two fifth year pupils shopping. She has pastoral responsibility for certain 'target' pupils – pupils who are particularly vulnerable socially and/or emotionally, and who need the reassurance that a 'mother-figure' can provide.

Contact with outside agencies is not particularly extensive, although relations are such that if the advice or assistance of a specialist agency is needed it is usually forthcoming. The area educational psychologist visits fortnightly for about two hours, during which time she will discuss general issues to do with the running of the department, consult with staff over particular pupils, carry out individual assessments as necessary, and liaise with staff who have pastoral responsibilities. There are weekly visits from a speech therapist who provides a specialised intervention for one boy. She makes available a programme of exercises for teachers to carry out between her visits. Members of the advisory service are in contact as and when necessary. A psychiatrist regularly sees one pupil from the department, but no attempt has been made to provide the school with information concerning this boy. A physiotherapist pays weekly visits to a girl suffering from muscular dystrophy. As regards social worker involvement, a very small number of pupils come under the supervision of a social worker or probation officer. While contact here seems reasonable, a cause for concern is the larger number of pupils and families whose circumstances, though perhaps less pressing, could nevertheless profit from specialist guidance or support. Teachers quite often find themselves having to adopt a role more befitting a social worker in spite of their ready acknowledgement that they are not equipped for such a role.

Accommodation and resources

The Basic Studies department comprises four open-plan teaching areas (used for English/reading, maths, social studies, and art and craft respectively), a heavy craft workshop, a home management area, a library/recreation space, a staffroom/office and toilets. It is reached by crossing a small quadrangle, though it is no more physically isolated from main school buildings than any other of the provisions that have gone up on the perimeter. Any disadvantage that might arise from having to go out of the main school building is more than overcome by the social facilities it contains, which are generally made use of by the school.

Capitation for its pupils is around 60 per cent more per head than for a pupil from main school. Although this is quite favourable – and the department was very generously resourced in the beginning – as equipment and learning materials have begun to wear out, Basic Studies have had to apply for additional resources just like any other department. Particularly costly learning resources (eg a reading laboratory, a mathematics scheme) are having to be acquired piecemeal over an extended period.

Curriculum

Great efforts have been made by Basic Studies staff to provide a relevant curriculum for the various client groups that they serve. There are two overriding aims: mastery of the basic skills of literacy and numeracy; and general enrichment, through supplementary options (art, craft, social studies, gardening, etc) provided within the department or in main school. Quite different programmes of work are provided for the various groups the department serves and the balance between the two aims may vary – in the case of slow learners from the main school, for instance, the basic skills function is predominant – but they are fundamental to its curriculum planning.

The precise programme that any pupil follows varies in accordance with his or her particular needs. The head of department maintains that continuous curriculum assessment and development together with individual programming (which necessitates individual timetabling) are the means of producing an enriching and educationally sound curriculum. What does this mean in practice? All new entrants to the department are put through the Daniels and Diack battery of tests. This, together with information from their previous school and the psychologist's report, and wherever possible direct contact between the head of department and pupils, provides relevant data for planning an individual programme. Pupils are given a degree of choice as regards the content of their individual programmes, the teacher in charge maintaining, "If you don't have the child's approval you're not going to get very far..."

However, there is a particular emphasis on the basics. While few newcomers will be non-readers, a remarkably high proportion are fairly weak readers. (At one stage 25 per cent of first year pupils had reading ages four years behind their chronological age, while 86 pupils in the main school had reading ages two years behind their chronological age.) Where reading is particularly weak the SRA Distar and Racing to Read schemes are drawn on, as well as the department's own phonics resource kit, supplemented by a wide range of cassettes, workbooks, reading books, synchrofax and so forth. The bulk of pupils need structured practice in order to acquire word building skills. Here the department's own reading scheme comes into play. This was developed by the head of department in the face of what he regarded as the limitation of existing commercial schemes, viz they were insufficiently structured for this type of pupil. The scheme is in two parts: the first is a phonics-based programme; the second concentrates upon comprehension. It is based on the principles of programmed learning. Pupils work on those aspects of the scheme which relate to their specific area(s) of difficulty. Again there is a wide array of learning resources (workcards, worksheets and language masters). Pupils whose spelling does not match their reading ability either follow a commercial scheme (Blackwell's Spelling Workshop) or a course is specially structured for them, drawing upon a spelling resource kit developed within the department and designed to facilitate self-help skills in spelling. Once literacy has been attained (defined as reading at the 9-10 year level), a range of associated skills is taught, increasingly with a view to the needs of adult life (comprehension, punctuation, interpretation and so forth). By the time pupils are in their fourth year the concern is almost exclusively with such aspects of the adult world as tax returns, form filling and job applications.

The department has similarly developed its own number scheme. Here the primary aim is competence in money and time. If and when these have been mastered, pupils go on to deal with weight, area and capacity. The scheme can encompass all stages on the achievement continuum. Those pupils still at the pre-numeracy stage (very few) will concentrate on such aspects as sorting, matching and recording. The next stage is based upon Fletcher Maths, supplemented with specially prepared workcards and materials intended to make this scheme suitable for the older pupil. Further progress leads the individual on to developing more complex arithmetic skills as well as being introduced to problem solving.

A common core of lessons in main school is normally followed by pupils with moderate learning difficulties and their mainstream peers alike in the first three years. This comprises drama, music, PE/games, design, art and library (first year only). Occasionally a pupil who displays a particular aptitude in another subject area (eg science, maths) may be integrated slightly more. "We operate on the basis of a continuum of special needs, whereby a pupil will attend as many mainstream lessons as offer him educational value and help satisfy his needs" (head of department). Over and above this, the Basic Studies department seeks to supplement – "broaden and balance". In the first three years there is a 'Basic Studies Curriculum' comprising: literacy (reading and writing), numeracy, social studies (sub-divided into 'the self' and a local geographical/historical component), science, woodwork, art, home management, rural studies and additional sport.

In years IV and V an options system comes into play. Midway through each pupil's third year staff consult with pupils and their parents, and possibly outside agencies, to help determine choice. A booklet goes out to all parents which describes the various courses offered for the final two years of formal schooling. Pupils are free to choose five of the ten courses they are required to take. Mandatory courses cover: English, maths, 'core' (games, plus a choice from RE, health education, music and careers), human studies and science. These may be provided within the department or in the main school. The department itself offers specific courses in the following areas: a specially devised leavers' programme (discussed below), social studies, child care/home management and literacy/numeracy. There are additional extra-curricular activities in woodwork, photography and car maintenance. Staff of the department maintain that the supplementary art, craft or home economics that they provide many pupils is an essential part of their education: "Rightly or wrongly educationists advocate more practical education for special children, these are the subjects the less able can achieve in." More particularly, "We develop their practical skills so that they have a slight advantage over the main school pupils and ... [to] make up for less insight."

Although our account concentrates upon pupils with moderate learning difficulties, other groups of clients are not neglected. For example, a pupil with specific reading difficulties is likely to spend considerable time within the department working on specially prepared materials. He or she may engage in art or craftwork within the department if interested, while maths, physical science and biology are usually taken in main school. Pupils with a slight general difficulty in learning will concentrate particularly on basic skills when withdrawn from main school and may well be included in the department's social or rural studies courses.

It may be noted that timetabling for the sort of flexibility being described here is a major task, and inevitably one that entails compromises. Individual timetables have to be constructed in the context of the complex organisational framework of a large comprehensive school and the multi-faceted nature of the Basic Studies department's activities. The head of department identified numerous constraints that came into play in constructing timetables: timing of main school lessons cannot be altered to accommodate individuals; range of options in fourth and fifth year; teaching commitments of department staff in main school – the department's own programme must take account of these; requirements of the department's programme, eg areas such as science, social studies and pastoral care which are organised on a year group basis, and aspects of the leavers' programme which are relatively inflexible; and the need for balance within each pupil's timetable.

Finally, a feature of the Basic Studies curriculum worth mentioning is the 'token economy' system in use. The thinking behind its introduction was that some form of extrinsic reward system would prove beneficial when dealing with pupils who may have experienced considerable frustration and failure in their previous school careers. Pupils are awarded tokens for work that is good by their standards and for evidence of an improvement in behaviour and/or attitude toward school. Tokens can be 'cashed' for rewards which pupils themselves helped to select (eg table tennis ball – 6 tokens; game of bar billiards – 10 tokens; felt tip pen – 25 tokens; plastic football – 100 tokens). The system, which has been in use for over three years now, was endorsed by staff, who were convinced that the lesson output of pupils had increased while behaviour generally had improved. The head of department expressed satisfaction at the more positive attitudes to school and school work that has resulted.

Preparation for adult life

The leavers' programme that has been developed within the department deserves examining in its own right. It is accorded a high priority in the curriculum of senior (Years IV and V) pupils. The intention behind one of the staffing posts was that the person appointed should develop this aspect of the curriculum. In point of fact the eventual appointee had had some prior experience of running a leavers' course in an ESN(M) school.

The scheme proper began in autumn 1978, although considerable time and energy had gone into its planning beforehand. Prior to this time there had been few leavers from the department. The programme has seven main components and is allotted some five and a half hours of school time each week (later increased to seven hours). It encompasses the following:

   i) Outside visits. This comprises visits to places of interest within the community (eg police station, post office, travel agency, factories).
   ii) Independence training. Pupils are set a series of practical tasks, graded in difficulty. They range from simple purchases to making quite complex travel arrangements.

iii) Practicalities of independence. Allocated 60 minutes (including the above). This is concerned with such everyday matters as paying bills, drawing cheques, filling in forms, applying for jobs.
iv) Careers/work experience. Careers preparation is assigned 40 minutes weekly. It consists of TV programmes and presentations on the various types of job open to pupils. There is a degree of liaison with the careers service but not as much as one might anticipate.

Work experience has only involved a small number of pupils (seven) so far (November 1979). It is restricted to fifth formers. It is arranged as either a day out of school each week over a 10-week period, or a block of a fortnight, depending upon which is more appropriate for the individual concerned. The organising teacher visits a pupil once in his or her placement. A variety of jobs have been undertaken. Of the pupils currently in the scheme, one is working in a tool hire firm; a second, in market gardening; a third is engaged in van delivery work; a fourth, general hotel work; and the fifth, shop work. Of the two who had work experience in an earlier year, one boy worked on the highways department of the local council, the second – less successfully – as a forecourt attendant.
v) Do-it yourself. An 80-minute period which seeks to prepare pupils for home life. (eg wiring plugs, fixing washers, painting and decorating).
vi) Basic skills. A continuation of the department's emphasis throughout on literacy and numeracy, with a focus on everyday living. Thus, maths might consider weekly budgeting; English might entail an analysis of job advertisements or newspaper content. (This component is followed also by some 15 pupils with learning problems in the main school – not necessarily pupils who have had extensive prior contact with the department.)
vii) Duke of Edinburgh Award. Assigned 80 minutes per week. It has three elements: community service; individual interests; and undertaking an expedition. The intention is to integrate the official DOE Award into the school's own scheme, ensuring that those who complete it receive some form of certificate.

A feature of note is the explicit attention to monitoring pupils' progress through the programme. Aside from the feedback to staff, the teacher who developed the course was also concerned that it should be taken seriously and should not be viewed as a means of containing pupils.

Accordingly, he devised a checklist in order to keep a record of what pupils had attempted and achieved.

It may be noted that all the leavers to date – ten in number – were successful in obtaining employment. They are working in a variety of jobs – as carpenter, caterer, machinist, factory worker, boat builder, window cleaner, trainee butcher. With the exception of one who was made redundant, they have held their jobs for some time. Several are engaged in further training related to their work.

Monitoring progress

There is a particular concern here that records should fulfil definite purposes. The head of department sees them as illustrating the academic, social and emotional development of pupils. Records are not to be passive documents: they should indicate areas where pupils need help and suggest particular aims for teaching staff.

Early in the history of the department, individual members of staff maintained records of pupils' progress largely for their own use. The relatively small number of pupils made it possible for each member of staff to get to know individual pupils quite well, while information or observations could easily be conveyed to other staff by word of mouth. As numbers increased and more members of staff were taken on, this approach became unworkable. At the same time there was a move toward structured learning materials which had an assessment component built in. For instance, when using structured workcards, progress sheets are drawn up for each pupil listing specific objectives which teachers can tick off once they have been achieved.

In the course of our fieldwork, staff held a series of discussions on monitoring pupils' progress and came up with a proposal for a seven-fold record outline comprising:

  i) the standardised primary school record form
 ii) report(s) of the educational psychologist
iii)
 iv) details of pupil's attainments in literacy and numeracy
  v) profile of social and emotional development
 vi) report of leavers' programme
vii) miscellaneous documentation (eg any review forms, annual school report).

The annual report consists in part of an assessment carried out by subject specialists at the request of Basic Studies staff. A form headed 'timetable notes' is circulated among the relevant members of staff. The form has columns for comments from both teacher and pupil, and ends with the request to 'please identify the special educational needs of the pupil and indicate how we might organise his/her timetable to meet these needs'. Should teachers feel it is necessary, Basic Studies staff will arrange a meeting to discuss any issues raised by this means.

Most recently a more formal annual review of each pupil's progress has been initiated within the department. The intention is to discuss two pupils' circumstances on one lunchtime per week, recording what each has achieved, what difficulties (if any) remain and appropriate teaching objectives for the next 12 months. In addition, pupils' circumstances are carefully considered by a wider multi-disciplinary group during their third year at school.

Academic integration

We have seen how pupils with special educational needs may take a variety of subjects and spend varying amounts of time in main school classes, depending upon individual strengths and weaknesses. The withdrawal principle is the basic organisational tenet. Thus, pupils with moderate learning difficulties are integrated for between 25-50 per cent of their time at school. Pupils with less severe problems may spend as much as 80 per cent of their time in ordinary classes.

We made some enquiries on how pupils with special needs fared when in main school, discussing their circumstances with subject teachers and observing some lessons. In particular we were interested in teachers' perceptions of what they thought pupils were deriving from the experience. In order to appreciate teachers' responses the organisational basis of the parent school should be noted. In the first year ability grouping is practised; thereafter a mixed ability system operates with increasing setting toward the last two years at school. Thus, in the second year setting occurs for English, maths and French. In the third year science is added to this list. In the fourth and fifth years an options system prevails, with setting for English and maths and for certain of the more popular options (eg social studies). One other important point is the intention of department staff that wherever possible there should never be more than two Basic Studies pupils in any regular class. Any year group (to date there have been 18 pupils at most in a year group) can be sub-divided such that one or at most two pupils go to one of six, seven or eight main school forms. (Staff accept that in future with as many as 25 pupils in first year then some forms may have to receive up to four pupils.)

The staff we spoke with were very willing to be involved in this way. "I am perfectly happy to have them"... "It is only sensible to have them wherever possible" ... "The problems probably have been less than people expected", were three typical comments. A fourth teacher was positive about this practice because it presented a challenge – these pupils were less sophisticated and more responsive in some respects than most pupils he taught. There were difficulties of course. There was a general consensus on the need for a greater degree of planning beforehand; the need for a highly practical approach to lessons, written work being kept to the minimum; and the much greater demand for direct personal contact from certain pupils – "not being able to give them enough attention" was frequently mentioned as a source of worry. Sometimes the class itself needed restructuring, perhaps dividing pupils into carefully chosen groups so that Basic Studies pupils would stand a good chance of being fully involved in the lesson.

While some teachers mentioned that they would like to take pupils with special needs as a group by themselves for part of the time – a music teacher, for example, felt this would then enable her to "push them a lot more" (music is mixed ability throughout, though recently a non-exam music option has been introduced) – it must be said that generally teachers did not seem over-concerned about whether pupils were making progress educationally. A science teacher, for example, observed that as far as he was concerned the primary benefit was "in terms of the social integration ... that's a good enough reason to be there". Some teachers seemed to view the pupils' educational development as solely the department's responsibility, and in some respects it appeared that its presence in the school – although absolutely critical – excused subject teachers from having to assume responsibility for pupils' progress in their particular subject.

Various indicators of educational development were referred to by subject specialists. Pupils' quite reasonable competence at practical tasks was frequently commented on. They were considered to derive an element of satisfaction from carrying out experiments (for example, in science) where they did not encounter problems. A drama teacher spoke extremely positively about pupils she had taught. Some had had their first taste of success in her subject and their confidence had subsequently blossomed. She considered that drama was particularly appropriate for these pupils as some of them "don't have the inhibitions that the intelligent ones have".

Difficulties, where they did arise, could usually be overcome fairly easily, and with sound advance planning could often be avoided altogether. Pupils were often lacking in confidence and tended to stick close to their friend from the department. The solution here was to team them with a sympathetic pupil from main school. A music teacher had noted on various occasions the pride displayed by some of the brighter pupils when a pupil they had taken under their wing had done something quite successfully. A home economics teacher spoke of one girl's clumsiness, and the fact that this presented an element of danger in certain situations. The same could apply in science. It meant that the teacher needed to maintain a closer watch on things, perhaps teaming the pupil concerned with a responsible pupil of higher ability. It was very common for these pupils to have difficulty in thinking ahead, assembling equipment in advance of when they actually had need of it and generally carrying out practical work in a systematic way. Not only did this make for slow progress, but also the teacher was obliged to take a more active instructional or guiding role than usual. Demand on a teacher's time was sometimes occasioned by sheer carelessness or lack of organisation (eg pupils who were continually forgetting pens, pencils or books), or where a pupil's concentration span was extremely limited.

The most commonly voiced observation concerned these pupils' difficulty with writing and to a lesser degree reading. Because of this it seemed that an easier regime prevailed for them. Teachers sought to simplify texts and to reduce their reliance upon them when they could not be avoided altogether. Thus, a drama teacher remarked, "[they] do not stand out except when they go to scripts". Written work was kept to a minimum, and concessions were made for those who had difficulties over writing. Some teachers would give them odd practical tasks while classmates were taking notes or writing essays. One home economics teacher, however, expressed unease that pupils sometimes appeared to 'see through' this ruse and feared that their self-identity might suffer in consequence. Other teachers stated that they paid little attention to Basic Studies pupils' written work. One teacher, for example, described how she would put a tick beside it and write 'good' if it was legible! A common assumption was that pupils would be unable to sit CSE examinations because of their poor writing ability. However, this is not necessarily the case. Although a pupil with poor handwriting could not realistically expect to sit CSE English, nevertheless five pupils will this academic year be sitting exams in certain practical subjects (science, woodwork) with the aid of readers and scribes.

Exercising appropriate discipline had been something of a problem when the integration practice was still in its infancy. A number of teachers with whom we spoke attested to this. They agreed they had tended to take the line of least resistance in some cases and accepted that some pupils had probably taken advantage of this. They admitted to having felt unsure about when to insist upon something and when to turn a blind eye. Undoubtedly their task was not helped by the somewhat easier – because of the closer personal contact – regime that operated within the Basic Studies department. With time, however, teachers had become more confident and skilled in handling difficult behaviour. Wherever doubts remained, there was a valuable safeguard in the form of the school's pastoral system. In the first instance a problem would be referred to the particular year tutor. If he or she felt unhappy about handling the incident the head of Basic Studies department would be consulted.

In addition to posing problems for the ordinary teacher it should be noted that the presence of pupils with special needs has resulted in professional benefits for them as well. Over a period of time, through having direct teaching contact with these pupils, teachers build up a facility in dealing with their learning problems. This is particularly so when as here information and guidance from specialist staff are readily available. This development is of benefit to all pupils in the school.

The social context

Attending an ordinary school is widely claimed to enhance the social and emotional development of pupils with special needs. On the evidence available this was the case for a good many Basic Studies pupils – though as noted below, there were some causes for concern. There are plenty of opportunities for contact with pupils from the parent school, both in and outside the classroom. We have seen how practically all pupils spend 25–50 per cent of their time attending ordinary classes. In some of these classes there will be other pupils who are receiving, or have in the past received, occasional help from Basic Studies. This means that the department is familiar and well accepted throughout the school, and no great stigma attaches to being based in it.

Outside of the classroom, the department is host to considerable numbers of pupils at break and lunchtimes, and before and after school, eager to use its varied leisure facilities (bar football, billiards, table tennis). The department also promotes itself as a haven for those individuals who perhaps find the boisterous nature of a large comprehensive school overpowering at times. These pupils – and others – are regular visitors, and while staff do not intervene to promote interactions, associations between the two groups do develop.

The consensus among both department staff and other teachers was that there was generally a high level of acceptance with active friendship in some instances. The extent to which pupils are assimilated depends on individual personality and the amount of time spent in the ordinary classroom rather than on the degree of learning difficulties. While there were pupils who were not particularly accepted (eg a boy characterised by his rather old-fashioned appearance and immature behaviour, a girl who was generally made fun of and incited to misbehave), nevertheless the reasonably well-balanced individual could expect to meet ready acceptance and might well establish firm friendships. The extent of acceptance was apparent also in teachers' comments: "there's no picking on them" ... "there's a good deal of helping out" ... "there's better understanding among main school pupils", who were now perceived as almost "too protective".

Similarly, there was a good deal of evidence to suggest that pupils were benefiting in terms of their social and emotional development. The head of department noted that more than a third of their pupils had displayed marked social and/or emotional problems at some stage (eg irrational behaviour, phobias, disruptive behaviour). In all but a few exceptional cases – where problems were exacerbated through pupils' presence in a large comprehensive school – these difficulties owed nothing to being in an ordinary school. In many cases indeed problems were alleviated and the head of department was confident that the majority had benefited from the exposure to normal behaviour. Various examples of this were offered. One father noted how his boy who had previously attended a special school had changed, become "a different kiddie" indeed, and grown in independence – "it wasn't until [school] that he really started to stick up for himself". Another boy who had previously attended a residential school for the maladjusted was considered by school staff and external agencies alike to have made 'marked progress in terms of self-control and social competence'.

Combating immature or disruptive behaviour is a very necessary part of the routine within the department. Early in our fieldwork this was a particular problem because of the presence of a small group of older pupils who were severely disturbed, to the point where they began to be a negative influence on other pupils in the department. It is fair to say that their presence taxed the skills of members of staff. The preference was to handle incidents in a low-key way so as to defuse them and avoid confrontation unless this was judged absolutely necessary. Naturally, this was not always easy when dealing with severely disruptive youngsters. One member of the department's staff felt at the time that pupils were sometimes allowed to get away with too much and that this was detrimental to their future life chances. Unless they "learned to conform", acquired basic manners and displayed appropriate behaviour in different social settings, they would fall foul of employers and many general situations when they left school. In the event the situation was eased with the transfer of the most difficult pupils to residential schools, coupled with the greater acquisition of relevant handling skills by all of the department's staff.

Parents

This is one aspect of his job that the head of department puts considerable store by, maintaining that any educational programme is more likely to be successful if parents are actively supportive. He notes from experience that "once the rapport has been established with the parents, many problems with the children disappear". In practice, this concern translates into seeking to establish sound, largely informal relations with pupils' families, keeping them informed of developments in their son or daughter's education and making them feel welcome in school at any time. Parents are not encouraged to involve themselves directly in their child's schooling. It is felt that sufficient academic demands are made on pupils within school to justify their not being expected to spend time at home on further school activities. (Accordingly, homework is only given where it is specifically requested, and even then with reluctance.)

An important factor in establishing sound relations is the early contact between school and home. In the term preceding a pupil's entry to Brightwell, parents are invited in for an evening. They are addressed by the head teacher, have a chance to talk informally with members of staff and are given a tour of the school. In the course of the first term they are invited to meet with form tutors and heads of department. The courses that their son or daughter is taking will be outlined and discussed. Parents' evenings are held annually and parents are given a choice of dates. Further, the views of parents are carefully considered when the time comes for pupils to determine fourth and fifth year options. In addition to these formal occasions, it is emphasised to parents that they should feel free to get in contact whenever they are concerned about something, however trivial it may seem. Also, parents of pupils who are going through a difficult period are urged to pay regular – usually weekly – visits in order to discuss the developing situation.

We interviewed the parents of six pupils who were receiving considerable attention from the Basic Studies department. All were unanimous in their appreciation of what the school was achieving with their children. There were various indicators of progress having been made: educationally – eg with reading and writing; emotionally – eg a marked increase in confidence; and socially – eg various mentions of more mature and 'normal' behaviour ("He started to act like normal children"). All were happy that their child was attending this school, and none wanted an alternative placement.

This is not to say that there have been no criticisms. Several parents were keen to have homework and two felt frustrated that they were not able to help more directly in their children's schooling. One mother felt there were "too many sidetracks" (from proper lessons) and felt that her child needed "to be encouraged to see it less as a play school". In fairness to school staff, it must be said that some of these parents had unrealistic aspirations. They also saw education narrowly in terms of basic skills – "needs more practice with his reading" – when teachers' professional judgement might be that a broader preparation for adult life was more in order.

Summary

Brightwell offers a good working model of how a comprehensive school can incorporate pupils with special needs into its educational provision. The Basic Studies department has developed into a highly effective provision dealing flexibly with a wide range of pupils who have special educational needs. It is responsible for some 60 pupils with moderate learning difficulties, providing a basic curriculum within the department and arranging for their participation in main school lessons. It also functions effectively as the school's remedial department, offering help on a withdrawal basis for a large number of pupils in the school. The department has become an integral part of the school and its work is highly regarded within it. In addition to considerable curriculum development (in the area of reading and a leavers' programme) and planning, the department can point to in-service training initiatives that have been useful and well received.

The main questions for the future have perhaps to do with maintaining and building on achievements to date. There are some further considerations however:

1. Will the department continue to function effectively as pupil numbers increase? Will it be possible to maintain the same flexibility in view of the growing complexity of timetabling and staff deployment?
2. Would it be desirable, or feasible, to involve parents more directly in their children's education?
3. It is intended that the school should cater for a greater number of pupils with special needs in its catchment area, ie not only those with learning difficulties. How will this development affect the department and the ways of working and relationships with the rest of the school that it has developed?
4. Will the department staff be able to consolidate and extend the training initiatives already developed?

2
Primary provision for pupils with learning difficulties

This provision comprises two separate centres, for pupils with moderate and with severe learning difficulties. It is located at a small (200+) junior school covering the age range 7-11. The two centres are adjacent to each other and stand some little distance from the parent school. The centre for children with severe learning difficulties incorporates a self-contained facility for 'special care' children. The provision, which is situated in a small town in a rural area, serves the catchment areas of a large number of primary schools in the district.

Historical résumé

This predominantly rural authority covers a large area and has developed its special education provision on an area basis. When provision was being developed, the decision was taken 'to establish small area units at local primary and secondary schools, thus eliminating long travelling distances for pupils which would have been necessary if the alternative course of action of building larger but fewer special schools had been adopted'. These area units are special classes or departments based in ordinary schools and providing for specified groups of pupils drawn from a wide catchment area. The number of pupils in these units varies according to prevalence of the handicapping condition but would not be sufficient to sustain provision separate from an ordinary school. The *de facto* integration achieved in this way was seen to be quite successful; when linked with more recent changes in educational thinking, it led to a stronger commitment to area unit provision on the authority's part.

The first development in this school was the setting up of a special centre for pupils with moderate learning difficulties. Seeking a suitable location in which to establish such a facility for primary age children, the authority was alerted to the fact that space was becoming available in a school which was losing its infant children to a new infant school in the vicinity. Other factors which added to its suitability included: its central location; a green field site with extensive playing fields; and various social and medical facilities ready to hand. So, in 1969 an area unit was opened to cater for up to 40 pupils with moderate learning difficulties aged 7–11 years. Though it was 'to all intents and purposes... to be considered to be the area special school' (head teacher), the underlying purpose was 'towards integration and a positive move away from complete segregation'. The premises were physically quite separate from the main school.

Two years later, LEA officials were confronted by a new problem, how to provide for those with severe learning difficulties following the passage of the Education (Handicapped Children) Act 1970. These pupils had hitherto been provided for in an all-age junior training centre. After considerable deliberation the authority opted to develop a second special centre on the existing junior school site. This would serve a wider age range than the present school, or the existing special centre, going from 2 to 11 years. A self-contained facility for those requiring special care, age range 2–16, would also be incorporated. This centre opened in 1974 with places for 35 children. It represented a highly innovative step to take at the time, being one of very few such provisions attached to an ordinary school in this country.

On each occasion when a specialist facility was established, the authority does not seem to have been involved in the detailed planning within the school once the initial arrangements were made, though we were unable to collect precise details about the initial arrangements because of changes of personnel, at both school and authority level. Integration was not a central concern at the time, and there is little evidence of any advance planning or preparation involving existing school staff. Candidates for the headship of the parent school which was vacant at the time (1971) were asked for their views on the second special centre. (The person appointed did in fact request – successfully – that a communal staffroom be included in the building plans on the grounds that this would aid staff integration.) Otherwise there seems to have been little consultation with existing staff or provision of some general introduction and orientation toward these pupils' needs. Various members of staff were disaffected by what they perceived as a lack of effective concern on the part of the authority. One LEA official agreed that some staff felt that they had been "saddled with the handicapped kids", while teachers themselves voiced bitter complaints about the lack of planning.

The significance of this is twofold. First, introducing such a substantial number of pupils with special needs into a small school (74 as against 222 pupils in 1978, a ratio of 1:3) does not make for easy assimilation, and success depends on involving the ordinary teacher. Secondly, it is important in any such scheme to clarify to all concerned, however limited their direct contact might be, the purpose behind such provision. Possibly the authority had no intention initially of going beyond locational integration (ie special provision sharing the same campus as an ordinary school). Certainly they did not dictate a definite policy on this, leaving the working practice to be determined by the head teacher and his staff. One can question whether this will suffice when the arrangements are as innovative and demanding as these were.

Organisation and aims

Each centre has its own teacher in charge. The two exist fairly independently of each other, although there has been considerable discussion between respective teachers in charge over policy and practice. Administratively, each comes under the control of the parent school and is answerable to the head teacher. In practice, both enjoy considerable autonomy, particularly the centre for pupils with severe learning difficulties. In part this reflects the specialised nature of the educational provision these pupils require – "our unit presents so many different kinds of problems..." – and the likelihood that main school staff have a limited understanding of these pupils' needs. It indicates also the head teacher's confidence in the teachers in charge and his belief that they must be given a free hand if they are to work effectively.

Relations with the parent school are distant on the whole – "We do tend to run very much as two separate units... We are probably functioning as a mini-special school" (teacher in charge). This is somewhat less true of the centre for pupils with moderate learning difficulties. Its pupils are perceived by ordinary teachers as more akin to slow learning pupils in the parent school.

Various factors that have contributed to this lack of closeness can be identified. Some have been mentioned in passing: the failure of the authority to spell out what was intended or give a clear lead on integration; the lack of consultation and preparation of the ordinary teachers; and the relative autonomy of the teachers in charge with the associated avoidance by the head of a strongly directive role. Other influences include: (i) The damaging effect of misperceptions, eg misunderstandings concerning the qualifications of specialist staff and what is demanded of them: "They say you can't call it teaching" (special teacher); or of the allocation of resources: "*They* get more of their share, all the toys, better food, Christmas plays.... I feel sometimes the normal children miss out on some of the advantages" (ordinary teacher). (ii) The perception among many main school staff that the severely handicapped are a strange group whose behaviour is highly deviant. This was considered to have led to a situation where there were "two levels of discipline" in evidence in the school. (A visiting special educator considered in this context that the inclusion of 'special care' children was a big mistake: "They provide an abnormal setting for the whole group... the more normal are going to be pushed aside.") (iii) The fact that not all members of main school staff accept the presence of this provision – "Some [teachers]... aren't interested in this side of things" (teacher in charge). This has led to an 'us and them' attitude on the part of certain teachers. "They're not interested in my problems so I'm not interested in theirs" (ordinary teacher). It should be stressed that this is by no means the attitude of all staff. Some teachers are positive and well disposed, but the presence of a sizeable number who are not so has created a distance.

As regards the aims espoused for this provision, each centre places great emphasis upon providing a firm grounding in the basic skills. Staff are unwilling to jeopardise this through clinging to the principle of integration. The teacher with overall responsibility for pupils with severe learning difficulties described her concern to "get a good blend of the two" (ie academic and social) but stressed, "I wouldn't like to drop down on the language [and] number work." Neither teacher in charge saw much purpose in integrating for the sake of it: "It's really got to benefit the kid a lot. If it's only going to benefit the child marginally, it's dubious." Staff were not concerned at the absence overall of classroom (or functional) integration; most of their pupils were considered unlikely to derive a great deal of benefit from this: "Borderline M and S children's basic need is four years of special education... What are the kids here for? They've not been diagnosed as needing integration but as needing special education." Writing about whether there might be more 'actual classroom integration', the head teacher emphasised that 'when it comes it will have to be selective'.

Apart from this concentration on laying the groundwork for future educational development, the need to work deliberately on children's general behaviour and train them in social skills was recognised. Another aim was to develop close working relations with pupils' families, seeking to provide educational guidelines as well as being generally supportive. This was because education for these pupils had to be viewed in a very broad sense, and also because any disturbance within the home environment could affect a child's school performance.

Pupils

This provision caters for a wide range of pupils, from those with mild learning difficulties or some form of emotional disturbance through to the multiply handicapped child. The clientele of the centre for children with severe learning difficulties is particularly diverse on account of the absence of alternative provision – "Where there aren't facilities that would be suitable we are trying to do something... we are twisting our provision." In addition to its primary clients it is increasingly accepting "questionmark children", children who might be functioning at a higher level but are not old enough for entry to the appropriate provision (which cannot accept children under the age of seven). Equally, they may be under five and "beginning to exhibit problems". Also the actual composition of the group fluctuates over time. For example, a recent intake comprised mainly infant age children with moderate learning difficulties, many of whom would transfer to the other centre at age seven. By contrast, the next intake is likely to be a nursery/infant group with severe learning difficulties.

The special care section, with places for 10 children, is intended for those who have severe mental and physical handicaps. It too accepts other types of children from time to time because of the lack of more appropriate provision for them locally. For example, a rubella child of two and a half years with severe deafness was accepted on the grounds that a period of time in special care was better than no formal stimulation at all. The difficulty sometimes found in diagnosing accurately the primary handicap at such a young age is a factor to be borne in mind.

The role of the centre for pupils with moderate learning difficulties is also broader than might be expected, having been expanded by the LEA so as to cater for some pupils with mild behaviour disturbance in addition to those with learning difficulties. This latter group has in the past included a sizeable number of children from deprived homes.

Placement is usually attendant upon completion of the necessary SE documentation, the final recommendation being made by the educational psychologist. For some time now the latter has been recommending that children be placed in the 'special units' rather than being categorised and given a definite label at an early age. Where the learning difficulties are suspected to be no more than moderate, the psychologist makes it clear that "he expects the child will transfer through [to the appropriate unit] at seven". The same applies to those children who have started ordinary infant schooling but met with early failure in their educational career.

In the past there has been considerable difficulty in identifying those children most likely to benefit from this provision. Screening is undertaken at 6, 10 and 14 months in neighbourhood clinics in the absence of a pre-school assessment/diagnostic centre, though the quality of the screening was described as rather poor in the past. Even when a child had been identified prompt referral to the school was not always forthcoming. Currently, the school is notified of the vast majority of pupils with severe learning difficulties; for those with moderate difficulties the proportion brought to their attention can be as low as 50 per cent. Much of the problem here was seen to lie in the reluctance of head teachers to refer children with difficulties in good time, and also a tendency on the part of some to make inappropriate referrals. Pupils with moderate learning difficulties were frequently coming to notice quite late in their primary schooling – "We are screaming it's late at seven... it's incredible when they come in at ten" (teacher in charge). At one stage there was recourse to a screening system carried out in conjunction with the educational psychologist, based upon Young's Group Reading Test and Raven's Matrices. This was administered to all top infants within the area, any child who failed to reach a set level being referred for more extensive psychological assessment. This system remained in use for a year or two before being discontinued. The remedial advisory teacher now screens the entire school population at age seven, and some children come to light in this way.

In an effort to deal directly with this problem a new teacher in charge sought closer relations with the local primary schools. She invited all head teachers in the catchment area to visit. To date 20 out of 29 have taken up the invitation. (A number of the others already know the centres well or are teaching heads of small schools who find it difficult to leave their posts.) They look round the centres individually or in groups of two or three, meeting the children, seeing their work and talking to staff. Many teachers in these schools have expressed interest in visiting though few have yet been able to do so. This contact is seen to give heads a much clearer idea of what the centres can achieve and help them make earlier and more realistic referrals.

Neither centre has any hard and fast rules concerning children they are unwilling to accept, though there had been dissatisfaction about some referrals in the past. The teacher in charge of the centre for children with severe learning difficulties did state that while she would not refuse admission for a hyperactive child such a placement would present considerable practical difficulties. Her colleague in the second centre noted that every child was carefully appraised on his or her merits. Particular consideration was paid to what they as educators could offer the child, whether it was in fact the most suitable placement available; and also how the child might fit into the existing group of pupils.

More worrying than unsuitable candidates being put up for placement was the poor notification of potential candidates in the admissions pipeline. This meant that children who were borderline candidates might be accepted just before a child with a clear need for specialist attention was put forward. The teacher responsible for the severely handicapped described how on several occasions, having a place available, she had accepted a child with moderate educational retardation, or one who had "a speech problem, delayed development and an unstimulating home environment", only to be notified, weeks later, of a child with severe learning difficulties in urgent need of admission. While no child for whom a placement was urgent had been denied to date, this was only by dint of a good deal of internal re-organisation on the part of the teacher in charge and her staff.

There is little movement once directed to either centre, other than in the case of those very young children placed in the centre for pupils with severe learning difficulties purely because of their age. These transfer to the other centre on or near their seventh birthday. Pupils who attend the latter centre are unlikely to be transferred away from the location, because their need for specialised attention is so considerable – by implication other primary schools in the area are not considered capable of meeting this need. Also, there are now improved links with the main school which can be availed of if a particular child displays the capacity to benefit from time spent in the regular classroom. The head teacher reports that at least one child has been transferred permanently into a regular class every year for the past nine years. The number transferring fluctuates from year to year. In the school year 1979/1980 no less than three children, all fourth years, finally moved permanently into the main school. At the time of secondary transfer all pupils from these provisions – with the exception of those requiring special care – transfer to a nearby comprehensive school which houses a similar area facility.

Staffing

The centre for pupils with severe learning difficulties has five teachers including the teacher in charge, whose role is essentially non-teaching, four ancillaries and a nurse. The staff–pupil ratio compares quite favourably with the ratio obtaining in special school provision within the authority. All members of the teaching staff have taken specific training courses either based upon mental handicap or with a substantial component on mental handicap. The centre for pupils with moderate learning difficulties has three teachers (including the teacher in charge) and a welfare assistant. In this instance the staffing ratio is considerably below that recommended in DES Circular 4/73. The teacher in charge has taken a part-time course organised by the authority and leading to the Certificate in the Education of the Handicapped Child. The two other teaching members of staff have either taken this course or are presently doing so.

Both centres have seen considerable turnover of staff in their time, particularly as regards the crucial position of teacher in charge. The centre for pupils with severe learning difficulties had two teachers in charge in its first three years of operating. The very necessary stability has been provided by the present appointee, who has held this position for the past five years. At the other centre there were four teachers in charge in the space of nine years. The considerable disadvantages stemming from such turnover – most notably, the lack of continuity, and the difficulty experienced in developing a coherent and consistent policy of operating – have been offset to a degree by the fact that two of the four (including the current teacher in charge) had been on the staff of the special centre prior to taking charge and thus were not new to either school or special centre.

Involvement with outside specialist agencies is something that has developed a good deal in recent years. Much effort has been devoted to it, especially by the teacher in charge of the centre for pupils with severe learning difficulties. Upon taking up post in 1975 she discovered that relations with Area Health and Social Services personnel were mixed. While there was a sound relationship with paediatricians at one hospital, at a second "relations were very poor". Contact with a field services officer who had specific responsibility for the mentally handicapped but only worked on a part-time basis was fairly limited. No physiotherapy was being provided on a routine basis, while provision of speech therapy was irregular.

There has been considerable improvement on this. The link with Social Services still seems tenuous, in part perhaps because the teacher in charge has a close interest in developing links with the home and possesses relevant skills and experience. (She is a former teacher-counsellor who has been involved in establishing pre-school home teaching programmes.) There is a close working relationship with the present field services officer, though where individual social workers are involved relationships are not as strong. Physiotherapy is now provided on a day a week basis – though only after great pressure was brought to bear. Speech therapy – mainly working on children's articulation – was considered adequate by the teacher in charge – "We get what we ask for" (a half-day per week for the two centres, shortly to be increased to a day per week) – though two members of staff suggested otherwise. The educational psychologist and a member of the LEA advisory service visit from time to time, usually on the occasion of 'panel meetings', where there are specific matters to be addressed.

Two areas of achievement stand out in particular. First, the three paediatricians involved have been persuaded to hold their clinics at the school. This has been extremely well received by teachers and parents alike. Not only do the paediatricians see children and their parents on these occasions, but there are opportunities for teachers to discuss a child's circumstances with the paediatrician and for the latter to observe the child within the classroom setting. Apart from disseminating information, developing a better understanding of, for example, the effect of drugs prescribed to control epilepsy, and leading to suggestions on child management, the exercise is considered to have significantly enhanced the development of a common policy as between medical practitioners, educators and parents. Tensions that had been evident in the past, between doctors and parents in particular, were now largely overcome. Secondly, meetings of the Review and Admissions Panel are convened every six weeks at which representatives from a range of disciplines meet to discuss a variety of matters, not simply to consider admissions, which was the original intention. Representatives from the advisory service, Area Health, Social Services, school psychological service and the two teachers in charge are usually present.

Accommodation and resources

Both special centres are purpose-built, though the premises occupied by those with severe learning difficulties are more extensive and better equipped. This may reflect the fact that the centre for children with moderate learning difficulties was envisaged as "an economy unit". The former consists of two large open-plan teaching areas (corresponding to nursery/reception and junior areas), a smaller self-contained 'special care' facility, a small therapy area, a small indoor play area, office for the teacher in charge, a large staffroom (which functions for the school as a whole), toilets and storage space. The second centre comprises two small classrooms separated by a foyer which doubles as a third classroom/general office, and toileting facilities.

The school to which the provision is attached occupies old premises. Both special centres stand a short distance from the main school. The playground is too small for the number of children on roll, though there are large playing fields adjacent which may be utilised in good weather.

The centre for those with severe learning difficulties was well equipped with basic materials and resources from the beginning; the other centre perhaps less so. Wherever additional everyday resources have been required the authority has been quite generous in providing them. For special items of equipment (eg larger play materials, language kits), money has to be raised by appealing to charity, and here the centre for pupils with severe learning difficulties has a distinct advantage: "It is much easier for us to raise money than the M's" (teacher in charge); the general public has shown itself more willing to give on behalf of children whose difficulties are readily apparent. It was pointed out that resources appropriate for those with moderate learning difficulties were of a different order: "A stack of books does not look as impressive as a stack of toys." Further, having a less favourable staffing ratio – most particularly as regards classroom ancillaries – meant that staff had less time for preparing materials and arranging classroom displays than their colleagues in the other centre.

In any account of funding the part played by a parents' support group convened by the head teacher should be noted. The majority of the most active members are parents of main school children, but there are some parents of children attending the special centres also. The group has raised sufficient funds to purchase a minibus, a variety of audio-visual aids and, most recently, the school's own swimming pool. Special centre pupils have their fair share of use of such resources – indeed, they are the main users of the minibus.

Curriculum

It is difficult to give precise information here. Staff were conscious of many difficulties and weaknesses, and various efforts were made in the course of our study to resolve them. The goal of a carefully devised curriculum implemented across the centres as a whole was still in the future. (A curriculum document was being worked out for pupils with moderate learning difficulties.) Both centres described a programme of individualised teaching with a strong emphasis upon the basic skills. For example, the nursery/infant teacher described how ideally the children in her care would be working through pre-reading and pre-number, with additional emphasis upon independence in regard of toileting, feeding and dressing. She drew quite heavily upon language materials developed for the young mentally handicapped child by an educational psychologist and a language adviser within the authority. A listening scheme – part of the Learning Development Aids scheme – is used to promote the ability to discriminate between different sounds and generally to develop auditory skills. Number work is based upon individual learning programmes developed by staff of Bennet House, a school for pupils with severe learning difficulties. At this age the social and academic aspects of the curriculum are closely interwoven.

Attempts have been made in the past to rationalise the curriculum. For example, when we first made enquiries we were informed of two areas of concentration: seeking "to form a basic curriculum" between the nursery/infant and junior departments; and establishing continuity between the nursery/infant department and the centre for children with moderate learning difficulties in regard of pupils who were likely to transfer at age seven. The preference of the teacher in charge was to encourage her staff to develop a suitable curriculum, rather than to impose her own ideas upon them. Some staff meetings were held to work out common approaches. It was difficult, however, to bring people together and meetings were also disrupted by differences of opinion between members of staff. It seems as if limited progress was made: "We are in a looking stage rather than a drawing it together stage" (teacher in charge). Some teachers felt that there was lack of unity among them and bemoaned their isolation: "If a unit staff were united we could work together more, like a special school staff. In a special school you've all got the same interests and experiences [so] that in the staffroom you can talk about your work and get support and advice... [Here] we are losing the detailed discussion and support that keeps you going." The teacher in charge did suggest, on the basis of her experience in special schools, that this was based on an idealised picture of special school where commonly there was no discussion of curriculum issues. In her opinion the central problem was the lack of time – staff spent any time free from teaching on lesson planning, preparing materials and marking work.

Monitoring progress

It is left to individual teachers to maintain their own records of pupils' progress. Those records we saw seemed relatively thin and unstructured. An attempt was made at one time by three members of staff from the centre for pupils with severe learning difficulties to develop a more formalised procedure for assessing pupils' strengths and weaknesses and recording any evidence of progress. They had discussed appropriate criteria, identifying six main areas: language development (based upon a language scheme developed for the young mentally handicapped child); social and emotional development; motor development; self-help skills; intellectual (pre-number and number, pre-reading skills, visual perception); and play skills. It had been agreed to complete record forms termly and forward them to the teacher in charge. In the event this procedure was not implemented in any general way, with only one teacher using it systematically.

Detailed curriculum-oriented records are maintained on pupils with moderate learning difficulties. Class teachers complete a detailed pro forma noting progress on specific aspects of phonics, reading and number work. These record sheets are passed on from one teacher to the next.

More formalised monitoring is conducted by the Review and Admissions Panel, though the panel's deliberations tend to involve only children with severe learning difficulties. The progress of other pupils is only reviewed (in the more formal sense) every 18 months or so, although the intention was to hold annual reviews.

Academic integration

Both special centres function as full-time base for the pupils on their roll. The extent to which there is any classroom integration is extremely limited. Staff claimed they were ready to integrate infants with severe learning difficulties wherever possible, but the lack of age peers in the school – something to be particularly regretted in view of the common belief that this is the best age to integrate this type of child – meant that it was not readily practicable. The children's particular needs and their limited attainments dictate the limited classroom integration, as does the lack of close association with the parent school. There is also the rather formal nature of educational practices within main school; in the words of one special educator, "the children in the units have failed in this [type of] set up and failed very badly... we can't just put them back in ordinary classes". A colleague noted that "our children have disrupted the formal situation before".

Such integration as there is for pupils with severe learning difficulties is of two main kinds: contact with pupils with moderate learning difficulties and links with an ordinary infant group in a nearby school. Certain of the older pupils have some interaction with age peers from the other special centre, mainly for art and craft and PE – later to be replaced by horse-riding and swimming. This also works in reverse in that the younger most backward children from the latter centre join their more handicapped peers for certain specialised instruction such as the Learning Development Aids scheme.

There have been attempts from time to time to develop links with a local infants school. Thus, at one stage in our study some of the more able infants started attending an ordinary infants school one afternoon per week. This was later extended to the whole infant age group. Parallel sessions of play and more focussed creative work were organised. The seven children involved were accompanied by three adults from the special centre. Later this exercise – described by the teacher in charge as having been quite successful – was abandoned. This was for various reasons: the enthusiastic teacher on the infants school staff whose class they joined left the school and was replaced by a supply teacher who felt she could not cope, even though specialist support was on hand; there were difficulties of timetabling and co-ordinating lesson activities between the respective classes; and transport was problematic, particularly in bad weather. There was also the feeling that children's time was being wasted – "Our kids, in an unstructured situation, tend to just wander and do nothing at all" – and could perhaps be put to better use in the special centre.

For pupils with moderate learning difficulties there is the possibility of association with the parent school. This takes place on an individual basis with individual pupils joining particular lessons. Thus, on the occasion of one of our visits two second year girls joined a mainstream class each afternoon for topic work, with an additional period of writing once a week. A teacher from the centre – who had previously taught in main school – took a needlework class in main school once a week accompanied by some of her pupils from the centre. A number of other pupils of various ages went swimming or joined in games with main school peers. Their teacher in charge observed that "some of them [ordinary teachers] are prepared to have them as long as the child can cope". Teachers were perceived to be willing for such involvement for only the occasional lessons, however: when she had broached the possibility of mixing a group of her pupils with main school pupils, staff were 'not so keen'. In this respect a development which offers hope for the future is the creation of a scale post for a member of staff from the special centre with a brief to promote integration. It is hoped to get the more able pupils into the main school each afternoon when creative and social activities are taking place.

The social context

To benefit from being part of the more 'normal' environment of an ordinary school there must be opportunities for contact with peers. In this respect a major disadvantage of the location is undoubtedly the absence of an infant department. A further disadvantage is the limited amount of contact time. The only real opportunity for social interaction arises at play and lunchtime. Pupils with severe learning difficulties are not included in main school assemblies on a regular basis, though they are of course present on special occasions. Assembly was considered inappropriate by the teacher in charge because of its rather formal nature: "It's not really geared for them ... our children would be a nuisance." Also, they often arrived late and would then only cause added disruption. As regards school dinner, those with severe learning difficulties were excluded in the early days on the grounds that there was insufficient space. Over the past three years all those considered capable – some 15 in all – eat in common with the main pupil body, being dispersed throughout the room. Some are still excluded because they are too severely handicapped (special care children), too young, on special diets or having feeding problems. As regards extra-curricular activities, opportunities at this school are generally limited, being restricted effectively to football and netball clubs, and taking place out of school hours. Apart from not having in many cases the requisite co-ordination and skills to participate in these games with main school pupils, pupils from the special centre would have difficulty in attending any activities after school since they are dependent on special transport.

Staff made much of the fact that in a special school these pupils would not have such extensive opportunities for mixing with peers. Our enquiry and observation would suggest, however, that this opportunity was hardly taken and that the nature and extent of interaction left a good deal to be desired. (It is not being suggested that there was a great deal of teasing or other negative interaction – there was no evidence that any such occurred – but that there was little positive contact.) Staff identified two forms of contact. First, "some more capable children will mix in and...play together in a very positive way". However, we saw little evidence of this. Secondly, certain pupils from main school "like to look after children in the unit" (usually the younger children, or those in wheelchairs). This 'playing with' children was more apparent. One member of staff spoke about this to us: "They play with them as though they are objects rather than playing at their own level." The absence of age peers at infant level must be noted, however, since this is where easiest contact might be expected.

There is somewhat more contact between pupils with moderate learning difficulties and peers from main school. They attend all assemblies, have lunch in common and use the same playground. They remain to all intents and purposes a distinct group, however. While this could be seen to confirm the claim that the presence of pupils with severe learning difficulties provided "an abnormal setting for the whole group", an alternative interpretation was put forward by their teacher in charge. She suggested that their preference for playing among themselves was a natural consequence of the limited classroom integration: it was only to be expected that they would want to mix in playtime with classmates.

An indication of what could be achieved was demonstrated by a visiting special educator. Concerned at the paucity of the interactions between the two groups he introduced a peer-tutor programme. The rationale underlying this was that "interaction doesn't happen on its own without some injection like this...their looks are against them...their communication skills... their limited ability to play". His nine-week peer-tutor programme entailed volunteers from main school being trained in matters such as how to facilitate co-operative play with peers who had severe learning difficulties, how to talk to them, and how to resolve difficulties that might arise. Peer tutors were allocated on an individual basis. Tutor and peer met up over 23 lunchtime sessions. Initially this was within the special centre (11 sessions) where various centres of interest were set up (construction toys, puzzles, doll's house and make-up box). Later, when relationships had been established, contact moved into the playground (12 sessions) where no special resources were provided. At the end of the period, the organiser repeated his initial playground observation. He reported a notable increase in the level of associative and co-operative play between the two groups, with a corresponding decrease in solitary play, engaging in attention-seeking activities, or being a mere onlooker. The intervention had demonstrated 'the ease with which attitudes can change' in a very short period 'provided guidelines are established'.

Without doubt this intervention stimulated relationships between the two groups in the short term. Staff did not seem to take the study too seriously, however, and there was little sign that they built on the insights and possibilities it offered. Generally, they carried on as before, making a minimum of intervention and in at least one case maintaining that the natural interaction between the two groups was adequate and any artificially promoted interaction of this kind was unnecessary. Accordingly, the possibilities for contact that exist tend to be ignored or under-utilised and the apparent disinterest on the part of some ordinary teachers continues. No effort is made to disperse pupils at lunchtime even though one special educator acknowledged that "you can separate them if you can be bothered". The overall impression is that many staff would go along with one teacher's comment, "There isn't much you can do about [social] integration."

Parents

The various teachers in charge have attached considerable importance to establishing links with parents, though they set about it in different ways and assign it different priorities in relation to classroom teaching. Two in particular sought to involve parents in their children's education. The teacher in charge of the centre for pupils with severe learning difficulties described an involvement with parents that lay outside the province of both health visitor and social worker, the two agencies most commonly involved with the home. This was in order to promote acceptance of a child's handicap; being supportive generally, especially as regards offering emotional support; liaising with professional agencies on the parents' behalf; and involving the home in the child's physical and educational development. An example of this involvement was when parents who were experiencing problems in managing their child were invited to visit school and come into the classroom where they could work alongside the teacher, "to see how we are *not* reacting to things".

It was also intended to introduce the Portage home-teaching approach, where relevant. In the event this was only used with one parent of a 'special care' child. It had not been taken very far because of the extremely slow progress which it was felt these children could make. With the particular mother in question they had had difficulty in getting her to take on any responsibility. It was claimed that mothers with social problems would find it difficult to complete the tasks set.

In addition, on two afternoons each month a toy library is held at one of the centres. This involves pre-school children, children in special care, and sometimes infants with severe learning difficulties. Staff use it as a way of working with parents, softening the ground in the case of those parents who are resistant to their child coming to the centre. The staff involved are from the particular area where children are drawn from, the teacher in charge (on the pre-school side), and perhaps child-minders and foster parents. A typical session will have up to six parents in attendance, with possibly one or two child-minders. Some 30 families are involved in all.

One of the teachers in charge of the centre for pupils with moderate learning difficulties attached great importance to home contact and was extremely active in the local community. Undeterred by criticism that that was to the detriment of his teaching commitment, he believed that he was meeting a genuine need and insisted that the children's problems could not be divorced from their home environment. Referring to an uncontrolled epileptic for whom the school had arranged medication, he remarked, "If we don't do anything about [medication] then it is pointless our trying to educate him." Speaking about the large number of pupils who came from deprived backgrounds he commented, "Where parents have not bothered then we have to ... Where the parent is bothered but inadequate ... then we do a supportive role." His was a more general family support role than that carried out by his colleagues. This role was continued, though somewhat less emphatically, by his successor who believed that her teaching role should be to the fore. She was no less predisposed toward visiting parents but insisted that home visits take place after school and not interfere with teaching time. (The centre was not in fact staffed to allow for home visiting during school hours.)

Summary

This provision catering for sizeable numbers of pupils with moderate *and* severe learning difficulties (and special care pupils) on the campus of an ordinary primary school is virtually unique in Britain. For various reasons the extent of integration has been relatively limited. Indeed, staff have not tended to see their role in integration terms; their function was to provide an appropriate education for the pupils in their charge, and the educational possibilities offered by the proximity to an ordinary school were at best a bonus to be availed of occasionally. The two groups of staff remained quite separate and, in the case of some main school staff, distant, and there was very little in the way of joint planning or teaching activity. Particular achievements of the special centres include the multi-faceted contact with parents, the excellent links with outside agencies and the range of visits and extra-curricular activities arranged for pupils.

Various questions could be considered in relation to future developments. They include:
1. There has been considerable development in thinking on integration since the centres were first planned. Staff may wish to consider whether the time has come to re-examine their goals and modus operandi. Would pupils' needs be better met for instance if the special centres became *functionally* part of the parent school, and there was a more flexible exchange of staff and pupils across all parts of the school? Would it be beneficial if there was a staff appointment with the specific brief of promoting integration?
2. Staff acknowledge the need to revise the curriculum and initiate more systematic means of recording pupils' progress. Will they succeed in these enterprises and, in particular, will they make use of recent developments, especially in the education of those with severe learning difficulties?

3. Would the extent of social interaction between the two groups, and the assimilation of those with learning difficulties into the parent school, be furthered by giving conscious thought to the matter and making planned interventions?

3

Secondary department for pupils with learning difficulties

This special department in a comprehensive school caters for pupils with a range of learning difficulties – mild, moderate and severe. The school is large (1100+), mixed and covers the age range 11–18. It is situated in a small town in a rural area. The department receives pupils from a wider catchment than that of the parent school. We concentrate here on those pupils within the department who had severe learning difficulties.

Historical résumé

The authority in question is predominantly rural, covering a large area, and has developed its provision on an area basis. This has reduced the need for travelling long distances, and in some cases for residential placement as well. A number of 'area units' have been set up. These are special classes or departments based in ordinary schools and providing for specified groups of pupils drawn from throughout the area. The number of pupils in these units varies according to the prevalence of the handicapping condition but would not be sufficient to sustain provision separate from an ordinary school. Some units were set up initially as an alternative to special schools for that reason. This de facto integration led to the developments described here.

The previous chapter described provision within this authority for junior pupils with moderate learning difficulties. By 1970 the first batch of these was reaching the stage where secondary transfer was imminent. Since there was no special school the authority had to make new provision. It was decided to transfer all pupils on to the secondary school to which other pupils in the junior school transferred. (At the time this was an 11–15 junior high school. In 1972 it became an 11–18 comprehensive.)

The head teacher was accordingly approached. He had no objections, seeing little difference between these pupils and pupils of very low ability already in the school. In 1971 the first batch of pupils was transferred. They were incorporated into what was, effectively, a remedial class. They spent much time with remedial teachers, though there were opportunities for taking subjects in mixed ability groupings.

At about this time the authority was faced with a new problem: making educational provision for children and young people with severe learning difficulties. Previously deemed ineducable, these became the responsibility of education authorities in 1971 with the passage of the Education (Handicapped Children) Act 1970. Noting the satisfactory placement of pupils with moderate learning difficulties in ordinary schools at both primary and secondary levels, the LEA was encouraged to make provision for this new group on a similar basis. The secondary school was approached once more to see if it would accept all pupils with learning difficulties no matter how severe (with the exception of those requiring special care). The severely handicapped were, at the time, housed in an all-age junior training centre. It was agreed that those aged 11 and over would come to the secondary school, while those aged under 11 would go to the feeder junior school which already provided for pupils with moderate learning difficulties.

However, the head teacher of the comprehensive regarded this second group of pupils as very different from the first, and felt that they could not be absorbed into the body of the school in the same way as those with moderate learning difficulties had been. He pointed to their untoward patterns of behaviour, "demands for physical contact" and so on which would be unacceptable in the main school and would make their assimilation impossible. He agreed to accept them but on condition that they had their own separate premises. Accordingly, a purpose-built special department was erected close by the existing school building; a short linking corridor was planned but never built. The first pupils with severe learning difficulties arrived in 1974 with the transfer of eight pupils and two teachers, one part-time, from the junior training centre.

Apart from having been consulted by the authority on his willingness to accept severely handicapped pupils, the head teacher had fairly limited contact with the authority. In retrospect, he felt that he would have benefited from "a briefing earlier on with someone who was knowledgeable [about such a novel practice]". At the time he considered "everyone [was] ignorant of what was needed". Some additional resources – both material and human – were provided by the authority, but other than that they had suffered from the general lack of awareness. Attempts were made to combat this from within the school by arranging a series of staff seminars, films and discussions with the existing pupils, meetings with parents and teachers, and preliminary visits to the school by the severely handicapped pupils. The head also visited several special schools in other areas.

There has been steady and considerable development since the early days. All pupils with learning difficulties are now part of a much larger department – the Slow Learner Department – which includes main school remedial pupils and those with specific learning difficulties, as well as those traditionally labelled 'educationally subnormal'. Within this department those with severe learning difficulties are in a somewhat separate position, occupying as they do their own physically distinct premises, unlike the others who are taught in classrooms in the main body of the school. Since the department does not assign pupils to rigidly defined categories and indeed deliberately blurs the distinctions between pupils, it is difficult to specify its clientele in terms of traditional categories. Roughly speaking, in January 1979 there were 13 pupils with severe learning difficulties who might be designated as ESN(S); 67 with moderate learning difficulties who might be designated ESN(M); and some 94 pupils receiving remedial help with English and/or maths. A further very much smaller group of pupils with specific learning difficulties were also receiving attention. This should be seen in the context of a large comprehensive school with over 1100 pupils.

Organisation and aims

The Slow Learner Department is a major department within the school, comprising a Unit for those with severe learning difficulties and special classes for those with moderate difficulties. It also functions as the school's remedial department. It has its own head, who is a senior teacher, and two deputy heads, one of whom is responsible for the Unit.

It may be noted that the department enjoys a higher status than many such departments in secondary schools. This was deliberate policy from the outset: "It is recognised as a major department in the school – a department I put to the fore" (head teacher). Administratively, it is part of the school, but in practice – as with other departments – it enjoys a high degree of autonomy. General guidelines are drawn up through close consultation in the first instance, and thereafter individual heads of departments assume a high degree of responsibility: "I like to know what's going on ... and I like to be involved in the original organisation ... but then I like the staff to work on their own initiative" (head teacher).

The operational aims can be considered at the departmental level or in regard of individual pupils. For the former there are a number of relevant dimensions. One of the most critical is the decision to blur distinctions between different pupil groupings (specific learning difficulties, remedial, moderate and severe learning difficulties). The reality of some differences is not denied – "we are aware that there are differences". The effort, however, is to play down their significance – measured intelligence, for instance, has limited relevance for educational programming – and, more especially, to communicate a view of the department as "a cohesive unit" providing flexibly for a range of pupils. The department has not eliminated these distinctions, particularly where those with severe learning difficulties are concerned; as noted, their education is carried out quite separately. Staff did point to considerable flexibility and crossing of boundaries, however. A number of pupils are in fact placed in quite different teaching groups (eg ESN(M) and remedial) according to their particular ability in different areas of the curriculum. Also, a pupil with marked social and/or emotional problems can be taken into the department for a time to receive specialised support even though there are no particular learning problems.

Secondly, there is an intention that staff should teach across the department as a whole rather than always remaining with a particular group of pupils: "If we are to make integration respectable then ... we have to integrate ourselves [within the department]" (head of department). This proved difficult to put into practice for many years. Not all members of staff were in agreement about its relevance or feasibility given the department's staffing, and it is only in recent years that progress has been made toward this goal.

Thirdly, it is the intention to seek active working links with the main school. This has tended to proceed relatively cautiously, with the emphasis on careful planning and setting up channels of integration which can be pressed into use wherever appropriate. There is no "blanket integration" of pupils with learning difficulties – and indeed very little anyway of those with severe difficulties. A previous head of department described the process in a written document as 'a planned and prepared absorption which recognises at once the need for separately taught skills ... and the possibilities for social mixing and common learning within a structure which does not make impossible emotional demands on the children involved'.

As regards the aims espoused for pupils, the main feature is the emphasis upon promoting social confidence and personal independence. The traditional academic targets are not ignored of course, and specific aims will vary with individual pupils. The 'socially acceptable product' is considered to be as relevant as academic achievement, particularly in the case of those with severe learning difficulties. To this end considerable time and effort go into helping pupils "to be able to hold conversations intelligently ... communicate generally", and to develop relatively 'normal' modes of behaviour so that they will not stand out or be ridiculed.

Pupils

The department provides for all secondary age pupils with learning difficulties within the area, with the exception of those requiring special care who remain at the special centre located in the feeder junior school. Pronounced learning difficulty is the primary criterion for placement, though some pupils with additional handicaps are accepted. Thus, the department has had emotionally disturbed pupils, but does not see itself catering for those whose primary problem is severe emotional disturbance. One such boy had in fact to be excluded eventually; in the interests of the majority it was not possible to give such pupils "the environment they need". The department has also accepted a spastic boy with learning difficulties who was confined to a wheelchair. Because he spent much of his time in a particular suite of rooms the mobility problems were reduced. He did have wider access around the school through the use of light alloy ramps which could be easily laid down and taken up, though it is unlikely that this solution would suffice in any general way.

The department's catchment area is more extensive than that of the parent school, embracing the catchments of a number of other secondary schools as well. At this stage in a pupil's educational career, admission is automatic since pupils transfer up from the junior provision. In addition, the occasional pupil may transfer from some other specialist provision, eg a special school.

Pupils with severe learning difficulties are automatically placed in the Unit. Thereafter, a system of continuous assessment ensures that any necessary adjustment is carried out as and when appropriate. This has happened in at least one case: a boy who started full-time in the Unit was spending half his time in a first year ESN(M) class by the end of the year; after two years he was nearly full-time with this group, and even attended mixed ability classes for art and craft.

Pupils with moderate learning difficulties are initially placed in an ESN(M) class. Continuous assessment again ensures that any necessary re-adjustment can be made – something that is more frequent with these pupils. As a general rule, the size of this group diminishes as they go through the school because of their increasing ability to integrate. All decisions are taken by the head of department in consultation with his staff. The educational psychologist may be involved, particularly in regard to formally reassessing a pupil.

Historically, pupils with severe learning difficulties have gone into Adult Training Centres some time after their sixteenth birthday. However, the department is in the process of developing a specific programme of training for post-school life, designed to facilitate assimilation into the wider community upon leaving school. Pupils can be retained at the school to the age of 19 while they undertake this course. This course is described in more detail below. Through work experience, careers guidance and preparation, it seeks to enhance young people's employment and/or further education possibilities as well as helping them to live as independent adults to the greatest extent possible.

Staffing

There are seven teachers and two ancillaries assigned to the department. Pupils with severe learning difficulties are taught largely by a team of three teachers and one welfare assistant. This area of the department has been fairly self-contained, though two of the three teachers now have other teaching duties, being responsible for a class of pupils with moderate learning difficulties. Only one other teacher has any formal involvement with pupils with severe learning difficulties. This person has registration duties with them and spends 20 per cent of her time teaching them. The remaining staff teach across the department. One of them has a particular responsibility for organising and overseeing the work experience programme.

The role assigned to the two welfare assistants is worth noting. One, a former nurse, works with severely handicapped pupils; her colleague, a trained nursery nurse, is deployed throughout the department. Both find themselves undertaking duties considerably in advance of what would customarily be expected from a classroom ancillary. In one case this arose fortuitously. In the early days there was only one full-time teacher. Whenever she was engaged in other activities, eg receiving a distraught parent or dealing with a crisis, and the part-time teacher was absent as well, then the ancillary found herself having to take charge. Since then she has always been used in a direct teaching way within the classroom – for example, taking small groups for pre-number or pre-reading work – as well as meeting pupils' physical needs.

When her colleague first came to the school, the then teacher in charge set her to work preparing visual aids and other learning resources. He also encouraged her to work with first year moderately handicapped pupils, hearing them read, providing specific skills work to the direction of the class teachers, and so forth. Later she was attached to a first year class for 50 per cent of her time, working to instructions from the teacher and assuming control in her absence. (This particular teacher was responsible for the work experience which meant that she spent each Monday out of school.) A further two periods were spent with a probationary teacher who had no previous experience of pupils with learning difficulties. Finally, six periods per week were taken up with work on pupils' speech. This came about because of an increasing need for help with their speech among pupils which – through pressure on the speech therapist's time – was not being met. Although not having any formal speech therapy qualification, the ancillary has served what, in effect, has been a practical apprenticeship. The speech therapist began by including her in therapy sessions. She would explain what she was doing and why. Later the ancillary took over the sessions, working to the therapist's detailed instructions. The therapist would correct mistakes in a matter-of-fact way, and suggest means of improvement. Although the speech therapist still maintains primary responsibility for diagnosing a pupil's specific therapeutic needs, with time the ancillary has come to contribute to this. The ancillary emphasises that what she does is not confined to speech correction – "there's a lot of other things going on too . . . A lot of it is language development . . . concept stuff . . . not just clear speech". She has been on a number of in-service training courses which have a bearing on this kind of remediation, most particularly a course concerned with a language development scheme that has been developed within the authority.

This degree of collaborative working was comparatively rare in the programmes we studied. A good deal of professional support was available from agencies based in the locality. This had not always been utilised however, and steps were taken in the course of our visits to derive more benefit from this expertise. Hitherto – with the exception of the school medical officer and speech therapist, who had been closely involved all along – involvement of outside professionals had only come about when a particular need arose. For example, the education psychologist only came in on problematic cases; on these he would typically conduct a formal assessment and report verbally to the head of department, giving an indication of the level at which the pupil was functioning and perhaps some general advice on management.

Other outside agencies were involved as necessary. For instance, two pupils were regularly seen by psychiatrists. A field-officer for the mentally handicapped had formal responsibility for pupils with severe learning difficulties. As and when necessary, form tutors liaised directly with this person, and indeed with any individual social worker who became involved with a pupil from the department. However, thoughout much of the duration of our fieldwork there was limited contact for the most part, to a degree the consequence of the head of department's concern that they as educators should develop closer links with pupils' families. Home visits by the head of department and members of his staff (normally the form tutor) were made as necessary. As regards advisory personnel, considerable use has been made of a remedial advisory teacher who can advise on reading matters and has reading resources at her disposal. There has been little contact with the adviser for special education. The senior adviser for special education visits termly but only in a general capacity.

One positive development that occurred during our researching was the holding of termly working lunches attended by a wide range of professionals – psychologists, psychiatrists, area special education adviser, remedial advisory teacher, social worker and representatives from the department. These meetings are envisaged as an opportunity of exchanging ideas on a variety of topics such as work experience, the curriculum for the severely handicapped aged 16+ and parental involvement. Individual pupils who are giving cause for concern may also be discussed, though ordinarily these would come up at a specially convened case conference, involving the educational psychologist and members of staff of the school who have had involvement with the pupil in question.

Accommodation and resources

The purpose-built section of the Slow Learner Department comprises three open-plan work areas, a small library, staffroom, office and toileting facilities. This is where pupils with severe learning difficulties spend most of their time. It is designed to be self-sufficient. The rest of the department incorporates five classrooms located within the main school although fairly adjacent.

With regard to resources, the department is in a very favourable position. The head teacher encourages all heads of departments to ask for whatever they need and strives to meet all reasonable requests. The Slow Learner Department has built up a good stock of specialist learning resources and pieces of equipment, and the head of department has a free hand in renewing or adding to this stock. In addition to tape-recorders, language masters and so on, the department has two colour television sets of its own and is able to utilise the extensive video equipment of the main school.

Curriculum

The various groups of clients served by the department are provided with a curriculum appropriate to their particular needs. For pupils with severe learning difficulties, considerable emphasis is placed on the basic foundations of learning – reading, writing and numeracy. Typically, each morning is given over to formal work, with practical and creative activities in the afternoon. In addition to basic learning there is also an emphasis upon equipping pupils for optimum independence in adult life. This has included exposing them to a variety of real-life situations: using the telephone, borrowing books from the library, obtaining assistance from the emergency services and so forth. The emphasis is upon providing "a mental preparation for leaving" – encouraging self-reliance, developing problem-solving skills, practising making decisions and so on.

For the older pupils, a significant new development was the introduction in autumn 1978 – after several months of planning – of a new programme, the '16+ Programme'. This is a curriculum opportunity for those pupils ages 16+ who it is felt would benefit – socially, emotionally or academically – from an additional two years' schooling. It is in place of the traditional move to an adult training centre (ATC). The programme (outlined in Diagram 1) covers survival and practical skills (eg

Secondary department for pupils with learning difficulties 55

MODEL FOR 16–19 YEAR PROVISION

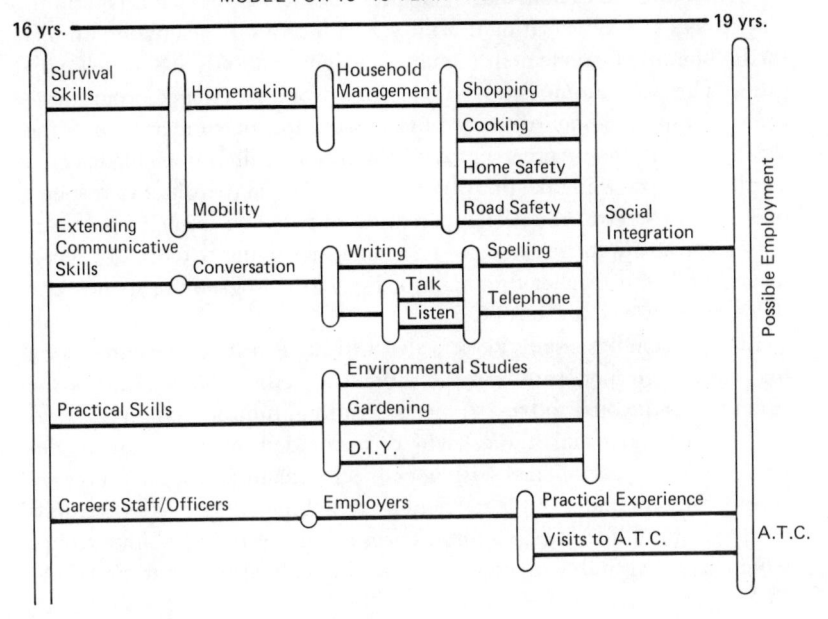

16 yrs. ———————————————————————— 19 yrs.

- Survival Skills — Homemaking — Household Management — Shopping
  - Cooking
  - Home Safety
  - Mobility — Road Safety — Social Integration
- Extending Communicative Skills — Conversation — Writing — Spelling
  - Talk
  - Listen — Telephone
- Practical Skills — Environmental Studies
  - Gardening
  - D.I.Y.
- Careers Staff/Officers — Employers — Practical Experience
  - Visits to A.T.C.

Possible Employment

A.T.C.

home-making, household management, mobility) and extends communication skills – conversational ability, writing, use of telephone and so forth. The practical element includes gardening and do-it-yourself activities. The programme is linked both to a work experience programme offered in main school (discussed below) and to work undertaken in the local ATC. While involvement with the former will only be for selected pupils, all those who take this programme will from their first year spend one day per week at the ATC, increasing to two days in their final year. To ease transition, but also to assist in introducing a more academic orientation, the teacher organiser of the 16+ programme spends one half-day per week at the ATC.

Emphasis on basic skills work is also a strong feature of the curriculum for pupils with moderate learning difficulties. About 50 per cent of the timetable is devoted to basic subjects (reading, number, language, cognitive skills and social studies) which is provided by staff from the department in a special class setting. Subject specialists from main school supply the remainder of the curriculum, teaching either classes of pupils with learning difficulties (eg for science, music) or mixed ability groups which contain pupils with moderate learning difficulties (eg art and craft, PE).

For remedial pupils or the pupil with a specific learning difficulty the specialised attention forthcoming from the department is more particularised. Remedial pupils, for example, receive additional help with their maths and/or English; pupils who experience difficulty in writing attend a handwriting clinic which is convened once weekly over a term, and so forth. The department also serves as a temporary sanctuary for disruptive pupils and school phobics.

During the course of our research a major attempt was made to revise the overall curriculum of the department. The impetus for this stemmed largely from the head of department who took over in 1977. He perceived a need to introduce a more systematised teaching approach, with individual members of staff working less in isolation and more as a team. Recent developments in thinking on how to go about educating the slow learning pupil were also influential – most particularly, the need for a structured teaching approach based upon specified short-term objectives. All members of staff of the department were involved, each being assigned a specific task to be undertaken in conjunction with one or more colleagues. The intention was to break down the various areas of the curriculum – notably, language, reading, number, social studies and practical social skills – into finely graded component parts. Each working party would report back to the group as a whole on what it had achieved. In point of fact this exercise – conducted in teachers' own time with formal review meetings held weekly – ran for several months before being abandoned. There was a feeling that the returns had been rather limited in relation to the effort expended.

Preparation for adult life

A particular aspect of the department's curriculum is its preparation for adult living. All fourth and fifth year pupils in the school, including those with moderate learning difficulties (but not those with severe learning difficulties who follow the 16+ programme described above) take a course entitled Education for Personal Relationships, as well as receiving some specific careers preparation. The former is directed specifically at adolescence and covers a wide variety of topics:

1. Making friends
2. Boy/girl relationships
3. Sexual relationships
4. Courtship, marriage and family
5. Development of the moral sense
6. Good manners – respect for other people and their ideas
7. Class and racial discrimination
8. Freedom
9. Leisure
10. Transition to outside world.
11. Provisions within the community.

This course seeks to help the growing adolescent to form relationships with others, bridge the gap between school and the outside world, and in general become a responsible adult. It is timetabled for two periods a week and is well supported with written and broadcast resource material.

Careers preparation provides information and guidance on the different forms of employment, and gives an indication of what might be a realistic choice of job and the skills involved in obtaining and holding down a job. The course content is the same for pupils with moderate learning difficulties as it is for their peers in main school, although adapted to their capabilities and specific needs as necessary.

A particular aspect of the preparation for post-school life carried out with pupils with moderate learning difficulties and other less able pupils is a work experience programme. This was organised initially on a one-day-a-week basis. Each participant spent one full day per week over a 10-week period in a working context. There are three different work placements over the year – "a job of their choice, one of my choice, and one agreed choice" (teacher organiser). More recently, the programme has been restructured to allow for a block period at work during one of the placements. Each session comprises: a preparation period; a day at the particular workplace for five consecutive weeks; and a full week at work. Throughout there are specific follow-up activities back in school. The purpose is to provide experience of different working environments – to "show them the range of work they can do . . . what working is like". There is no intention of obtaining employment, although offers of work sometimes arise incidentally. Considerable emphasis is placed upon the socialising aspects and developing personal relationships. It is possible for pupils on work experience to go on to a link course provided at a nearby technical college.

Though the programme was devised initially for pupils with moderate learning difficulties, it was being offered to those pupils with severe learning difficulties who were judged likely to benefit from it. To date two such pupils have been included in the programme, with considerable success. One boy received an offer of employment, while the second went on to a link course at a nearby technical college. Two further pupils have now been included in the programme, which has been adapted somewhat to meet their needs. Given the emphasis in their case on mobility and social training, each pupil attends the workplace for mornings only for five weeks. At the end of this period, if their work rate has been satisfactory, they attend for one full day per week.

After the first 10-week session the teacher organiser invited the six employers involved (the number of firms was later to increase to 12) to lunch, together with the careers officer, and representatives of the school. In fact three sets of employers attended. They raised two particular issues: first, they wanted such meetings *before* pupils came to them so that they would be more aware of pupils' difficulties; and secondly, they asked if pupils could attend for a block of time so that they might see different aspects of a particular job. The latter request presented the organiser with something of a dilemma. Under the existing arrangement participants met up the following day to talk about what they had done – "a collective experience". It also allowed of any specific follow-up that was necessary – resolving problems that had arisen, reinforcing particular areas of need and so forth. However, she agreed to explore the possibility of a more sustained period of work on one of the two remaining work experience sessions.

Monitoring progress

A formal annual screening is undertaken which draws upon Tansley's (1967) general work in the field of remedial reading and, more specifically, on reading and assessment materials prepared by Jackson (1971) and Neale (1958). Otherwise, subjective impressions are documented – no useful purpose is seen to be served by "testing for testing's sake". All assessment is internal; and the psychologist is only called in on problematic cases. The official records are not particularly extensive, in part a reflection of the fact that the psychologist, when involved, only gives verbal reports. There is the intention that the curriculum revision when completed will have assessment procedures built into it. While this remains unfinished, however, the emphasis is on the individual teacher's own appraisal, supplemented by observations from departmental colleagues.

Academic integration

A wide range of possibilities exist to be availed of depending upon individual strengths and weaknesses. Thus, remedial pupils are based in main school and withdrawn for specific remediation (either in specific class groups for English and/or maths or in the lowest sets). Pupils with more marked learning difficulties are in particular class groupings for a substantial part of their timetable, ranging from 25 periods (out of 40) within the department in the first year to around 18 periods in the fifth year. The extent of time integrated into main school thus increases with age. Integration is either as a class group for music and science – taken by a subject specialist – or in mixed ability classes for craft and games. While these pupils are with subject specialists, the remedial pupils avail of teaching facilities within the department. Pupils with severe learning difficulties remain for the most part within the purpose-built premises. Those considered socially and emotionally capable can join their peers in main school. PE is one subject where a degree of functional integration has existed in the past.

An issue that is highly germane to this particular location concerns how subject specialists cope with teaching pupils with moderate learning difficulties. Our enquiries revealed a remarkable degree of willingness for such involvement. The consensus was that good organisation, backed by liaison with members of staff from the department as necessary, was sufficient for the ordinary teacher to be able to cope. It was imperative that work be pitched at the correct level so that all pupils could succeed. Practical activities such as art and craft were considered to enjoy an advantage over more theoretical subjects, in that a task could easily be set which all could do but to differing standards. One of the greatest areas of difficulty concerned work rate. Pupils with moderate learning difficulties had to have work they could do, otherwise there were endless demands for attention, such that, as one teacher pointed out, "It's the high flyers that suffer in teachers' time spent with them." An art teacher who noted the same tendency of stopping after each stage and awaiting further guidance suggested that pupils needed "two bites at the cherry", and argued that a double period of art in a mixed ability setting ought to be followed by an additional period in a small group (of pupils with similar ability) where specific reinforcement work could be done. In certain subjects (notably science, but craft too depending upon the particular activity) the possibility of physical danger may pose problems. One science teacher, who believed in an element of calculated risk – "I don't really think there is any point in removing the danger completely" – spoke of how he was constantly "making a big fuss out of clumsiness".

There was widespread agreement on the need to talk more about tasks set, making sure pupils fully understood what they had to do. Emphasis was placed upon getting pupils directly involved in some activity rather than giving them lots of factual information. Theory was deliberately kept to a minimum. Some teachers pointed out that they did not expect any written work from these pupils. All were agreed that close attention needed to be paid to their work – "I would expect to see everybody every two minutes" was one teacher's comment – something that could present considerable practical difficulties in a class of 18 or more pupils.

What value were pupils deriving from these opportunities? "I have had to expect less and less of them . . . I realised it was more and more hopeless to expect any kind of scientific understanding" was one science teacher's reaction. He had learned through experience what it was appropriate to emphasise: "[Pupils] will enjoy themselves – they are getting the feeling that they are getting some science . . . It's new experiences . . . new vocabulary, a lot of drawing and writing practice, *related to something they have actually done* . . ." In addition, there was the opportunity for learning how to establish working relations with other pupils – in woodwork for example, "he does the bits he can do and learns to cooperate with other children".

Social development

While there are opportunities for functional integration which some pupils from the department are able to capitalise upon, it is the social benefit that is more generally realised. Clearly, this is closely related to the opportunities for interaction that exist. How then do the various groups of pupils fare in this respect?

Pupils with severe learning difficulties, though more or less full-time in the purpose-built premises, nevertheless know their way around the school and make use of its facilities. They attend lower school assembly twice weekly, and dine in main school on a daily basis. They use the school's swimming pool under the supervision of sixth formers. Those of fourth year and above participate in the youth club activities open to senior pupils in the youth wing each lunchtime (five pupils take advantage of this on a fairly regular basis). At play and lunchtime, while they may join other pupils, the majority spend their time in a self-contained play area which is out of bounds to pupils from main school. An element of contact from *within* occurs through pupils from main school coming into the premises either on a formal basis, as part of a community service course, or less formally to offer general assistance with craft activities, hearing pupils read and so on.

Other pupils in the department spend considerably more time among the main body of pupils of the school, and are claimed by staff to be largely indistinguishable from their peers. When we ourselves sat in on lessons we had difficulty in differentiating them from the main body of pupils. However, there were various indications that pupils from the main school had no such difficulty – "the other kids seem to know" was the verdict of one teacher from the department. There were various signs – "they are not confident . . . are very socially immature, it is always the remedial K. is and the M's that socialise . . . They like to help the caretaker, like to feel they are needed." There were various references to the 'Mong Wing', that area of the school used extensively by pupils with moderate learning difficulties. We heard of older pupils from main school who, when coming for remedial help, would wait until the corridors had cleared at change of lesson before approaching these classrooms, and how they "hated the lower chairs and that smell of infant schools".

Nevertheless, these pupils, especially those with severe learning difficulties, are benefiting from being surrounded by normal modes of behaviour. Their teacher in charge declared that "they are much more confident in themselves, much calmer, not as aggressive... We don't get this artificial shyness." The benefits were claimed to extend beyond the department's pupils to the pupil body as a whole where a more tolerant attitude was found to prevail. One teacher's observation echoes comments by several colleagues: 'There is no proof – but one feels that their presence... helps to develop and sustain the generally caring attitude found in this school – the attitude of the majority of pupils towards any pupils found to be in a minority situation.'

We talked with a number of pupils from main school who had specific involvement with pupils from the department. What were their perceptions of how these were viewed by the school as whole? "A lot of the people try to ignore them." "There's just not enough people interested." These were two comments, referring particularly to those with severe learning difficulties. The impression conveyed was that there were no particular strong feelings against – or for – the department's pupils. There was a certain pride in the realisation that "our school is one in a hundred" (in having these pupils); there was a good level of tolerance, and as a group the special pupils were an accepted part of the school. Contact between individuals was limited, however, and close friendships that crossed the department's boundaries were the exception rather than the rule.

We heard of only occasional instances of teasing. There had been one serious incident when a group of severely handicapped pupils were physically attacked in the playground, but staff insisted that this was a very isolated occurrence. This view was corroborated by a pupil from main school who pointed out that it was only the new arrivals at the school who took undue notice of them. Though this could on occasion be excessive – "They crowd round them and shout out, 'Look at those Mongs.' Some of them hit 'em, sometimes they get them to fight among themselves" – they soon got the message that this kind of behaviour was not acceptable and they quickly acquired the prevailing tolerance.

Parents

Parents are welcome to visit school whenever they feel the need. This is in addition to the customary open evenings. The head of department is increasing the amount of contact with parents, making home visits in some cases. Contact is largely for the purpose of gathering or disseminating information. Parents are not involved in the education of their children, whether through systematic reinforcement of school work or otherwise.

We interviewed two sets of parents whose children had severe learning difficulties. Both commented positively, emphasising the progress their child had made. One father had noticed a marked improvement in his son's arithmetic, reading and writing, particularly in comparison to his achievement as a junior school pupil. The mother of the second felt that being in a more 'normal' environment had definitely benefited her daughter – particularly as regards her speech. They also noted greater competence and independence – "She cooks, makes tea, does lovely woodwork which at one time we couldn't imagine [her ever] doing." Both sets of parents were highly satisfied with the assistance that had been forthcoming from school: 'Very satisfied, no complaints"... "We've been very fortunate that they're here". Both noted how they were always made to feel welcome whenever the need to contact the school authorities arose.

Summary

This secondary school is virtually unique in England and Wales in attempting to educate pupils with the full range of learning difficulties, even of the severest kind, in an ordinary school. The Slow Learner Department, which is responsible for them, has become a major department within the school. The curriculum offerings of the department are highly differentiated according to individual need. Pupils receive a good grounding in basic skills and in some cases have access to a wide range of curriculum opportunities in the main school. Curriculum development has been an explicit concern of the department, though – with the exception of the 16+ programme and the excellent work experience programme – progress has been limited. There is a fair amount of integrated teaching; main school staff are positively disposed toward this, though some would like more guidance and support. Social interaction between pupils with learning difficulties and their peers is unproblematic if limited in extent. It may be noted that the present level of operations has been reached without a great deal of help from outside agencies. There has been contact with the latter, increasingly so in recent years, but the dynamic for the development has come throughout from the department and its staff.

Various questions may be noted for the future:

1. Will the work experience programme be able to cope with greater numbers and in an increasingly difficult employment situation? Will it be able to build on its initial successes with pupils with severe learning difficulties and extend its opportunities to others?
2. In view of the concerns expressed about the basic curriculum within the department and the availability of specific teaching skills outside it, will it be possible to tackle the whole question of the curriculum for pupils with learning difficulties in a concerted way and work out a common philosophy and common strategies across the school as a whole?
3. Are staff satisfied with current means of monitoring progress, or is there need of a more systematic approach, perhaps related to more precisely stated teaching objectives?

4
Special provision for children with severe learning difficulties

This is an account of one LEA's approach to making suitable educational provision for nursery and infant age children with severe learning difficulties. Unusually, the LEA opted for special class rather than special school provision, and during the early 1970s five special classes were opened in four ordinary primary schools.

Historical résumé

Under the Education (Handicapped Children) Act 1970 responsibility for the severely mentally retarded child passed from Health to Education. Education authorities were required to provide facilities for the education of these children over the age of three who had previously been deemed ineducable. This particular authority, seeking to discharge its newly enjoined statutory duty, was influenced in its thinking by various factors, among them: a shortage of existing places; the concern that Education should pursue a specifically educational approach with these children, rather than importing from Health an approach with little educational reference; pressure brought to bear from the local Society for Mentally Handicapped Children who called for an expansion of the opportunities for education within ordinary schools; and the example of existing provision within the authority. It was claimed that the Brooklands experiment (Tizard, 1964) was a potent factor: parents 'wished their children between the ages of three and eight to be provided with the rich environment and the stimulating experience of the kind provided . . . in Brooklands' (assistant education officer). (Brooklands was an experimental practice which ran for two years in the late 1950s. In essence, it was an attempt to apply to severely mentally and perhaps physically handicapped children in residential care 'the principles of child care that are regarded as meeting the needs of normal children', rather than perpetuating the traditional largely custodial approach. Thus, staff paid direct attention to speech and play activities as well as dealing with incontinence, promoting independence and modifying disobedient or anti-social behaviour.)

A particularly decisive influence was the fact that an appropriate model already existed within the authority. This was the infant Opportunity Class, which had been in operation for over eight years and was well proven. This provision was developed for hyperkinetic, disturbed and backward children aged five to seven. It was conceived as an extension of day ESN provision (this commenced at age seven) but with one critical difference: the facility for extended assessment – a period of time when teachers could carry out sustained observation within an educational setting, thereby arriving at a much better understanding of a child's problems. By 1971 there were five of these classes providing for some 50 pupils. A further model came from the workings of a diagnostic and assessment class attached to an ESN(M) school. This class took in and provided education for children who would otherwise have been deemed ineducable. (Some though not all of these did in fact transfer to junior training centres at age seven.)

These provisions served as a prototype, as it were, when children with severe learning difficulties had to be catered for. The first classes were opened in 1971, two attached to infant schools and a third to a primary school which already contained an opportunity class. A further two classes, in separate schools, opened in 1973. These classes were located in schools chosen for particular advantages. Thus, the first school selected had suitable classroom space in an attractive setting, and a recently appointed head teacher who was extremely enthusiastic about the venture. An added advantage was the base of the school psychological service close by. Other schools selected were noted for their good infant practice and had some spare space. A factor that has significant implications for integration is that none of the schools has a nursery department so that three and four year olds in the special classes are without age peers. (Nursery provision within the authority is limited; only three schools in total have nursery classes attached to them.)

Aims and organisation

The purpose of the provision – beyond meeting the LEA's statutory duties – is to provide the early stimulation that is so important for the severely retarded child. The classes seek to provide this stimulation in a structured and professional way. This is tied into a long-term assessment function. Rather than submitting young children to a once-for-all – and probably static – psychological assessment and deciding on special school placement on the basis of it, any such decision is postponed until the age of seven or eight. By then the child will have had the chance to demonstrate his or her capability and to benefit from specialised teaching, and the decision arrived at will reflect the detailed knowledge of the child and his or her working that the teacher will have built up.

Under this provision teachers seek to make available an education appropriate to the special needs of children with severe learning difficulties within the context of the ordinary school. A general aim is to treat them like other children as far as possible. The individual learning approach arises directly from the child's developmental level, which itself is arrived at through a mixture of general observation, setting specific tasks and seeing how the child manages them, some specialised assessment, and discussion between teacher and educational psychologist. Good infant practice is considered to be at the root – there is little or nothing of the tightly structured behaviourist approach pursued by some special schools with this type of child.

Administratively, all five classes are subsumed under the parent school, though in practice each enjoys considerable autonomy. The classes are staffed generously: each has a teacher in charge and two welfare assistants to a maximum of 10 pupils. (In one case an assistant is shared with the opportunity class.) In addition, a relief teacher is available for two sessions per week (equivalent to one full day) in order to release the person in charge from her teaching duties. Such a favourable staffing complement facilitates the highly individualised approach which is followed. It also encourages flexibility in teaching and makes integration possible. Should a child demonstrate a capacity to benefit from being with ordinary children for some activities, then he or she can be accompanied into the regular classroom by an adult.

A further level of flexibility is available in one school which has an opportunity class as well. In some ways this represents an intermediate point between the special class and ordinary classes, and it greatly expands the possibilities of exchange and movement out of the special class. Unfortunately this arrangement only obtained in one school.

It may be noted that because of the organisational arrangements teachers are relatively isolated. There is little professional exchange with colleagues in the parent schools since the nature of their work is so different, and opportunities for professional development through regular contact with colleagues are non-existent. There is a valuable programme of in-service training, as described below, but this cannot make up for the isolation imposed by the organisational format.

Pupils

The intention is that this provision should serve all children within the authority aged three to eight years who have severe learning difficulties. Although many will have additional handicapping conditions the learning problem should be the *principal* difficulty. The paucity of pre-school provision in this LEA should be noted, however; also the fact that opportunity classes do not accept children under the age of five. These two facts, together with a third feature, viz that there is no formal admissions policy – admissions criteria "have not been established as such" (psychologist) – mean that in practice the classes cater for a diverse group of children. Officially, children are placed for "psychometric reasons or developmental delay", but there have been instances of the classes being used to house children for whom no other provision was available even though they were not well suited to meeting their needs.

While the range of handicapping conditions varies from year to year, the majority have Down's Syndrome or have been diagnosed as 'brain damaged'. Many have slight to moderate additional handicaps. The only type of child likely to be excluded is the severely multiply handicapped child who is not mobile. (These normally attend either a residential or a day hospital school, or special care units attached to two ESN(S) schools within the authority.) Some classes contain several disturbed children or children with marked language problems. While there was some question about the capacity of staff to deal with such pupils, it was felt that it was "reasonable to expect staff to cope up to a certain level" (psychologist), aided perhaps by specialist expertise from outside agencies.

Many children who come into this provision will have been known to the educational authorities for some time through attending a playgroup for the mentally handicapped. Placement depends largely on the recommendation of the school psychological service and Area Health. The assistant education officer (special education) "always retained [the right to] the ultimate decision", having considered "the advice of the psychology service". This right is justified on administrative grounds – eg the practicalities of transportation, the composition of the class. Sometimes the process is short-circuited where there has been medical notification of a Down's Syndrome infant: "I wouldn't delay the admission of a child if I hadn't got [a psychologist's report] . . . if he was SSN" (assistant education officer). School staff are not consulted about the children to be placed in their classes, though in recent years they usually see them before admission.

Various developments are possible after the child has spent a period of time in the special class. Very occasionally a child will make such exceptional progress that he or she can be transferred out of the special class. The system of continuous monitoring in practice makes this possible. This occurred in two cases at one school, the children concerned transferring gradually into a main school class. One of these was a girl who moved into main school infants. She was described by her former teacher as "not the slowest in class"; socially she was "no problem". More typically, however, children will be retained until after their seventh birthday, and their current circumstances fully appraised at that stage. The admissions panel – which is also responsible for determining the forward placement – has four options to choose from: day ESN(S) school (there are two of these); day ESN(M) school (there are three of these); an appropriate residential placement; or a private school of some description (eg Rudolf Steiner). (When these classes first opened, the possibility of similar provision at junior level was not ruled out but rather deferred until some working experience had been obtained: 'We are working near the limits of our knowledge and experience and do not wish to prepare for junior classes for a little longer.' In the event, it seems unlikely that junior classes will materialise.) The procedure followed is for the teacher to complete an SE form on each leaver, commenting upon educational progress made in the areas of reading, writing, number, creative and physical skills and play activities. An educational psychologist will then carry out a detailed assessment prior to discussing the case with the principal psychologist. Rating profiles completed twice yearly by teachers are a further source of information. There follows the panel meeting, attended by educational psychologists, representatives of Area Health and Social Services, a representative of the LEA administration, and the heads and class teachers of the children being considered, should they so desire. Although the child's case may well be discussed, in many instances the actual placement has effectively been decided in discussions held prior to the meeting. The case conference functions as a forum for true decision-making only where a child's circumstances are particularly problematic.

It became evident to us that there were tensions underlying these decision-making processes. It was apparent that psychologists' and medical officers' reports carried more weight than those of teachers – even though the latter have a more detailed knowledge of any child as a result of their close working involvement. Some teachers were dissatisfied at this and felt that their professional knowledge was being undervalued. Some commented critically about other professionals "who feel prepared to comment on a child that they know very little about". As against this, there was a view from one head teacher who noted that "teachers . . . are not as objective in their assessment as outside professionals, as they [teachers] know the child and have seen the changes". Some psychologists felt that teachers were at risk of becoming "too emotionally involved" with their children and overestimating their capabilities. While teachers might be subject to limitations and biases in their observations, the principal educational psychologist noted, however, that 'both parents and teachers knew the children more intimately than the educational psychologists could ever hope to, had greater opportunity for prolonged observation over a longer period of time and could describe the children in great detail'.

Staffing

The first point to make is to reiterate the very generous staffing ratios which apply across these classes (teacher in charge and two welfare assistants, all full-time, to 10 pupils). Additionally, a part-time relief teacher visits four of the five classes for the equivalent of one day a week, thereby releasing the class teacher for other duties, eg preparing learning materials, undertaking home visits and – occasionally – teaching in main school. Both this and the favourable staffing ratio are the outcome of early planning on the part of the assistant education officer. He was concerned that staff should not become too bound up with handicapped children: "I don't want these teachers losing contact with normal children."

When the classes were first developed there was little or no concern to appoint staff with previous special education experience – indeed quite the reverse. The dedicated special educator was at risk of using school "as a substitute for life". The emphasis instead was on acquiring experienced nursery and infant teachers, people with "a rich and rewarding life outside school", who were "warm and outgoing, able to work with two others in a small group", and not likely to be put off "by the sheer messiness of the job". The lack of specialist training was not considered a serious drawback, as it was believed that any necessary training could be provided once in post.

The staff appointed display considerable variation in their respective backgrounds. Two of the five had in fact taken the NAMH Diploma, a specialist diploma in the education of the mentally handicapped. (This is no longer available.) Both had worked in junior training centres prior to their appointment. The other three teachers had all had ordinary teacher training. Two were infant trained, the third junior – though she had had considerable teaching experience with infants. Two of the three had no previous contact with handicapped children.

There are 10 welfare assistants working in these classes, mostly on a full-time basis. Three are NNEB trained while a fourth started the course but did not complete it. Another is a qualified primary teacher who was unable to obtain a teaching post. The remaining ancillaries are either SRN or Norland trained or had worked in a voluntary capacity in special playgroups.

The teachers in these classes are appointed to a Scale II post in the first instance and may well be promoted within a year or so. The assistant education officer seeks to arrange a Scale III position "as soon as they have shown they can do the job". There has been concern throughout about the career implications for the teachers of taking charge of special classes which might keep them outside the mainstream of education, and efforts have been made to guarantee promotion prospects for them. (Indeed, two teachers from the classes have moved on to senior posts within ordinary schools.) Related to this is the encouragement given staff to go on courses – not necessarily restricted to special education.

A particular training initiative in this authority is the in-service programme provided for *all* staff working with pupils who have marked learning difficulties in special classes and schools within the authority. This training is organised by the principal educational psychologist through the school psychological service. On one day each term all special classes are closed for this purpose. This facilitates the attendance of class teachers and ancillary staff. Heads of schools which house special classes are also invited, as are members of the various medical and paramedical support agencies. Usually the day is organised around a central theme with outside speakers being brought in to present relevant matter. A wide range of topics has been covered, some of them stemming from direct requests by the teachers. They include: the nature and availability of support services; teaching early language, communication and attention skills; the various dimensions of parent/teacher involvement; developing the concept of number; problems of diet and feeding; the Portage approach to service delivery; use of drama techniques to explore different facets of group relations and group work; causes of retardation; and monitoring systems in special education.

The primary aim of this programme is its professional content, but there is also the valuable opportunity it affords practitioners to meet colleagues from outside their schools. (Teachers repeatedly stated that they felt isolated, with no-one else on the staff sharing the same concerns or even appreciating what these were – "The things that make me excited or depressed don't mean anything to the other teachers".) Setting up and maintaining this programme has been a major achievement – and there was general endorsement of it – but there were some difficulties. Some teachers felt that the balance between formal presentation and informal discussion was tilted too much toward the former. They greatly appreciated the chance to exchange notes with a colleague or colleagues from other classes but sometimes had no time to do so in a tightly structured training day. Another difficulty stemmed from the inclusion of ancillaries. While commendable in many ways, this did make for difficulties in finding a common base for discussion in view of the diversity of professional background and theoretical understanding. It was felt that on at least some occasions it would be more productive if the two groups were organised separately. Also, there were certain critical areas of special class practice (eg the importance of structured play, knowing how to handle disturbed behaviour) which had not been covered in the training which some classroom ancillaries had had, and there was need of specific instruction for them.

In addition to these termly training days, various other in-service activities are organised. These include a voluntary course of 13 seminars held after school ($1\frac{1}{2}$–2 hours' duration), covering aspects of the education of children with severe learning difficulties. It may be noted that some staff are assiduous in seeking out and attending short courses to further their professional development.

As regards the role undertaken by welfare assistants, their primary responsibility is for the general welfare of the children, toileting and feeding in particular. They are not restricted to this, however, and work closely with the class teacher in group activities. Indeed, many of the teachers set work which the assistants supervised while they provided one-to-one tuition. Assistants also undertook specific duties such as hearing children read or assisting with writing practice. Whenever children go into an ordinary class they are accompanied by an assistant. The importance of ensuring that ordinary teachers did not feel imposed upon was recognised – 'I believe that infant teachers cannot be expected to take on this extra responsibility without additional help' (AEO). However, it is not the intention that they should provide full-time support for the integrating pupils; rather, the ancillary should keep an eye on how they are managing and ensure that they are gainfully occupied, but strive also to be of general assistance to ordinary pupils.

Contact with outside agencies has been relatively limited, due in large measure to staff shortages. The main agency involved is the school psychological service. This service has been overburdened – four psychologists (later increased to five) for a school population of around 49 000. As a result, contact with the special classes was limited for much of the duration of our fieldwork. This improved later and in several of the classes psychologists were visiting every two or three weeks.

The psychologists had traditionally seen their work in terms of individual casework and in-service training. As noted, the latter was accorded high priority and involved regular joint activity. The amount of individual casework done was quite limited. As psychologists became involved more closely, they spent time observing children, talking to teachers and counselling parents. They made little direct input to the curriculum, even though this was an area where teachers felt they could benefit from more explicit advice and guidance. The one exception was behavioural disturbance where psychologists sought to provide help so that teachers were not prevented from teaching.

Another agency with a fair amount of contact was speech therapy. The frequency of visits varied considerably from class to class – from fortnightly to every three to four weeks. However, only one teacher stated that the frequency of visits was very unsatisfactory – in a class which a therapist visited on four afternoons per term: "We really need them every week." There would appear to be quite reasonable collaboration between therapists and staff for the most part. In one class the therapist did tend to work with children on her own, but in the others there was mention of exercises and special programmes of work being devised by the therapists; these would be given to teachers and ancillaries along with advice as to how they should be put into practice on a regular basis.

The involvement of a physiotherapist was mentioned by two teachers. In one case visits concerned a particular child whose physical condition had been appraised and a series of exercises devised for the welfare assistant to carry out on a regular basis. In the other, although again only one child had been involved, the class teacher felt that many more pupils who faced considerable difficulties with co-ordination could perhaps have benefited.

Apart from the school psychological service, there is no source of specialist educational advice in this authority. There is nobody with the relevant expertise in the advisory service, and no effort has been made to draw on the experience of staff in the special schools. The assistant education officer who was involved in setting up the classes and has administrative responsibility for them is responsible for primary as well as special education.

From the medical perspective, circumstances seem satisfactory for the most part, though there was a complaint from staff at one school that medical practitioners were unwilling to provide details of children's physical conditions. (Since then a system has been initiated whereby a school can obtain on request a card listing essential medical information on a given pupil.) At most classes the school medical officer visits twice termly and on request. Several classes have had contact with specialist centres outside the authority. In one instance a hospital-based physiotherapist had followed up one of his patients and given useful advice on physical handling and exercises. In another example there had been contact with a specialist assessment centre, while experts in behaviour modification had visited from the Hilda Lewis Centre to advise on the management of children with severe behaviour problems.

Finally, it may be noted that there was little interdisciplinary working on the part of the professionals involved. Although the services of a range of professionals are available, it would seem that as far as these special classes are concerned the agencies operate independently of each other. There is some informal contact relating largely to passing on information or administrative matters but little working involvement focussed on individual children.

Accommodation and resources

In every case the special class occupies an existing structure, and in most instances the degree of adaptation necessary was fairly minimal. Instances of modifications carried out included: withdrawal area for individual attention; appropriate toileting and installation of sluices; and access to a covered patio and garden area. Attention was also given to ensuring that part of each classroom reflected a homely atmosphere by being equipped with curtains, carpets and so on. Though for the most part the quality of accommodation was quite acceptable, there were problems in one school where two classes had been housed in huts which the head teacher regarded as sub-standard; the roof of one of these was later to cave in, making it necessary for the classes to double-up on accommodation for a period of three years.

The location of the special classes in their parent schools was quite another matter. While in one case the class occupied an extremely central position – opening onto the dining area and with head teacher's office and staffroom close by – in other instances classes were on the periphery of the school, if not actually separate from it. Though one teacher was unperturbed by this – "Some people feel we are rather tucked away but I prefer it, it's quieter and [children] are not so likely to be knocked down when going to the toilet" – the consensus was that it was a considerable drawback. In one location, for example, it meant there was quite a journey between the special class and the reception class in main school. This tended to rule out spontaneous and short-term association between the two groups. In another case the physically separate nature of the hut was seen to hinder free movement of both staff and children in inclement weather, while staff tended to remain within the hut rather than going into the main staffroom.

There is also the question of resources to consider. Most classes were quite well resourced. A wide variety of equipment and materials for play was considered essential – large mobile toys, Wendy House furniture – as well as specifically educational resources – art and craft materials, books, language masters, puzzles and small table apparatus. The authority was considered to have been quite generous both in their initial outlay and in the subsequent capitation allowance for books, stationery and equipment. The latter stands at twice that of the ordinary infant child and is subsumed within the overall budget of the school. However, even though each class had access to the resources of the parent school the money available, although sufficient for classroom consumables, did not extend to covering larger items of equipment such as language masters, television sets or tricycles. One school engaged in fund-raising, though with reservations: "You must be very careful when using these children for fund-raising" (head teacher). The problem was one of finding a balance between excessive sentimentalising and ensuring that adequate facilities were available.

Curriculum

As stated earlier, the guiding idea behind the curriculum adopted by these special classes is an enriched version of nursery and infant teaching practice: an abundance of learning resources, a stimulating learning environment, and the ready availability of individualised attention – both in relation to children's general difficulties in learning, and with regard to specific difficulties (eg developing speech and language).

Teachers aim to cover the basics – reading, writing, number and language – every day with each child. Other activities such as painting, shop, and playing with large, wheeled toys take place twice weekly. Reading begins with the children's own names, progressing to matching words using flash cards. Children may produce their own books, the teacher or ancillary writing a sentence which the child has to copy and make a suitable drawing. Number work begins with counting objects, recognising numbers, using songs and finger plays. Children also learn to sort, count and recognise numbers. Language work is particularly emphasised. It is strongly individualised, with children encouraged to name objects by pointing to them and saying the appropriate word. Teachers do not have recourse to any of the specialised language schemes that are now available (eg Peabody Language Development Kit, Distar Language).

Decisions about the curriculum rest in all cases with the teacher in charge, although there may be consultation with classroom ancillaries. Given that the teacher is answerable ultimately to the head of the school, the latter will be kept informed of what is going on; there may even be joint discussion between the two. Nevertheless, the special classes probably enjoy more autonomy than any other class in the schools. As one teacher in charge stated: "Other classes work to the same basic schemes of work and curriculum but the [special class] has independence in deciding and planning work for individual children."

One might ask in what respects the curriculum these children receive differs from that provided for the ordinary child. Any differences are not so much a matter of content as of where emphasis is placed, together with the actual delivery of the content. The importance attached to developing language and understanding has already been mentioned. Certain children receive individual speech programmes prepared by a visiting speech therapist. Another aspect that is strongly emphasised is music and movement, provided by a peripatetic teacher who is herself the mother of a Down's Syndrome child.

Naturally, all teaching is presented at a slower pace, and with a premium on varied repetition. In addition, learning needs to be planned much more than for the ordinary pupil. Each teacher will typically draw up termly aims for every child in each of the following areas: self-management; pre-number; pre-reading; speech and language; constructive and creative. Also, opportunities for teaching extend beyond the customary classroom activities. For instance, toileting sessions can be capitalised upon for the purpose of teaching the various parts of the body; lunchtime is an opportunity for teaching socially acceptable eating habits. A lot of time needs to be spent with these children, and teachers need to be aware of the very fine discriminations that must be made. Also, the teacher needs to have a great deal of patience, since progress in most cases is extremely slow. As one person involved observed: "Teachers who like to depend on results might get a bit frustrated because the results take so long to come. You've got to be satisfied that you're doing the right thing yourself without getting the results, until eventually you do." The importance of close supervision – which the generous staffing affords – was strongly emphasised. As the infant adviser wrote, 'It is not enough to provide and encourage participation in [for example] play situations; the adults must be on hand to exploit with the individual child the first glimmer of a materialising association, be it visual, aural or kinaesthetic.'

Broadly speaking, all pupils spend most of each morning in the special class. In part this reflects the belief that this is when they are most receptive to learning. It should be noted of course that this is the time when reception classes will also be following more structured activities. Apart perhaps from watching TV or participating in assembly, it is considered that retarded pupils would be unable to cope with integration at this time of the day. The afternoon, when reception children are engaged in art and craft and play activities, is regarded as an altogether more appropriate time to seek to integrate, primarily for the social benefit.

The typical school day for a child in one of these classes might be as follows:

0900/0920	Children arrive in minibuses or with parents.
0920/1000	Formal directed activities (eg number and colour, language, music with peripatetic music teacher, television (integrated)).
1015	Toileting, milk and biscuits.
1030/1145	Individual workbooks, creative activities, music and movement (integrated)/assembly/cooking (each one day per week).
1200/1245	Toileting and lunch.
1245/1330	Free play. Helpers from top juniors come in to play on a voluntary basis. Adults only intervene as necessary.
1330/1400	Television (integrated); peripatetic music (one day per week).
1430/1500	Singing, PE, drama.

Monitoring progress

Teachers have recourse to both formal and informal measures in order to monitor pupils' progress. The former is an Observation Rating Scale developed specifically for severely retarded children by the then senior educational psychologist. The scale is based largely upon a content analysis of teachers' reports, extended and extrapolated by drawing on existing developmental scales and general psychometric experience. It is completed twice yearly for each child by the class teacher. The scale consists of five main areas: general presentation (eg appearance, attitude, general behaviour); independence (ability in regard of self-management and mobility); language development; social development (eg the nature and level of individual play and group participation); and learning aptitude (eg attention level, manipulatory skills, ability to discriminate). The instrument is described as 'an observation tool with a classification system to monitor developmental process and guide teaching and management', also 'an objective, comprehensive, and structured teacher's report'. Some reservations were expressed about the instrument: it took a great deal of time to complete, and some teachers felt that the psychologists' reports based on it told them little they did not already know. On the other hand, it did assist them in structuring their observation of a child and ensuring that significant aspects of behaviour were not overlooked. Also, by virtue of its detail it had direct curricular implications which were taken up in some instances.

The teachers themselves set greater store by the more subjective school-based records that are kept. Some psychologists too accepted that these represented a better instrument for monitoring purposes. Although the standard LEA record of a pupil's progress is not maintained for pupils in the special classes, most teachers note down any indications of progress, difficulties encountered, relapses, and so forth on a fairly regular basis. A more formal updating occurs every six months or so. One teacher maintained a daily record of what she had done with her children, eg activities under the headings of pre-reading, reading and language; number; stories, music, poetry; PE/drama/movement; nature, science and special interests; art and craft. However, this was primarily for curriculum planning purposes; she only updated records on the children every six months or so, arguing that their very slow progress did not warrant anything more frequent: "You don't get much progress and it's not fast enough to do a report every term." Even when updating records she claimed that there was "nothing very much when you come to write it down".

A second teacher, who was disposed to recording any sign of progress, however slight, regularly kept a series of check-lists covering the following aspects: social behaviour and play; hearing and speech; posture and large movement; vision and fine movement. She had developed her own check-list based upon the Observation Rating Scale and the Stycar Chart of Developmental Sequences (Sheridan, 1975). She also recorded children's mobility, independence, communication, interaction and music development in another book. Two other teachers maintained weekly notes for their own use and, in addition, filled out a detailed report twice yearly with comments under the following headings: appearance and personality; general behaviour; independence; play; intellectual development; language development; and physical development. Their head teacher noted that, apart from the Observation Scale, there was no ready record form geared specifically to this category of child. Consequently the basis of the records that were maintained varied from one class to another and was continually evolving.

Finally, some of the teachers maintained a home-school book. This had been abandoned by one of the classes, the teacher in charge stating that she preferred to telephone or speak to the parents directly (she claimed she saw all parents on two or three occasions each term). In a second class this system was utilised daily. In a third it was maintained weekly, being envisaged as a source of basic information rather than as a means of actively involving parents in their child's education.

Integration

One of the assets most frequently claimed for this provision is its proximity to ordinary education and, in particular, the possibility it affords of integrating children into regular classes as appropriate. While all teachers espouse the aim of integration, they stress that they do not feel under any compulsion to be seen to be vindicating what is still for many educationists a contentious practice – particularly in regard of children whose learning difficulties are so severe.

The extent of integration fluctuates quite naturally in accordance with the age and characteristics of the children in a special class at any particular moment. It is recognised that "integration has got to be planned", and that care must be exercised in order not "to over-programme it". The teacher making this last comment referred to a girl who had spent each morning in a regular class. It was not long before she had to be brought back to the special class – she seemed to miss the secure environment and was not completing her basic skills work. Where it does occur, integration is customarily into a reception class since it is felt that this is the most appropriate age level, with its emphasis upon the basic skills and creative/play activities. It is also the case that the developmental gap between ordinary and special children is narrower at this age than subsequently.

The principal benefit of integration is envisaged as social – seeing normal models of behaviour: "From the work angle they don't integrate at all" (teacher). In order to be able to integrate a child typically needs to be toilet-trained, able to play with and generally fit in with ordinary children, capable of communicating well enough to be understood, able to eat with a knife and fork and have sufficiently good table manners so as not to stand out unduly when eating.

There is considerable variation between the special classes in regard of the nature and extent of integration. This is partly a reflection of factors referred to above, but also the consequence of differing degrees of emphasis placed on it by teachers and head teachers in the various locations. In general, there is integration for certain well-defined activities: music and movement; PE; dance; television; singing; assembly; and all school events such as school plays and trips. In some locations children are integrated for their lunch and in the playground at break and lunchtimes. In addition, certain carefully selected pupils may integrate into the general activities taking place in reception classes, either fitting in with whatever is going on at the time or taking work with them.

The following account of what occurred when severely retarded children joined regular classes is taken directly from field notes:

'Two children... Stuart and Herbert, eight and seven respectively, joined a reception class (for $\frac{3}{4}$ hour). There were 29 children in the class in all... Stuart has been going to lessons with this class on his own. When Herbert goes however Harriet, a welfare assistant, goes too. Herbert still needs support in that he feels insecure if there is nobody there he knows... There were three adults [present] – the teacher, a welfare assistant and the welfare assistant from the special class.

'The class was doing group work. One table was designated for art work, another for maths, and the rest of the groups were doing creative writing. Stuart was working at the art table with four other children, painting the shapes of a teddy bear puppet they were making. Herbert was at an adjacent table with Harriet cutting out the puppet shapes. There were two other children on this table doing creative writing.

'The children in the class seemed to talk to Stuart but I didn't notice many speaking to Herbert... most of the children were chatting fairly easily although one child [appeared] rather condescending.

'When Stuart had finished painting the teacher asked for someone to take [him] to wash his hands. Quite a few children volunteered. When Stuart came back he got a book which was his from the normal class pile and took it to the teacher. I noticed that he jumped a huge queue of eight children! The teacher wrote a sentence for him at the top of the page and he had to draw a picture. Stuart took his book and joined a table of children all doing [this task]. Harriet was not there but he chatted quite happily with the other children.

'When Herbert finished his painting a child was asked to take him to wash his hands. When he returned he was given a book... (he obviously hadn't had one before as his name was put at the top). Again the teacher wrote a sentence for him which he had to copy and draw a picture. He went and sat at the same table as Stuart although there was a child in between them. Harriet sat beside Herbert. Although Harriet never really moved far from Herbert's side she did chat to the other children... and they would go to her and ask for words they couldn't spell. The [other] welfare assistant stayed in the corner of the room for the whole lesson listening to children read. She had no contact at all with the special class children.'

The social context

As stated previously, the main benefit of integration is envisaged by teachers and head teacher as a social one – being surrounded by normal modes of behaviour, which it is hoped the severely retarded will acquire. As one teacher says to colleagues in main school, "All I say is it's social, don't worry if you can't give them any work." (One might judge that this is setting expectations too low in some cases where children could benefit from properly guided teaching in ordinary classes.) As with integration in the previous section, the nature and extent of opportunities for interaction vary from class to class. This in turn will affect the amount of social contact that actually takes place. We look at this here in the context of three key social aspects of the school day: assembly; break and lunchtime play; and school dinner.

We consider assembly first. In all four schools although there is assembly daily the special children usually attend only once a week. They are at a disadvantage in arriving later, and leaving earlier, than ordinary pupils because of the dictates of the transport arrangements. At one school assembly had been rescheduled on one day a week in order that they might be present. One head seeks to make helpful mention of the special children wherever possible, taking care to do this naturally – "it must not be a forced situation" – and not to overplay it.

Some extracts from field notes taken during assemblies in the schools paint an encouraging picture:

'The children seemed quite well accepted; there was some amusement at their antics but it seemed good natured and quite acceptable. The children did a percussion number of their own...'

In the second:

'Three children accompanied Sharon [welfare assistant] to assembly ... During [this] there was quite a bit of staring at the children by those close by. One of the children...sat quite still throughout; we gathered subsequently that he is extremely introverted... The other two moved about quite a lot, sliding up and down the floor at the back, stroking other children and generally hugging each other and other children within reach. Nobody seemed to take too much [notice];... Sharon made occasional, fairly casual interventions.'

Even though the children themselves might have had very little idea of the content of the assembly, their presence can be justified on the grounds that this is one of the few occasions when ordinary pupils will be made aware of their presence. Certainly in one of the schools – and perhaps in others too – it is the case that most ordinary pupils see very little of them otherwise because they arrive late and depart early, occupy a separate playing area at break and lunchtime, and so on.

Breaktimes present a slightly more diverse picture. In one location there is no formally scheduled break – classes take time out as and when convenient. If a child with special needs happens to be in the regular classroom at that time then he or she will remain with ordinary children. Otherwise the special class may well stay in its own separate playing area. At two of the schools, although breaktimes coincide, the special classes have their own play areas. In one this practice was justified on the grounds that "they are very little and [would] get hopelessly lost" in a large playground. At the other the nursery play area was on the opposite side of the school building. At the fourth school the head teacher was intent on promoting social contact – "they shall take part in every activity" – and the special class children were encouraged to use the main playground, even though they had their own fenced off area.

One other point to note here is that in some schools older pupils come into the special class at lunchtimes to play with the children there. The two groups of pupils are largely left alone; there is no formal supervision, adults only intervening when it is absolutely necessary. Having observed such activity in one location our feeling was that children were played *with* – perhaps not surprising given the difference in age and developmental levels:

> 'You couldn't really call it playing. The [junior] girls tended to emulate adults with... rather condescending voices... conversation [in the main] seemed to consist of "No, don't do that". The only activity they did was to rock either [of two retarded children] in a barrel. The rest of the time they tended to stand around [rather] self-consciously, not knowing what to do. All the contact was with these two children [the others present had no contact at all]' (field notes).

We believe this underlines the need for adults to seek out opportunities to intervene rather more, perhaps to structure play and deliberately set up occasions that will lead to meaningful social interaction between the two groups. It must be noted, however, that the absence of nursery departments in these schools meant that pre-school children did not have age peers.

School dinner again presents a rather mixed picture. At two schools the older children dine in main school; this is considered inappropriate for nursery age children, who lack the necessary feeding skills and table manners. At a third, one child each day takes lunch with children from an opportunity class in the main dining area. The special class teacher here noted that her children ate faster and used a knife and fork properly when dining out in the main school. In the fourth school the customary situation is reversed – selected pupils from main school are invited into the special class to eat. Not sending children out into main school was justified on various grounds; notably that they needed a rest, and that the noise and greater scale of everything in main school would upset them.

By way of summary, it would seem that social benefit does accrue to these children from their general presence in the mainstream of education and from the specific classroom involvement which some enjoy. They are surrounded by normal behaviour, mix to a degree with ordinary pupils, and are not teased or considered 'odd' to any noticeable extent. One head teacher claimed that in her school there had not been "one incident of unkindness involving the handicapped children". This must encourage their self-esteem, while having to subscribe in some measure to mainstream norms should foster independence. This is further enhanced by the wider outlook and experience which being in the mainstream of education brings. There are benefits too for the ordinary child. Teachers pointed to the improved understanding of handicap, more accepting and helpful attitudes, and the dispelling of the fear of children who look or behave somewhat differently from themselves. This was encapsulated by one adult who observed, "If these children had been in my school I'd have understood and not had that fear..."

Parents

Since this provision was developed partly in response to parental pressure, it is not surprising then that parents have been a supportive force throughout. They would appear to derive considerable satisfaction from seeing their severely handicapped children attending ordinary schools. They are considered also to benefit from being better able to put their child's handicap in perspective, and through acquiring guidelines for their own child's development from seeing in what respects they differ from ordinary children.

Although many parents live a considerable way from the schools they are encouraged to feel that the school their child attends is *their* school. The schools have sought all along to establish and maintain close links with parents. All of the special classes hold termly open evenings. In addition, four of the five hold coffee mornings or afternoons which, apart from being an opportunity for general socialising and informal contact with the class teacher, frequently will have an educational orientation. Outside speakers such as a speech therapist or dance teacher will be brought in to talk about their work. Parents are invited to all school events (plays, galas, etc) as a matter of course. Some parents fetch their child to and from school; in some classes the teacher in charge encourages them to feel at home in the class, stressing that they can stay for as long as they like, and on occasions has had them helping out in the classroom. It is made clear to all parents that they are welcome to telephone or call in whenever they feel they have a problem or feel the need to talk to someone.

Some schools have paid particular attention to informing the parents of ordinary pupils about the presence of these classes. One head teacher wrote to the parents of infant children before the special class opened, expressing the hope that they would join in activities wherever possible. She also suggested that should they have any doubts or queries on the matter to come and discuss these with her. Thereafter, the parents of each new intake have been invited in and informed of the existence and the purpose of the class. Another head reported considerable interest on the part of main school parents; one mother saw it as an advantage 'that her infant children were fortunate to have the opportunity to learn about "handicap" from firsthand experience'.

In other locations, school staff have been somewhat slower in realising that it is up to them to take active steps to promote the necessary understanding and involvement. A recently appointed teacher in one special class, herself a parent of the school, stated that, prior to her appointment, she had known very little about the provision other than that it existed. In another school staff had sought to overcome this problem by initiating, toward the end of our researching, coffee mornings for the parents of the latest intake to the school. Children from the special class, their parents and special education staff were also invited. The hope was expressed that this would become a regular event.

A particular feature of this provision is the 'day-off' built in to the provision for each class teacher. This is time free from teaching and is for the purpose of facilitating a range of activities, including making home visits. In point of fact, two of the five teachers did not make home visits. One stated that this was because she felt able to have sufficient contact with parents at school. Of those who did visit the home it was recognised that this could be overdone unless caution was exercised. Home visits usually were once a term, more frequently where there was a specific need. While in some cases these were essentially social visits, to maintain parental interest and encouragement, one teacher had used the visits for quite specific purposes. These included advising a parent about her child's feeding; getting across ideas about effective child management; and in one instance arranging for a psychologist to give a mother specific advice on how to control disturbed behaviour. One teacher had also been involved in teaching the Makaton signing system to some parents.

We interviewed two parents of children attending the special classes. Both were extremely enthusiastic about the placement – "Going in at three was the biggest thing that happened"... "Couldn't have done more for him than they have done". Being retained within a normal environment was considered to have rubbed off on the children's general behaviour, while their contact with ordinary pupils and the assistance forthcoming from these had been particularly advantageous. Both were happy with the amount of contact they had with teachers; though this was very different as between the two cases, it seemed to be adjusted to the level of contact parents wanted.

Summary

This provision for pre-school and infant age children with severe learning difficulties is highly unusual in the British context in that the children are being educated in special classes attached to ordinary schools rather than in special schools. Children have the benefit of a good staffing ratio and receive teaching appropriate to their needs. The emphasis is on providing a stimulating learning environment and lots of individual attention. There is some interaction with other children, mostly unstructured and occurring outside the classroom. Most children transfer to ESN(S) schools at the end of the infant stage, though a small number have gone to ESN(M) schools.

Questions that might be considered for the future include:
1. Can the opportunities for integration be used more systematically? Would a greater level of professional interaction between special

class and main school teachers make it possible for the pupils to spend more educationally structured time in ordinary classes? Would greater intervention increase the level of social interaction?
2. Will it be possible for the various professional agencies involved to give more time to the classes, and work collaboratively with each other and with special class staff?
3. Would children benefit if ways could be found of involving their families more systematically in the effort to meet their special needs?
4. Will any further thought be given to extending this form of provision beyond infant schooling?
5. Is there any possibility of establishing nursery provision in these schools so that pre-school children in the special classes can associate with normal age peers?

Part Two
Provision for Pupils with Physical Handicaps

Specialist provision for the physically handicapped has traditionally centred on special schools. The concentration of resources and trained staff allows a level of attention that would not be feasible in ordinary schools. Gulliford (1971) noted in the early seventies that some form of integrated schooling was available to a very small proportion (less than 2 per cent) of the physically handicapped population. The benefits claimed for special schools are not without drawbacks, however, and there have in recent years been both a greater public airing of the drawbacks and a consideration of alternatives.

Elizabeth Anderson's (1973) *The Disabled Schoolchild* stimulated early interest. More recently, Cope and Anderson (1977) demonstrated the viability of unit provision, offering evidence that in some respects it was the better alternative. Anderson and others have demonstrated that physically handicapped pupils without neurological abnormalities do not present specifically educational problems. They may have extensive care and therapy needs or require special means of access to the curriculum (through special equipment, building alterations and so on), but there are usually no *educational* reasons for excluding them from ordinary schools. So those with mild physical handicaps can be placed in the ordinary school with little or no special help, while pupils with more serious handicapping conditions can often be educated in the ordinary school so long as the requisite physical and therapeutic support is forthcoming. In this way those who have spina bifida without hydrocephalus, those who are disabled as a result of thalidomide and many others can be educated satisfactorily in the ordinary school.

Where there are attendant learning difficulties – as often with cerebral palsy, spina bifida with hydrocephalus and so on – specific teaching expertise may be required. It should be noted that the nature of the physically handicapped population has changed significantly over the past 30 years. Medical advances have virtually eliminated some causes of physical handicap such as polio and tuberculosis or made it easier for some pupils, eg those with congenital heart disease, to attend ordinary school. The commonest physical handicaps (cerebral palsy and spina bifida) now are congenital ones. With cerebral palsy, the motor disability is frequently complicated by additional problems – learning difficulties, sensory and speech impairment. The pupil with spina bifida may well have hydrocephalus in addition and can present a major care problem in school. In summary, while there has been a growing realisation that some physically handicapped pupils do not present an educational problem, there has been a concomitant growth in the number of those who have additional learning problems.

This may explain in part why the growth of integrated provision has been relatively slow. Cope and Anderson (op cit) conducted a survey into the extent of LEA provision for physically handicapped pupils in ordinary schools. By 1975 12 (out of 105) LEAs had units at primary level – with places for perhaps 150 pupils. This did not of course take into account the – limited – provision for physically handicapped pupils attending ordinary schools on an individual basis. At secondary level there was rather more provision, and a good deal was being planned, as the accompanying table shows.

LEAs making provision for physically handicapped pupils in ordinary schools at secondary level, 1975 (Cope and Anderson). (Numbers in brackets refer to provision which was being planned.)

In ordinary classes	14	(5)
Special classes/units	4	(9)
Special school sharing campus with ordinary school	11	(6)

By 1977 there were 543 pupils attending designated special classes (primary and secondary), a figure to be set against 13 964 in special schools.

In this section we present an example of each of the three categories suggested by Cope and Anderson. The example of individual integration operates principally at primary level though a small number had reached secondary stage at the time of our study. The special centre we studied is in a secondary school. The special school described is an all-age one but the main thrust of integration has been at secondary level.

5
Individual integration of physically handicapped pupils

This is a programme of integration for severely physically handicapped pupils that operates in part of a large rural authority. At primary level pupils attend the local or other neighbourhood school. Secondary provision entails an element of grouping in designated comprehensive schools. The programme currently comprises 20 pupils in 15 primary schools and six pupils in five secondary schools. A further 30 pupils described as moderately handicapped also attend ordinary schools.

Historical résumé

This authority is a large rural one whose population is dispersed across hilly terrain where communications are difficult. The bulk of the population is in fact concentrated at one end òf the authority. There is a large number of physically handicapped pupils to provide for, with for instance an incidence of spina bifida nearly four times the national average. Severely physically handicapped pupils had traditionally gone to residential special schools, initially in a city some distance away and, since the mid-sixties, more locally in an inter-authority special school. The latter was not in this authority, however, and was well away from the main centre of population so that most placements were still residential and pupils had no contact with their neighbourhood schools.

Change came about as a result of efforts by medical officers to place physically handicapped children in ordinary schools and in response to parents' wishes, within a context created by the operations of a hospital pre-school centre. The main centre of population (of the authority newly formed in 1974) has had the services of a spastics unit for many years. This is a day centre attached to a general hospital and had originally kept young people up to the age of 16. In the mid-sixties its clientele changed as special schools opened and the more able physically handicapped were placed in the latter. So it was decided to concentrate on pre-school provision with a strong emphasis on building family links – the paediatrician in charge "had been against residential care even then [in the 1950s]". Also, the centre widened its remit beyond cerebral palsy, accepting in particular the growing number of spina bifida children who were – due to surgical advances – surviving beyond infancy. There was a strong emphasis on establishing links between home and the professionals, and making professional interventions – medical, therapeutic, educational – on a daily basis so as to retain the child within the family environment. This provided the "opportunity to observe over a prolonged period the child's ability to function in the community".

A further strand was the medical officer's involvement with the families of handicapped children. Through a programme of regular home visiting as soon as the infant left hospital, particularly in the case of spina bifida, she established and maintained close contact with the families. She became convinced of the inappropriateness of separating young children from their families when they reached school-going age. (Many of them attended the hospital day centre until then.) Though not an educator, she professed unease about the educational strengths of the residential placements available and claimed that many parents did not want to send their children away to special schools. All of this led to a consideration of the possibility of education being conducted in other than the special school setting. All that was wanting was a trial run.

The opportunity presented itself in 1969. Mary suffered from spina bifida and was severely physically handicapped. She was bright, however, and her parents were determined not to accept a special school placement for her. They were also articulate middle-class parents who worked within the educational system themselves, and to the medical officer it was "a chance not to be missed". Accordingly, she approached a local infant school head teacher who agreed to accept her. Mary transferred from there to an ordinary school and indeed received all her education up to school leaving age in ordinary schools.

Further development was slow at first and it was three years before another child was integrated in this way. Numbers were small in the early stages as only selected pupils were placed in ordinary schools. These were cases where there seemed to be a fair likelihood of success and where parents were intent on an ordinary school placement. The latter was for a variety of reasons: unwillingness to consign their child to a residential placement; dissatisfaction with the educational provision of the special school – two parents withdrew their child from it; and the knowledge, from existing examples, that integration was possible. In the course of time, it became standard practice in much of the authority for physically handicapped children, even the most severe cases, to attend ordinary schools so long as they were not considered educationally subnormal and there were no overriding reasons against it. In fact, very few physically handicapped children from the area have been placed in a special school in recent years. These are children who are very severely handicapped or for whom there are socio-emotional reasons for a residential placement.

This integration programme developed in a relatively piecemeal way through individual initiative and parental pressure. Though "the time was not propitious" and the result was "imperfect provision", the prime mover insisted, however, that "you've got to start somewhere". It became established as the primary educational route for physically handicapped pupils in much of the authority in a de facto way rather than as the result of a formal LEA policy decision. Indeed, the LEA maintained a background role for many years, acting in response to representations made or pressures applied. It acceded readily in most cases, formally making the placement requested and arranging for the necessary ancillary support and adaptations to buildings. The LEA took up a more active role when pupils had to be considered for transfer, initially to junior schools and more recently to secondary level. The first few pupils to reach secondary age were placed in a particular comprehensive school. The plan to concentrate secondary provision at the school, with all pupils being transported to it, did not materialise. An LEA working group (November 1979) felt that while in principle all neighbourhood secondary schools should have access to handicapped pupils it was not feasible for all schools to have specialist facilities and permit access to all areas of the school. The plan being considered was to concentrate on two 'key' schools, chosen to keep transport requirements to a minimum; modifications would be made to these and special facilities provided as necessary.

Organisation and aims

This provision started on the basis of individual initiative; children were placed in their local primary school or, if that was unsuitable for any reason, in a nearby school. The local school was automatically considered as the first option, but would sometimes not be chosen because of the amount of physical alterations required or, exceptionally, because the staff in another school were considered more receptive. In the early days medical staff joined with education staff in approaching a school, assessing its suitability and generally overseeing the placement. In the course of time, these roles were taken over exclusively by education staff.

A systematic procedure for making the approach to schools was devised in the early days. This was not followed in full in every case, but it does represent the steps considered necessary. It comprised the following stages:

(a) The medical officer and the adviser for special education/infant organiser (prior to 1974 the area was part of two different counties each with its own working practices) made a joint school visit to discuss the possibility of a trial placement with the head teacher; they described the child's condition and management in detail, surveyed the physical characteristics of the school and noted the possible need for toilet adaptation, ramping and so on, and discussed the need for ancillary help.

(b) The head arranged to discuss the matter with staff.

(c) The head and reception class teacher visited the hospital day centre to meet the child and observe what went on at the centre.

(d) A formal recommendation was made to the Director of Education who, if in agreement, undertook to provide ancillary help and effect the building alterations.

As noted, this is the idealised procedure and not always the case in practice. Especially in the early days, stages were omitted or were carried out poorly and many schools reported considerable dissatisfaction with the manner in which they had been informed of the placement and the initial arrangements made. In recent years some educational psychologists have become involved in the process.

Transfer from infant and junior schools to the subsequent stages of schooling was always the primary responsibility of education staff. Attendance at the neighbourhood school and individual integration both proved harder to pursue here. Whereas most infant and many junior schools could be readily adapted to accommodate physically handicapped children, this was not the case at secondary level. This matter was under active discussion at the time of our visits. No totally satisfactory solution seemed to be available. It was generally accepted that the ideal of individual integration with pupils attending their neighbourhood schools would have to be forgone, despite misgivings about creating secondary units which might defeat the object of integration. As noted above, the thinking was moving toward developing provision in two designated schools and transporting pupils to one or other of these.

Broadly speaking, the aims of this provision are to enable physically handicapped children and young people to live with their families and have the same access to ordinary schooling as their able-bodied peers. These aims were viewed differently, and given different weightings, by the various parties involved. Also, the LEA tended for many years to see the provision in administrative/placement terms: it had to provide education for certain pupils – the special school placements proposed were not acceptable to some parents – no other arrangements were available within the authority – and this provision offered a means of discharging its statutory duty.

As might be expected, the removal of the need for residential placement was at the forefront of parents' minds. This was also a major target of the medical officer primarily involved, who considered that the effect of boarding education, particularly for younger children, was "to compound handicap with emotional separation". It often led to isolation within the community and difficulties in making the transfer from school to some form of independent adult living. So a primary aim of the integration programme was to avoid the disadvantages of isolation, dependence and emotional immaturity that were allegedly associated with special schooling, and to secure for disabled youngsters the emotional support and maturational benefits of living with their family and belonging to their local community. This meant redefining 'normality' for these youngsters and seeking a normality for them that was closer to that of their able-bodied peers. Where previously it was normal for a severely physically handicapped child to attend a special school, effectively disappearing from the local community, the aim now was to minimise the need for separateness and emphasise rather what they had in common with other pupils.

A related aim was to ease parents' burden and help them come to terms with their child's handicap. The medical officer in question felt that parents saw a stigma attaching to special schools and were distressed when their child was placed in one. By placing them in ordinary schools "you give them hope"; "the hurt and resentment of the parents really only starts being healed when the child starts [ordinary] school". Speaking of a girl who died at the age of 10 after a period of normal schooling, she affirmed that "even if only for that case it was all worth it; the parents could hold their heads high, she went to an ordinary school".

It was also the intention to provide disabled pupils with the same access to educational opportunities as their able-bodied peers. As noted, the medical officer and some parents believed that the special school placements available did not do this. The former was adamant that where the primary handicap was a physical one the educational needs were no different in kind from those of other pupils and were best met in ordinary schools. If anything, there was need of a greater degree of intellectual stimulation to enable young people to compensate for their disabilities – "those who are most handicapped have to make the most effort to keep up". So, "if you are physically handicapped... you must be stretched to the utmost intellectually". This goal was seen as most likely to be achieved if pupils attended ordinary school.

Pupils

This programme of integration extends to all of the authority's physically handicapped pupils. Not every physically handicapped pupil is included of course, and there were – and are – different views as to who should be included and who excluded. The most radical stance is taken by the medical officer who has been associated with the project from the outset: the problems of handicap are primarily problems of management, and these do not on their own necessitate removal from the ordinary school; the latter is justified only for socio-emotional reasons, when family support is lacking – "where the home is not conducive to the child being exposed to the rough and tumble of the ordinary school" – and so on. A colleague stressed the possibility of "dignity and self-respect": in addition to privacy for toileting, there must be a reasonable likelihood of acceptance. He instanced the case of a boy who was quite deformed looking and was physically weak, so that it was unlikely that he would become a member of the school community in any sense. The psychologists' concern was whether the child would be able to cope academically. One psychologist said that if IQ was below about 80, it was then a question of looking very closely at how well the child would be able to cope socially and manage the classroom situation. Learning difficulty was also the critical factor as far as the adviser was concerned: if a child's learning difficulties were such that he or she would be classified ESN(M) that child was not a candidate for integrating. A research physiotherapist who was closely involved for a time affirmed that most spina bifida and many cerebral palsy cases could go to ordinary school but drew a distinction based on the need for physiotherapy: if their condition was such that they needed specialised physiotherapy on a frequent – ie daily – basis, then they should not be at an ordinary school.

All of these children come to notice virtually from birth, being noted on the appropriate handicap or observation registers. There is regular home contact through visiting by the senior clinical medical officers. Many of them attend the hospital day centre mentioned above and/or the associated child development centre. School placement is usually initiated by a senior clinical medical officer or the hospital day centre bringing a child to the notice of the school psychological service. An educational psychologist then assembles information on the child and carries out an assessment. This stage is frequently done hand in hand with surveying the local school or schools. When this is done and practicalities worked out in relation to a given physical site, a formal recommendation for placement is made to the director of education.

Of 89 physically handicapped pupils attending ordinary schools within the authority (figure based on questionnaire returns from schools, 1979-80) a total of 20 at primary level and six at secondary level were described as severe. A further 24 and six respectively were described as moderate. The severely handicapped group included nine cases of spina bifida, four cerebral palsy, two muscular dystrophy, as well as a number of bone deformities, accident cases and other handicapping conditions such as Still's disease and heart defects. Many of them were incontinent and had mobility problems, by being confined to wheelchairs and/or requiring walking aids. In 14 cases out of the 26 pupils described as severely handicapped, building modifications had to be effected. (Building modifications were necessary also for 10 of the moderately handicapped group.)

Most of the pupils were described as of average intelligence by their teachers. On a five-point scale (1 = superior, 5 = very limited), the following distribution was obtained for the severely handicapped group:

Scale	1	2	3	4	5
Frequency	0	2	16	8	0

Staffing

As this is a programme of individual integration with pupils placed in existing classrooms, the main staffing considerations have to do not with teachers, but with care staff and physiotherapists. Accordingly, we look at these two groups first before turning to other staff involved.

Ancillary staff
The main input to the programme from the LEA has been the provision of ancillary help, which has been on a generous scale. Every pupil has the services of a welfare ancillary on either a full-time or part-time basis. Generally, this meant providing the school with an ancillary extra to establishment, though cover was provided by doubling up in some cases where there was another physically handicapped pupil at the school or by utilising existing staff where there was an adequate number of nursery assistants. In one case, a school requested – and was allowed – a half-time teacher rather than an ancillary.

The ancillary is clearly a key person in a provision of this kind. Many of the younger children are incontinent or need assistance with toileting. In one school which did not have an ancillary the toileting had to be done by the class teacher; this proved too burdensome and the child had to be removed from the school even though she had integrated well and was independent in her splints. The availability of a welfare ancillary has been important for reasons over and above the actual work they do. Many schools were initially reluctant to take on a severely physically handicapped child, and the offer of an ancillary was a concrete token of the LEA's support for the venture. This is not a negligible factor as schools and individual teachers sometimes feel that they have problems dumped on them and are left to cope as best they can. (One person observed that the context was one where cut-backs were affecting teacher attitudes and reducing their tolerance for special pupils.) In several important respects teachers were not given adequate support, but the generous provision of ancillary help promoted acceptance and led to more positive attitudes than would otherwise have been the case. Moreover, many ancillaries were available to help out in a general way in the school. Particularly when they had care of only one pupil, their formal duties did not engage them full-time and they were available for a range of helping tasks. In this sense the presence of the special pupil was seen to redound to the school's benefit.

The roles assigned to welfare ancillaries and the duties carried out by them varied considerably. They included: providing basic physical care and mobility; supervising swimming, walking and other exercises; implementing physiotherapy programmes; monitoring equipment and physical condition; basic, ie non-teaching, classroom support; teaching involvement; general ancillary duties unrelated to handicap.

A main part of their job for all ancillaries is to attend to the pupils' physical needs. A typical day might include: receive child from taxi and transfer to wheelchair; place in calipers and remove as appropriate; tend to toileting needs throughout day; transport around school; assist with eating as required; prepare for taxi at end of day. It is to be regretted that in a small number of schools the ancillary's role did not extend beyond this level. Whether this was for lack of thought or for personality factors it was not always possible to say. The result was the same, however – the ancillary was under-utilised, sometimes to a point of extreme frustration, and an opportunity for enhancing the school's activities lost.

Many ancillaries supervise pupils at play, assist with walking exercises, attend to posture, and increasingly in recent years implement a structured programme of physiotherapeutic exercises under a physiotherapist's instruction. Some are able to take their pupil swimming. These activities were little in evidence during the early days of the scheme. Many staff, teachers as well as ancillaries, were unsure about handling these pupils and had little idea of their physical capabilities. The tendency was to over-protect and see risks where none existed. Pupils were not being stretched physically; the importance of upright posture, regular walking and other exercise was, with few exceptions, not appreciated. This changed when physiotherapeutic advice and support became available, and many ancillaries now play an active part in promoting the pupil's physical development.

A further activity arising out of the physiotherapist's involvement is the monitoring of equipment such as wheelchairs and calipers and looking out for sores, points of discomfort and so on. Without training, ancillaries do not know if equipment is suitable, properly adjusted, likely to cause discomfort and so on. With a modicum of training, however, they can be sensitised to make relevant observations that will lead to appropriate remedial action being taken in good time. This is an important part of the ancillary's job and while there would seem to be room for improvement there has been considerable development since the early days of the scheme.

Some ancillaries spend a great deal of time providing basic classroom support. This can be acting as amanuensis for a pupil who has difficulty in writing or preparing materials, distributing books and doing other tasks so as to free the teacher for teaching. On occasion, however, there seems to have been a policy of having the ancillary on hand just in case anything went wrong. In one case this was justified through the child's poor manipulative control – "needs somebody with him all the time"; the ancillary just sat by the child in the classroom, without a particular function – when she was not attending to his physical needs.

A small number of ancillaries functioned in effect as teaching aides. This included hearing children read, correcting work, helping in a remedial department with children working on their own and so on. These activities were not of course confined to the handicapped pupils. One ancillary was talented artistically and encouraged to use her skills with the children. Another, working in a secondary school, assisted with 'living skills' – making tea, simple cooking, ironing and sewing.

Finally, various general tasks not connected with the handicapped were assigned. Some of these have been mentioned. Others included: typing for the school; doing dinner duties; and assisting with first-aid.

The least satisfactory aspect of the ancillary role has been the absence of suitable training. The LEA has a general ruling that classroom assistants have an NNEB qualification, though some have been appointed without it. This does introduce an element of training, albeit a somewhat irrelevant one, since the courses available comprise very little on handicap. (This is particularly so at secondary level where, as the ancillaries themselves noted, the duties and orientation of a nursery assistant are hardly relevant.) It was quite clear that there was considerable need of training, and many ancillaries themselves acknowledged that this was so – "we don't know if we are doing more harm than good". Several ancillaries contacted the hospital pre-school centre for advice and information. Others picked things up from parents and medical officers, while most learned a great deal from the physiotherapists eventually appointed. The glaring need, however, is for a formal custom-built course. In fact, a course has very recently been set up for nursery assistants working with children with special needs. This is organised on a regional basis within the county and comprises 10 hour-long sessions once a week after school. It was devised initially with assistants working in special schools in mind, but those working with the physically handicapped in ordinary schools were invited as well. The course was not specific to physical handicap but did include some material on it as well as other relevant matter on speech therapy, play, music and movement, and so on. More recently, there has been discussion on the possibility of adapting the local NNEB Diploma course to include a component on physical handicap.

Physiotherapists

For many years after the integration programme started no physiotherapy was available in the schools. There had been physiotherapists in post prior to local government and health service reorganisation, but their services were not retained after 1974. Their work was of course confined to special schools, and pupils attending ordinary schools did not receive physiotherapy. One set of parents managed to make their own arrangements with a hospital-based physiotherapist, but most of them were unaware of the continuing importance of physiotherapy after their child had been discharged from hospital. This was a major weakness of the programme, and pupils' needs in respect of toileting, physical activity and equipment maintenance were poorly met in consequence. A research physiotherapist working from a nearby hospital visited a number of the schools and noted:

> 'Many of the staff appeared unsure about handling and had no idea of the physical capabilities of these children. There was an attitude of protection and sympathy... Toileting procedures had been coped with by trial and error and urine bags often leaked because the necessity for regular emptying had not been recognised... No one was aware of the physiological importance of daily standing, walking and exercise on the bladder, bowels, soft tissues, spasticity, respiration and circulation in paraplegic children and the inadvisability of sitting in a chair all day... Some children did not use their splints at all as the parents had neglected to send them to school, others used them spasmodically. Frequently, when a class had a physical education lesson, the physically handicapped child sat in the chair and when the class went swimming the child was left behind... Training in walking and activities of wheelchair transfer were also neglected. Wheelchairs needed adjustment, adaptation and repairs, there was no routine maintenance and no one to contact even if the problems had been recognised... Brakes... very often were found to be unsafe or broken.'

A report to the Area Health Authority detailing the difficulties and possible solutions added pressure to the case for providing physiotherapy by exposing the need very sharply and by "providing ammunition". In September 1978 a peripatetic physiotherapy service was established, with three physiotherapists being appointed eventually. They worked in special schools as well so that their commitment to the integration programme was in effect part-time; at the time of our fieldwork they spent respectively 24, 18 and 22 hours (out of 35) working in ordinary schools or at home with parents. Within 12 months they were seeing 59 physically handicapped pupils in ordinary schools. The workload has continued to expand to a point where the people in post affirm that it cannot be adequately dealt with in the time available.

Each physiotherapist visits the pupils she is responsible for on a rota basis, usually every few weeks or termly with review cases. More frequent visits – two or three times a week – are arranged for those who need more intensive physiotherapy, eg post-operative or where a child is being trained in new orthoses. The main components of the physiotherapist's role are: treating individual pupils; training and working with ancillaries; and monitoring equipment. The balance between these will reflect the individual pupil's needs, but a key factor from the outset has been the amount of delegation involved. This was necessitated by the number of pupils to be seen in a limited period of time and the distances to be travelled. It was made possible by the availability of care staff and the flexibility of working on the part of the physiotherapists appointed.

The standard pattern on a first visit is for the physiotherapist to see the pupil alone initially, and later in both the classroom and general school context (corridors, toilets, playground, gym, etc). She will check for any problems of physical management that the pupil presents, and for any difficulty with mobility that he or she experiences or might be expected to experience. Sitting in on PE lessons is regarded as particularly crucial, to see whether the pupil is included or not, and to advise on routines or activities he or she could cope with using existing or perhaps additional equipment. In the classroom the physiotherapist concerns herself with assessing such issues as what would be the best form of movement, taking account both of pupils' mobility and obstruction to others. By the close of the visit the therapist will have worked out specific reinforcing exercises for the ancillary to carry out informally on a daily basis. Seeking minimum disruption to the pupil's education is paramount. Presented on workcards these exercises – to be used "as a guide" – are explained to both ancillary and teacher. These may be walking exercises, practising transfer from wheelchair to splints, or specific physical exercises.

Subsequent visits by the therapist typically will comprise: a period of individual treatment for the child, which the ancillary always attends – a form of ongoing induction; discussion of any problems that may have arisen with teacher and/or head; possibly some guidance on specific exercises; advice on miscellaneous aspects – the pupil's posture within the classroom or the appropriateness of classroom furniture; and the checking of orthoses and wheelchairs to ensure they are in proper working order.

It is clear that establishing the peripatetic physiotherapy service has made a considerable difference to the integration programme. Quite aside from the manifest benefits to the pupils, both teachers and ancillaries are far more aware of their physical needs and better equipped to meet them. They have a better understanding of their conditions and have built up skills in dealing with them. Attitudes too have improved: the previous overprotectiveness has diminished greatly and staff are far more confident in their dealings with the pupils. Welfare assistants have benefited in particular and have responded very positively to the extra dimension in their care for pupils. The pupils themselves have gained through having a far more normal experience of schooling.

Other staff
Many different professionals are of necessity involved in a programme of this nature. Besides care staff and physiotherapists, particular mention needs to be made of teachers, medical officers, educational psychologists and the special education adviser. No extra teaching staff were considered necessary, though it was intended to recruit teachers with a specialist background in physical handicap for the projected secondary developments. Pupils joined existing classes, in some cases a remedial class or department, but otherwise an ordinary class within the school. Head teachers professed to taking great care in selecting appropriate (ie sympathetic, mature and so on) teachers to receive these pupils, though it must be accepted that the range of choice in a small primary school was usually limited.

Considerable dissatisfaction was expressed by teachers at the lack of guidance and support. They were not looking for specialist training courses so much as basic instruction and access to expertise when necessary. While teachers acknowledged that in the main they had the requisite teaching skills, a recurring concern was whether pupils were being stretched academically. They did not know whether lack of concentration, for example, was due to laziness or the result of some physical factor and consequently were unsure how to deal with it. One head teacher who had several pupils with hydrocephalus was quite uncertain as to what it was reasonable to expect of them and worried lest too much pressure would be harmful. This uncertainty – on the part of otherwise experienced teachers, it must be noted – went along with a sense of isolation: "Other people must have had dealings educationally with these children... [If only I could] talk to them... to know what to expect." Teachers were most aware of the *educational* consequences of their lack of expertise, but there were other deficiencies too relating to physical handling, toileting and care aspects where their total lack of experience meant they were unaware of many problems.

These training deficiencies were commonly acknowledged to be a major drawback of the programme. They reflected in part the piecemeal and ad hoc way in which it had developed and in part the absence of suitable personnel. Medical staff had always sought to brief the school in detail when a child was first placed. This did not cover the educational implications, however, and sometimes did not include the class teacher. In any case, the pupils would often move on to other teachers in following years. Moreover, the system sometimes broke down; one school, for instance, claimed that because of the requirements of medical confidentiality there had been considerable difficulty in getting details on some pupils' physical conditions. As the programme developed, teachers (and ancillary staff) were invited to visit the hospital pre-school centre. The problems on the handling and care side which persisted in serious measure for many years were not resolved until the appointment of community physiotherapists as noted above. On the educational side neither the advisory service nor the school psychological service was staffed at a sufficient level to provide the necessary support. Some teachers had done a considerable amount of reading and private study. A plan was mooted to appoint specially trained teachers who would provide specialist peripatetic support, but it did not come to fruition. A positive initiative was reported from a secondary school recently involved in the integration programme: this entailed a joint presentation to the entire school staff by the adviser, medical officer and educational psychologist. This was considered useful and led to positive follow-up activities.

As regards the medical services, the hospital pre-school centre has played a significant role, as noted above, and there has been considerable involvement on the part of the community child health service (and the school health service which it succeeded in 1974). Mention has been made of the key role of the latter in initiating the programme. For many years the medical officer most closely associated with it was instrumental in approaching schools and giving such guidance and information as schools received. As time passed and Education adopted a more active role, Health moved from the forefront though still retaining a considerable involvement.

Various aspects of this continuing involvement have been detailed above and can be cited briefly here. Much of it flows from the fact that physical handicap is in the first instance the concern of the medical profession; it receives first notice of individual cases and – with the possible exception of health visitors – is the first professional group to impinge on the family. So, candidates for placement are usually brought to notice by the medical service. While formal assessment and recommendation are the province of the school psychological service, the medical service will have known the child for much longer and makes a major input to placement decisions, either informally or through participation in case conferences. Medical officers pay regular visits to schools to advise and inform and to monitor progress. This is necessarily confined to medical and some physical matters but has been greatly valued by the recipient schools. There is likewise a continued involvement with families.

The school psychological service is involved in this programme primarily through its formal role in initial placement. Individual psychologists conduct assessments on children presented to them by the medical services. Referral is nearly always at pre-school stage (sometimes as young as two and a half years but mostly around four) and children are usually seen at home. The psychologist assembles background information and does some testing to get an idea of the child's intellectual functioning. The decision on placement 'depends not only on the physical handicap but also on the child's mental abilities and social and emotional factors' (psychologist). The psychologist discusses the placement possibilities with parents to ensure that they realise why decisions are taken. (In some cases, for instance, it has been necessary to explain to parents why the integrated placement suggested by other professionals may be extremely problematic.)

Having assembled information on a child and established that attendance at an ordinary school may be appropriate, the psychologist visits the potential receiving school(s) to check on suitability – mainly the attitudes held by teachers and any physical constraints. The next step is to liaise with the senior adviser over the administrative arrangements. Parents are informed of the outcome. The psychologist then convenes a meeting at the school with the senior clinical medical officer, senior adviser, head teacher and, if possible, prospective class teacher. The psychologist also arranges for the head to meet the child and parents. If all has gone well, the psychologist then makes a formal recommendation to the director of education.

When placement has been made there is usually no further involvement either in the way of curricular guidance or reviewing of progress. This is a function of the pressure of work attendant on a poorly staffed service – ratio of 1:12 500. Psychologists seek to make one visit early on to talk to the class teacher, but subsequent contact is on an informal basis when they are visiting the school for other purposes. One psychologist noted that all she could do if she was unhappy about a placement was to put it on her review list and consider the case in a month's time. Beyond that there will be no further contact in the ordinary run of events. Reviews are of course carried out on request and on the occasion of transfer from infant and junior school.

The formal involvement of Education in the programme was through the advisory service, in particular the senior adviser for special education. As the programme developed, Education took over the co-ordinating role, developing working relationships with the medical services. The senior adviser had administrative oversight of the programme, being responsible for placing children and liaising between the schools and other agencies involved. More recently, he has been involved in trying to set up relevant training opportunities for both teachers and ancillary staff. Because of pressure of time – for most of the period of our involvement he was the only special education adviser in post – he was constrained to see his role purely in administrative terms and acknowledged that he was not in a position to give any advisory support to the schools involved. Beyond overseeing the initial placement his role was confined to troubleshooting and maintaining a general oversight of the programme.

Accommodation and resources

Building modifications were often the most manifest sign of the presence of a physically handicapped pupil and so attracted a good deal of attention. The LEA undertook to provide access to the school and sanitary facilities as needed whenever a physically handicapped pupil was placed at an ordinary school. Costs incurred were relatively minor as schools where the requisite modifications could not be made easily were rejected from consideration and also as the provision made was often at a basic level. (It should be noted that the adaptations had to be paid for out of a limited minor works budget.)

In most cases, the work carried out comprised the provision of ramps at one or more entrances to the school and adaptations to a toilet. Minor ramping was usually sufficient to permit access, though in one case the ramp had to be at the back of the school by the kitchen entrance because there was not enough space at the front of the school. This acted as an isolating factor for the pupil in question since access to the playground – which was in front – entailed a trek right round the school. Changes of level within the school were another matter. The schools involved at primary level were all single-storey but some had minor changes of level as well as raised thresholds and other obstacles to wheelchair users. In some cases nothing had been done about these – either because the site made it difficult or no thought had been given to it – with the result that whole sections of the school were out of the – unaided – reach of the physically handicapped pupil.

As many of the pupils were incontinent and had to be changed or had urinary bags which needed regular attention, the provision of adequate space for toileting in private had a high priority. The usual approach was to adapt a section of the school's existing toileting, though on occasion a separate facility within the school was constructed. The arrangements we saw ranged from the perfectly adequate to the barely acceptable. It was argued that Victorian buildings did not lend themselves to the requisite alterations. Be that as it may, the conditions under which some pupils saw to toileting needs were far from ideal – inefficient use of space, insufficient or no storage, unattractive décor, inadequate disposal arrangements and so on.

This did not apply to all schools by any means and some had achieved quite satisfactory arrangements. It must be noted that even here, however, some schools reported major difficulties in getting the necessary alterations made. It was not clear whether this was due to penny-pinching on the part of the authority or poor communication between the parties involved, but the effects were clear – substandard arrangements or arrangements that were only put to rights after prolonged agitation by the school, and diminished enthusiasm for integration. Furthermore it should be noted that modifications did not usually extend beyond toileting and ramping. Lowered thresholds, vision panels in doors, non-slip surfaces and so on were not considered save by way of exception. Also, in at least one case there was a worry about fire risk as the only means of escape from the classroom was along a narrow corridor which would be blocked by a wheelchair; it is unlikely that a fire officer would have sanctioned the arrangement. As far as resources went, pupils were following the same curriculum, broadly speaking, as their peers and had access to the same curricular materials and resources. Specialist educational equipment, adapted typewriters and so on were little in evidence. Pupils were well equipped with orthoses (calipers, walking aids) partly due to the proximity of an orthotic research unit and the involvement of a research physiotherapist who was using schools in the area for development trials of new orthoses. When the community physiotherapists were appointed they were able to monitor the use of orthoses and make sure that pupils progressed appropriately, eg from rollator to crutches.

Curriculum

The primary aim of this integration programme is to give physically handicapped pupils the same access to ordinary schooling as their able-bodied peers. Accordingly, children enter the ordinary reception class in infant school and participate in school activities wherever possible. They are withdrawn initially only for management purposes – toileting, transfer to and from wheelchairs, and so on. Many of the children have learning difficulties, whether because of factors associated with their physical condition, limited learning experiences or other reasons. It is the aim to meet the needs arising from these difficulties in the same way for these children as for able-bodied children with similar difficulties. Thus in one junior school two of the three physically handicapped pupils spent much of their time in a remedial group, while the third, who was more able, belonged to an ordinary class. Elsewhere, pupils followed individual programmes while staying within an ordinary class and following its timetable. Several pupils were a year behind their age peers because they had missed a lot of schooling through illness or hospitalisation.

At primary stage teachers claimed that they had little difficulty in exposing pupils to the normal school curriculum. Lack of fine motor control and poor handwriting imposed a restriction in some cases, but otherwise pupils were being taught alongside peers and made good progress. While many pupils were doing well it must be noted that their access to the curriculum was limited through the lack of specialist knowledge on their teachers' part, as some of the latter acknowledged. This was evident in unduly low expectations, lack of awareness of specialist equipment and techniques, and uncertainty as to how much pressure to apply. One very clear example of the narrowing of curriculum was in relation to physical education. As noted earlier, the tendency – almost universal in the early days – was to assume these pupils could take no part in PE and effectively to exclude them from it. This example highlights too the importance of having, or having access to, relevant expertise since this situation only improved with the arrival of physiotherapists on the scene.

Secondary provision was still being worked out at the time of our visits. The oldest pupil, Mary, was in her fourth year by this stage. She had followed exactly the same curriculum as her peers in the first and second year. In her third year she dropped science and geography to make time for cookery, as well as a little typing and some walking exercise. She had been having difficulty with these subjects, but they were chosen also because they coincided with times when there was least pressure on the domestic science facilities and cooking instruction could be readily arranged. In fourth year Mary dropped English literature in order to make time for 'consolidating' work in other subjects; it was felt too that the demands of getting round school, seeing to physical needs and so on all pointed to a need for a somewhat reduced curriculum. She was also at this stage devoting one morning a week to 'life skills' – essentially cookery and some needlework, done in conjunction with an ancillary. A younger colleague was less able and followed the usual programme of the remedial department, replacing music with typing and one period of social studies with cookery. She also had a walking period as well as extra swimming and needlework.

Preparation for adult living was still at a very tentative stage. Increasing attention was being paid to the development of life skills, although the focus was rather narrow. The head acknowledged that the existing resources of the school's careers department would need to be expanded if they were to provide effective careers preparation for physically handicapped young people.

Monitoring progress

There is no formal systematic review of pupils' progress or the success of their placement, other than that carried out by the school. The absence of regular review by the LEA reflects in part the piecemeal way in which the provision developed and in part the fact that the advisory service does not have the resources to do it. As far as both adviser and educational psychologist were concerned, their involvement had to be restricted to crises and particular difficulties – "a placement is successful if you hear no more about it". The medical officers paid regular visits to some schools to monitor progress in the areas that fell within their competence.

Physiotherapists' work was, as noted, tied in with close and systematic observation of pupils' physical development.

Pupils' educational progress was of course recorded by class teachers and individual schools in whatever ways were customary within the schools. These showed great variation, with about half of pupils rated below or well below average. Schools completed a questionnaire for the LEA on pupil attainments, relative to their age group, in English and maths. The results on a four-point scale (1 = above average, 2 = average, 3 = below average, 4 = well below average) for the severely handicapped group were as follows:

Attainments in English				
Scale	1	2	3	4
Frequency	1	12	8	5

Attainments in maths				
Scale	1	2	3	4
Frequency	2	10	7	7

The social context

An important aim of this integration programme was that physically handicapped youngsters should through associating with able-bodied peers become independent, mature in social and emotional terms, and generally acquire the behaviour patterns appropriate to their age. Considerable success was reported in this area. Most teachers, including some who admitted to having initial reservations, were very positive about the social adjustments and assimilation of the physically handicapped pupils. This picture was corroborated by limited observation on our part. Comments from teachers included the following: "A very cheerful girl who has fitted in well" – "No different from any other child" – "Well balanced". A good many instances of excessive attention and mothering were reported at the outset. One little boy in a wheelchair had classmates fighting to sit next to him! One teacher had found it necessary to monitor this closely. Apart from creating an unnatural social situation for the pupil – and reinforcing the singularity resulting from his physical disability – it deprived him of opportunities for growing in independence. Pupils found it all too easy to accept having doors opened, books fetched and so on. Generally, more normal attitudes and behaviour developed with the passage of time. Sarah is a case in point. At the start she was never on her own: "Groups took it in turn to look after her ... you could look across the playground and always see Sarah in the middle of a group." This gradually stopped and it was possible to see Sarah on her own without anybody feeling a need to rush up and talk to her.

A number of teachers referred to the immaturity that some pupils displayed, stemming, in effect, from being spoiled. These were children who expected instant attention, both in the classroom and outside, and "they need to be trained out of having their demands met immediately". A difficulty for teachers not versed in physical handicap was that they did not always "know what is an emergency and what isn't". This may have been related to the variations in practice here: some teachers made lots of exceptions for the physically handicapped – perhaps because they "can't let off steam like other children" – while others made a minimum of exceptions and insisted that they followed the same disciplinary procedures as other pupils. Thus, a rule in one school that pupils queue for lunch on the left was enforced for wheelchair users as well.

By no means all of the physically handicapped pupils were social successes. They included their share of isolates and social misfits and it would be unrealistic – as well as mistaken – not to expect the normal rules of pupil interaction to apply. Even in the case of one girl described as a "bossy little miss" who tended to push people off and was in consequence fairly unpopular, "they [other pupils] have tried with her". Generally, when physically handicapped pupils were unpopular or rejected by their peers this was attributed to personality factors considered unrelated to their disability. Teasing has not been a particular problem. One parent was aware of an isolated instance that had been hurtful, but otherwise parents and teachers concurred in the view that teasing had been no more than one would expect of any other pupil.

A number of teachers spoke about the positive effect on other pupils from having a physically handicapped pupil in the school. "Has done an awful lot of good for everybody – we have gained a lot from her." Several strands to this were identified: it gave pupils a sense of perspective and made them realise how fortunate they were; it provided an object for charity; and it made handicap 'normal' and part of everyday reality.

Parents

The general impression of strong parental support for the integration programme was corroborated from our own contact, by questionnaire and interview, with five sets of parents. These were in favour of the integrated placement both for its normality and the scholastic progress their child made. They strongly endorsed the schools' efforts on behalf of their children – "school has surpassed all our expectations" – "school has been particularly helpful and co-operative" – "have done everything possible". All were either 'very satisfied' or 'reasonably satisfied' with their child's progress at school. Most of the pupils were below average in ability, some well below, but the parents' general view seemed to be that the schools "are doing the best they can".

All parents interviewed were happy with the amount of contact with the school, though the actual contact had varied considerably both in extent and kind. It ranged from occasional telephone conversations with the head and possibly visits on open evenings to regular face-to-face contact with the ancillary and/or class teacher. In three cases parents were involved in transporting their child to school, so that informal contact was readily available; in one case this was acknowledged to be a considerable benefit for the personal contact it gave the mother and the improved attitude toward her child's disability. The other sets of parents affirmed that they felt able to contact the school at will – "We're at liberty to go over when we want" – "If I'm worried I just go". This facility was particularly appreciated by one set of parents whose child had previously attended a distant residential school where casual visiting was just not feasible.

The one dissatisfaction expressed about schools expressed related to the lack of continuity from year to year. Over the course of a year the class teacher and ancillary would, often with instruction and assistance from the parent, build up an adequate understanding of the child's condition but quite fail to communicate this to the following class teacher so that once again the child was subjected to innappropriate overprotective handling. Otherwise, the main complaints from parents related to transport. We heard a spate of stories about unreliable taxis, incompetent escorts – one child was let fall right out of his wheelchair – and bureaucratic bungling. (It should be said that we were not in a position to check out these stories, but they unfortunately sounded all too plausible.) Transport was generally provided in private cars which were unsuitable in the case of some wheelchair-bound pupils. Some operators were unreliable or unconcerned for the length of the school day: parents talked of rushing to get ready in the morning and "you're still waiting there at 10 o'clock"; in other cases pupils had to finish school early in order to fit in with transport schedules. Complaints and representations to the Education Office had only a limited effect since transport was organised by an independent department. Some parents were convinced that major upsets and difficulties over schooling were directly attributable to problems with transport. Two sets of parents felt constrained to lay on their own transport.

To sum up, these parents were strongly committed to an integration programme which they themselves had helped to establish – by their reluctance or refusal to accept special school placement and by their demonstration that integration was possible. It should be noted that though the population is dispersed parents are well organised, many of them having active membership of voluntary societies. Faced with inadequacies in the services provided, they have tended to respond by trying to provide the service themselves – whether this be organising physiotherapy independently of the school, laying on their own transport, or 'training' school ancillaries in toileting procedures – rather than withdrawing their child and looking to a special school placement where the services could be taken for granted.

Summary

This provision for physically handicapped pupils has built up from tentative beginnings over a 10-year period to a point where it is the primary educational route for physically handicapped pupils over much of the LEA. Development has been slow and fitful, suffering in particular from a lack of relevant expertise, and it was a long time before Education joined the venture with the same enthusiasm as Health. There can be no doubting parents' enthusiasm – or that of their children – for the programme. Likewise, most teachers involved have endorsed its efficacy and appropriateness. Children have followed the same curriculum as their peers, and gained clear benefits in terms of social development.

The further development of the programme will depend in part on the answer to five major questions:
1. What arrangements will be made at secondary level, encompassing specialist careers training and preparation for adult living in addition to regular curriculum? Will the requisite specialist staff be

appointed, and how will they be deployed? What use will be made of existing school resources such as pastoral care systems? Will the concentration of provision in designated secondary schools weaken pupils' links with their own communities? Will the benefits of individual integration be lost as numbers build up within the one school?

2. Will arrangements be made to monitor arrangements in a systematic and comprehensive way? What support if any can be made available in case of difficulty?

3. How are the manifest needs of teachers and ancillaries for training or access to expertise going to be met? Formal courses? Peripatetic specialists? Flexible deployment of secondary specialists? Can teachers be made more aware of the resources available to them within the school health service and the school psychological service?

4. Are the different agencies involved likely to come together other than for the initial placement? In other words, is there a prospect of inter-disciplinary working focussed on pupils' actual education?

5. Can the transport difficulties be resolved, taking account of the new situation at secondary level where a number of pupils will be coming to a single location from a relatively dispersed region?

6. How will the programme be affected by the opening of a new special school in a neighbouring authority which opens up the possibility of *day* special school placement? (This has financial implications as well since the authority is committed to supporting the longer established special school, and taking up places in the new school would entail in effect an element of double payment.)

6
A special department for the physically handicapped

This department for pupils with physical handicap is part of a large (1200+ pupils) mixed comprehensive school in a compact urban authority. It comprises a purpose-built suite of rooms attached to existing school buildings with places for 60 pupils, though currently catering for 40.

Historical résumé

Traditionally physically handicapped pupils in this compact urban authority have been educated in an all-age special school within the authority. A newly appointed head teacher set about tackling the problem of overcrowding upon assuming control in 1969. He judged that he had inherited 50 pupils of secondary age who could have managed in ordinary school. Convinced of certain disadvantages of special schooling, especially for older pupils, eg the lack of contact with able-bodied people – "We were sending them out with multiple problems at 16... they were pretty well educated but they hadn't really had the experience of relating to other people" – he set about making some changes. First, he sought to transfer these 50 pupils to their local schools. After strenuous effort he managed to place some 30 of them but faced increasing difficulty, particularly with regard to access. LEA officials argued that on economic grounds it was not feasible to provide access facilities in all the authority's secondary schools. However, the necessary physical adaptations could perhaps be carried out in a particular school, and it was agreed to seek out a suitable location.

At the time a first, middle and upper school system had just been adopted by the authority with transfer at nine and 13. Transfer at age nine was felt to be too early for integration. Many physical conditions were such as still to require medical or physiotherapeutic attention, while some pupils were having surgery, so that pupils should be retained in the special school since it could better accommodate the disruption entailed in meeting these physical needs. It was decided accordingly to have transfer at 13+, retaining the special school for pre-school and primary age children.

Finding a suitable location did not prove very easy and the school eventually chosen was in fact the third choice. Two other schools had to be abandoned on first political and then economic grounds. Although the third choice, this was by no means a last resort. In preliminary discussion the then head teacher had been extremely positive about the proposed venture, and there was space for quite extensive premises. (In fact, resources were subsequently cut and the provision that was built was less extensive than had been intended.) The one major disadvantage was the split-site nature of the school. It is on two sites about a quarter of a mile apart, one site occupied by third year and sixth form pupils, the other by fourth and fifth years (because entry was at 13+ there were no first or second years). The physically handicapped are based in the first of these two sites but because of the integration programme need access – and transport – throughout both sites.

Advance preparation within the school appears to have been limited. Possibly it was assumed there was little need to inform and advise ordinary teachers in any deliberate way since the physically handicapped pupils that would be integrating into their classes would all be academically able. As for existing pupils of the school, there was a Community Studies course already running which all fourth and fifth year pupils took. This contained a component on handicap, which would have given pupils some understanding of peers who had special needs. The intention otherwise was to avoid drawing attention to the physically handicapped group or singling them out unduly. In retrospect, it seems likely that a general orientation on the nature and educational consequences of physical handicap would have been useful for teachers. One (specialist) teacher acknowledged that there was "probably a greater demand than we imagined [for some specialist knowledge]".

Aims and organisation

Staff of the special department seek to ensure that all pupils on roll pursue educational aims that are broadly similar to those of their peers in the main school but with individual needs being fully recognised and appropriately met. In addition, there is a concern to promote a more normal social and emotional development. Many of these pupils come to the comprehensive as immature and naive 13-year-olds in comparison with their able-bodied peers. Apart from seeking to combat the effects of prolonged education within the sheltered confines of a special school, there is also the need to help pupils cope with the normal problems of adolescence, which in their cases are often exacerbated by the physical handicap.

The special department functions for all physically handicapped pupils aged 13 + within the authority except for those who have severe learning difficulties. (Some of these latter were placed in the early years, but this was not judged to be successful.) This means that a wide range of ability is represented. As a result the department operates in a two-fold way as far as teaching is concerned: as an educational provision in its own right for those pupils whose learning difficulties are more serious; and as a liaising agency securing appropriate integrated placements, part-time or full-time, for its pupils and facilitating their education in the main school. It should be noted that it is a full department of the school, and its head, who is a senior teacher, reports to the school principal.

The advantages of the location are seen at their strongest for pupils of average or above average ability: a wider range of subject options; access to subject specialists and a wide range of curriculum materials; and the opportunity of taking subjects to examination level. The emphasis is on their *educational* development – "they're here to get their education first and foremost". For the less able pupil a similar concern to prepare them for adult life is translated into a different practice: "We concentrate on pushing literacy, numeracy... opportunities for integration will come as second to that". As regards pupils' social and emotional development, the proximity to the able-bodied is perceived as affording the opportunity to come to terms with the physical handicap and to learn to appraise their strengths and weaknesses realistically: "Top dogs in special school are made to feel their limitations here."

Physically handicapped pupils are attached to the department and integrated on an individual basis according to their capabilities. The needs of a substantial number – eleven in all – for much of the duration of our fieldwork were met for the most part within the centre itself, largely by one particular teacher. The others split their time between main school and the department in varying ways in accordance with their particular needs.

Pupils

It is intended that this school provide for the vast majority of physically handicapped pupils of secondary age in the authority. It also provides for a number of pupils from neighbouring authorities, these comprising about 20 per cent of the total. Those with minor physical disabilities would of course go to other schools of their choice wherever possible. (Secondary schools in this compact authority do not have formally designated catchment areas.) So, a wide range of handicapping conditions is encompassed, the major ones being spina bifida, cerebral palsy, muscular dystrophy and heart defects. A number suffer from epilepsy in addition. Some have toileting problems. Many have mobility difficulties, being confined to wheelchairs or dependent on walking aids.

The pupils span a wide range of ability including some who are very able and coping with A-levels as well as those who have moderate learning difficulties. Since physical handicap is frequently associated with brain damage or impairment of cognitive or social functioning the latter constitute a sizeable group. Indeed, staff felt that there was a danger that they would end up running an ESN(M) unit within what was essentially envisaged as an integration programme. Some pupils with severe learning difficulties joined the department at the start before any proper screening procedures were set up, but there was neither space nor resources to cater for them and it was decided that their needs would be better served in existing segregated provision. There was the further consideration that these pupils were felt to carry a certain stigma which was to the detriment of the others – "The whole project is at risk if people get to thinking all physically handicapped are like that."

As this provision comes quite late in pupils' school careers, no formal admission procedures are necessary. For most pupils transfer onward from the special school they will have attended during junior and middle schooling is automatic. By way of exception some pupils will join the department who have attended ordinary middle schools or who come from other authorities. All pupils remain at the school until they reach school leaving age. Some leave at 16, but others stay until after their eighteenth birthday. So far no pupil has had to be transferred elsewhere, although deteriorating physical conditions do sometimes put considerable strain upon the individuals concerned and on members of staff. It was intended initially that the department would provide for 60 pupils, but this figure has not been reached. From an initial batch of 13, the numbers on roll during our study varied from 33 to 45. The present total of 40 includes 15 in the sixth form – claimed to reflect the fact that there are few alternatives for them.

Staffing

Eleven posts have been added to the school's staffing to take account of the presence of the physically handicapped pupils. Six of these are formally assigned to the department. These have primary responsibility for the physically handicapped *in* the department – as opposed to those placed in ordinary classes – but they also teach classes in the main school. Some indeed belong to other school departments, such as the English department, and attend departmental meetings. In return, some main school staff contribute to lessons within the department. The other five posts are used to augment main school staffing ratios. There are five full-time welfare assistants plus a sixth who works part-time; these are untrained. It may be noted that obtaining the requisite number of ancillary staff involved something of a campaign which went on for a long period. There is also a full-time nurse.

Three members of the department upon being appointed were in their probationary year. Two teachers – the head of department and his deputy – had previous experience of teaching in a special school and were qualified in some aspect of special education (physical handicap and educational subnormality respectively). (Two others were in the process of completing part-time BEd degrees.) However, this lack of specialist qualifications was not regarded as a disadvantage; rather, the greater problem was considered to be one of finding teachers who were able to cope with the very different ethos and approach required in main school and special department respectively.

In this particular location the special schools allowance is *not* paid. The principal of the school is insistent that it is a divisive mechanism: "You can't have integration for the children and separatism for the staff ... you put up a great barrier ... it becomes harder to get everybody to opt in." By way of compensation there are extra allowances for particular expertise, relevant experience and so forth.

The involvement of outside agencies to date has been mixed. The educational psychologist visits about once a month to carry out assessments on individual pupils but is otherwise little involved in the running of the integration programme. The advisory service was involved in the early days when the department was being set up but has not been directly involved since. Medical coverage is good. In addition to the nurse on site, the school medical officer visits for a half-day every fortnight, reviewing individual cases and dealing with any emergencies. On the therapy side, the department has the services of a physiotherapist for six half-day sessions per week, and of a speech therapist one half-day per week. Physiotherapy provision would seem quite reasonable – although the therapist herself felt that in the time available only a limited service could be offered. Speech therapy provision, by contrast, is inadequate. In the three hours or so available each week the therapist sees four pupils regularly, with a further three seen on a review basis. The therapist feels that the pupils have attained their potential, although her view is not shared by teaching staff who press for more of the therapist's time. Given the shortage of speech therapists this is not possible. The therapist does work closely with teachers, leaving speech exercises for them to cover with pupils in between her visits.

Overall, the impression is one of the various outside agencies working in isolation from each other and from teaching staff. There were some instances of collaborative working but no general move to interdisciplinary working in a concerted way. This was acknowledged by one member of the teaching staff: "Each [professional] has his own little bit of information, and we must get together."

Accommodation and resources

The special department is purpose-built though, as noted previously, the economic recession has meant that the premises are less spacious than was intended. With a relatively high proportion of the pupils on roll spending a considerable part of their time within the centre it tends to be overcrowded. (This has meant, incidentally, that one of the arguments against bringing remedial pupils from main school in for particular lessons is that there is not the room.) The premises comprise two open-plan craft areas, a central area for general use, a small library, three classrooms, small office, physiotherapy room, room for the nurse, staff-room, and toileting facilities. Adjoining the centre is a large well-appointed swimming pool which was built at the same time and contains special facilities for the physically handicapped.

As regards the buildings in the main school utilised by the physically handicapped, considerable adaptations have been made but major obstacles remain on one site. Non-ambulant pupils are confined to the ground and first floors at the stipulation of the fire officer; as a result various specialist classrooms are inaccessible to them. The only curricular areas excluded in this way are technical drawing and pottery, though it was affirmed that the demand for these from the physically handicapped has been very slight. Otherwise, access to the curriculum has been maintained by re-locating specialist subject teachers. A science laboratory has been set up in a specially ramped hut which, though small, is fully equipped. There are lifts in both sites to give access to upper floors, though they do not help in the matter of fire regulations. One was purpose-built to a high standard and with the needs of the physically handicapped in mind. The other is an old service lift that is too small to hold a helper along with a wheelchair. The separation of the two sites is a major practical constraint. Two ambulances with drivers are available throughout the day to fetch pupils between buildings. This constitutes a considerable extra cost as well as a major limitation on pupils' freedom of movement and opportunities to socialise with able-bodied peers.

From the point of view of resources, the school in general fares quite well. The department has a well-equipped physiotherapy room with a good stock of wheelchairs and walking aids, and well-resourced cookery and craft areas. It has a plentiful supply of standard items of equipment, being allocated a reasonable sum of money and having a free hand in how it is spent. There have been difficulties over more sophisticated items such as electric typewriters which it was considered that a special school would acquire on the strength of charitable donations or money raised. In fact, a fund-raising campaign had to be mounted in order to acquire some equipment which was not forthcoming from the authority. The principal was not happy about this situation; while the need for the equipment was accepted, the campaign to acquire it underlined the singularity of the group in the special department and so went counter to what they were trying to achieve within the integration programme.

Curriculum

When discussing the curriculum opportunities open to pupils based in this department it is necessary to distinguish between two groups: those who spend much, if not all, of their school day alongside able-bodied peers; and those pupils who in addition to their physical handicap have some other handicapping condition, most notably marked learning difficulty, and spend much of their time within the special department. The former, the more academically able pupils, pursue individual subjects just like any other pupil of the school, taking exams and generally having an equal part in the academic life of the school. Their curriculum is essentially that of the mainstream and is determined by individual ability, inclination, career orientation and so on just as it is for other pupils.

The slow learners or those with specific learning difficulties who spend much of their time in the department follow a custom-built course. This has developed considerably in recent years and is still evolving. At first, provision seemed patchy and ad hoc – "no reading schemes, no material at all". Responsibility for improving matters was assigned to the deputy head of department, who had considerable experience of ESN(M) education. At one stage the thinking was to bring together the slow learning physically handicapped pupils with remedial pupils from main school, whose curriculum opportunities were fairly restricted. However, some staff saw difficulties with this. They pointed out that the remedial pupils tended to be considerably more able than the physically handicapped pupils retained within the department – "they'd be swamped" – and that in any case remedial classes were too large. An alternative would have been to bring remedial pupils into the department had there been sufficient space.

The curriculum of pupils based in the department is broken down into basic subjects – English, maths – plus various supplementary activities – science, craft, home economics, typing, PE and swimming. PE, as a specific activity, was only introduced relatively late in our research, with the appointment of a PE specialist who had had some experience of adapting the subject for handicapped individuals during her teacher training. Opportunities for taking lessons in main school were gradually extended to these pupils. Social studies was one of the first subjects for fourth formers and above, although a mixed drama group ran for a year before being abandoned due to difficulties over staffing. Midway through our fieldwork there were formal moves to build a bridge between main school remedial provision and the department's provision for its slow learners. Remedial classes were broken into small groups and physically handicapped pupils were introduced into them, with the teaching being shared between remedial and department staff. Thus, six fifth form pupils were split between two main school classes, joining them for six periods a week of English and maths. They took a further three periods of social studies – giving a minimum of nine periods per week (out of a total of 25) in main school.

Preparation for adult life

Preparation of pupils for post-school life has tended to be on an ad hoc basis, with the emphasis on careers guidance as opposed to careers education. The numbers involved to date have been small and other problems were seen to be more pressing than developing a formal leavers' course. A great deal of guidance and assistance is of course given to individual pupils in selecting further education courses, considering university places and finding jobs. Much of this individual counselling is done by the head of department, who is available to pupils in a flexible and open way.

A plan was mooted to place careers guidance on a more systematic basis. A newly appointed specialist careers officer drew up a programme of careers preparation comprising three components: group discussion – talking about employment generally, seeking out pupils' own aspirations; pre-vocational guidance – for specific counselling of individual pupils and their parents, commencing in the fourth form; and vocational guidance. This plan has yet to be implemented. It may be noted that detailed vocational assessment is at the moment available only to the occasional pupil who is sent on a Spastics Society assessment course.

Those pupils who integrate quite extensively are incorporated into the general careers programme of the school. In the past this has been a six-week-long slot in a community studies course, but it is now integrated into other subjects. Nothing specific is done to take account of the needs of the physically handicapped in this, and while it is informative in a general way it is, by common consent on the parts of both special department and main school careers staff, of limited practical usefulness for them. The school's work experience programme is not as yet open to the physically handicapped. This was introduced only recently and is still quite limited. The decision was taken to confine it to the able-bodied until it was better established. "We've particularly excluded the physically handicapped until there are definite links; we feel its unfair to ask a lot of the employers ... and we are having problems already trying to get a foot in the door" (school careers teacher). Also, setting up and monitoring placements for these would take a great deal of time – which was not available.

A more systematic approach is being worked out for the less able physically handicapped with the development of a specific course within the department. This started with a small group of sixth form pupils who were being taught separately by three members of the department for maths, English and social studies, all under the guise of integrated studies. It was decided to pool resources and develop a joint curriculum between them. The Design for Living Programme that resulted covers: personal hygiene and appearance; interpersonal relationships (though not sex education); household management; entertainment and use of leisure; social and public services; the community and local places of interest. Emphasis is placed on practical work, with lots of visits to shops and relevant institutions. The three teachers divide the various aspects of the course between them. One concentrates on cookery, together with some community care work; a second on basic mathematics (eg household budgeting); and the third on personal and social aspects. A science teacher is used for the section on hygiene.

Monitoring progress

This is an area that has seen considerable development. At first, the information available was relatively sparse and of limited educational relevance. Individual pupil records were maintained along traditional lines. Thus, while varying considerably in their particulars, most contained medical details and a report of an assessment undertaken by an educational psychologist. Some older pupils had details of their handicap charted by the Pultibec system. (This is a four-point scale for rating children's functional disabilities devised by Lindon, 1963, and described also by Anderson, 1973.) This system of recording was abandoned when it became apparent that some of the statements made were not appropriate to the pupils in question. Subsequent records relied more on teachers' impressions. The extent of information, particularly of a current nature, was fairly limited at this stage.

A record sheet subsequently developed assembles a good deal of information on a cumulative basis. This comprises: standardised test scores, conducted within the department; reports on school subjects from relevant staff; family information, from the head of department; medical information, from the nurse, plus a section on 'disorders likely to affect performance' completed by the deputy head of the department; external exams taken; notes on further education, employment, training or other post-school information; and a general section on hobbies, interests and so on. This is intended to be completed throughout a pupil's career and should give a comprehensive if concise overview of progress and attainments over the period. In addition, a timetable for each year is attached, giving a breakdown of subjects taken and amounts of integrated and non-integrated time.

Academic integration

The amount of time spent taking lessons in main school is determined by the pupil's academic capability and the degree of acceptance on his or her part of the physical handicap. As noted previously, in the early days it was the academic benefit of integration – eg access to subject specialists, being able to sit public examinations – that was emphasised, and only in exceptional cases did medical or physical factors enter into consideration. In November 1979, 25 of the 40 pupils on roll were following a range of academic courses: two upper sixth formers were taking A-levels (in economics, sociology and English; French and sociology, respectively); four of the eight lower sixth formers were following academic courses; 11 out of 14 fifth formers were being integrated; three out of the five fourth formers were integrated for 80 per cent of the timetable; and five of the third year entrants to the school were in the process of being integrated.

Originally all pupils considered capable of being extensively integrated were registered with a main school form group. However, this practice was revised when it came to light that the school's system of pastoral care was failing a small number of pupils. There had been odd instances of threats and minor harassment which staff felt would have been picked up sooner and dealt with more satisfactorily if the pupils in question had been registered in form groups with special department staff. Henceforth, each new intake was enrolled within the special centre, being integrated only gradually. The more able pupils will ordinarily join a main school registration group by their fourth year.

The integration of the more academic pupils was acknowledged by special education staff as "the easy bit ... so far the demands on the main school staff have been slight ... our problems start now ..." (ie when considering how best to integrate less academically able pupils). Hitherto, their contact with able-bodied pupils had been restricted to breaks and lunchtimes. Over an 18-month period a sustained effort was made to extend the possibility of integration to these. It should be noted that not everybody was in favour of this move: some staff were anxious about the size of the teaching groups in main school and the reduced possibilities of individual attention, and worried about jeopardising pupils' educational development.

Initially, they joined main school remedial groups, for social studies and drama, though the latter option only ran for a year as "the success ... outstripped the staffing opportunities" and preferences were given to pupils from main school. Existing main school remedial groups were broken into smaller groups for maths and English, and the physically handicapped accompanied by a member of staff introduced into them. This approach first involved fifth year pupils and was then extended. By the time of our last visit there were very few pupils who were not experiencing some integration. Seven of the most recent intake of 12 pupils were not – much of the first term is spent in assessing the new intake, and for those who are not academically able this goes hand in hand with teaching them; some three fifth formers – "low ESN" with additional difficulties in speech and writing – were not integrating; and four sixth formers were following a course designed specifically for them.

The social context

There was general agreement that the physically handicapped pupils had become an accepted part of the school and were deriving considerable social benefit from being there. Some had social and/or emotional difficulties, as is occasionally the case with physically handicapped teenagers. Staff considered, however, that the number of pupils with such problems was relatively small, and in any case those problems that did occur were not attributable to the integration programme. Indeed, pupils' presence in the more realistic environment of an ordinary school had enhanced their social and emotional development in considerable measure.

All pupils including those who do not take lessons in main school have the chance of making contact with the able-bodied at break and over lunch. The latter is particularly relevant, since able-bodied pupils come over from main school into the special centre to use its social facilities. However, two slight drawbacks with this are that it only involves younger pupils (older pupils are in a separate part of the campus), while a number of those who come in are the isolates and social inadequates. At least one member of this department felt this was a potentially invaluable opportunity for interaction but one whose potential was not being realised. He pointed out that interaction did not happen spontaneously: "It gives a façade of being integrated but I don't think it really is ... At present it's completely unstructured and the able-bodied kids dominate it ... We [staff] just see if it happens, where we could structure things."

Physically handicapped pupils we talked to were without exception positive about the benefits that this placement brought – without being blind to the fact that there were costs. Advantages mentioned included: being treated as an ordinary individual – "At [special school] you were a handicapped person ... [here] you are a person with a handicap"; being expected to assume responsibility for onself – "There is a very dependent atmosphere at [special school]"; the opportunity to strike up associations and friendships with the able-bodied – "If you are willing to go out and talk you can eradicate that [wheelchair] and it doesn't exist, it's the person in it [that matters]"; the enhanced motivation – "We want to prove to other people we can do just as well" ... "I can gain credit for the school ... *that* is the motivating factor"; and the opportunity of overcoming social misperceptions – "In their [society's] eyes you weren't just physically handicapped, but mentally handicapped as well. Here they see you with the able-bodied and to some extent that stigma is removed."

The possible costs that were recognised mainly concern the greater demands made on the handicapped individual, together with the fact that it is the academically able pupil who stands to benefit most, as the practice currently operates. It was physically and emotionally more demanding – "It is up to you to make friends ... you have to be a bit of an extrovert" ... "You have got to push but once you have pushed the help is there". In other words, while these more able and articulate pupils appreciated the benefits of being obliged to become independent and make their own way, they implied that some might miss out with this approach. In addition there were various practical difficulties (not all to do with social factors): missing out on specialist careers education; not being informed of changes of timetabling or room changes; and the fact that ordinary teachers were rarely friends as well as teachers, unlike special department staff.

We talked with able-bodied pupils too. What were their perceptions of the handicapped? Did they feel at ease in their company? What kind of interactions did they have? The sample was a small and possibly untypical one, but some common strands emerged. Overall, it would seem that the presence of the physically handicapped pupils in the school is accepted as a matter of course – a considerable achievement, and one not to be taken for granted – but that close relationships were the exception rather than the rule. One fifth former attributed this to the lack of opportunity for contact: he felt physically handicapped pupils could be out more in main school; and that facilities in the sixth form common room needed to be improved so that handicapped pupils could be tempted away from the special department. This particular boy described to us how a progressively more sympathetic attitude had developed with increasing familiarity. His initial reaction had been one of "why couldn't they stay in their own place and leave us alone", but now he accepted them as part of the school.

One sixth form girl stated that she had been extremely apprehensive – "I had never been with them before and you don't know what they are like". Naturally, there were some negative comments, eg about the peculiar way that some pupils ate their meals, the fact that they were granted privileges such as not having to queue for lunch and that you could not speak or fight back against them even when they were at fault – "They say stuff to annoy you because you can't hit them back". There would appear to be some teasing – mimicry, name calling and, on occasion, minor physical skirmishes.

While a few able-bodied pupils, particularly the older girls, had made friends with handicapped peers, the main benefit would appear to be one of greater understanding of their circumstances, allied to developing more tolerant attitudes – for example, thinking about the consequences of a particular action for other people. In this context mention should be made of a Community Studies course which incorporates a component on handicap. This is taken by all fourth and fifth year pupils, including some of the handicapped. This component lasts for a term and covers the various handicapping conditions. It is an innovative course that serves as a comprehensive introduction to handicap as a topic to learn about, and possibly led pupils to a view of handicap as a part of 'normality'.

Parents

The department has the strong support of parents. Of six sets of parents interviewed all were 'very satisfied' or 'reasonably satisfied' with their child's progress and were strongly in favour of him/her attending an ordinary school. This satisfaction was expressed in various ways; "Smashing ... marvellous" and "1000 per cent better (than special school)" were two of the comments. Parents made repeated reference to academic and social gains. Evidence of the former ranged from having made great strides in reading and writing through to taking A-levels, the ultimate indicator of success. The schooling generally was regarded as more rigorous; "Not much education at [special school] – they're too busy with the physical handicaps, she wasn't being stretched there" was one mother's comment. As for social and emotional development there were repeated references to the greater degree of independence that was demanded and fostered: "At [special school] they were a bit too helpful. For quickness they would do it for her. At [this school] she has to stand on her own feet ... which is a good thing." One mother spoke very enthusiastically about how her daughter had "come out more ... among ordinary children".

There were problems of course. Indeed parents' endorsement of the integration programme gains weight from being maintained in spite of the various difficulties that obtained. There was widespread concern about the future. One set of parents were so worried that "we try not to think about it". Such concern is not peculiar to integration programmes, but some parents felt that there were particular factors at work here that did not help the situation. There was concern about the lack of careers education and what was seen as insufficient involvement on the part of the specialist careers service. There was specific criticism of the latter for alleged unrealistic attitudes and, in one case, "wild ideas" about what a particular youngster might be able to do.

While parents did note benefits on the social side, there were costs as well. Two parents mentioned the difficulty their child had experienced in adjusting to a large secondary school, having come from the intimacy of a small special school: "It is such a big change – she is still adjusting now [after seven months at school]." This perhaps suggests a need for more advance preparation of these pupils. Coping with teasing had been a problem in at least three cases. Lack of close friendships with able-bodied pupils was another source of disappointment. Only one mother claimed that her child had a particular friend from main school; by contrast three others made a point of stating that their child's friends were also disabled.

As noted, parents were very happy with the academic progress achieved. There were several mentions of problems with recording, however. Two of the pupils whose parents we interviewed had difficulty in writing. Both mothers referred to the fact that at the special school the children had been introduced to typing. This had not been continued in the present school, and parents were concerned about it, claiming not to know the reason for it. This may well reflect a gap in communication rather than in academic organisation.

Contact between home and school was in fact relatively limited, as is perhaps the norm for secondary level. Also, some parents lived a considerable distance away. (In some of the latter cases, persistent difficulty with transport was reported.) All parents interviewed, however, said that the amount of contact was sufficient. They visited on open evenings and the like, and felt able to pick up the 'phone and make an appointment to come in if something was bothering them. One set of parents noted that "if there is any change in the flow of her education" the school would invite them in to discuss it. The example they cited was when their daughter's A-level courses were too demanding and there was need to re-think them. In another case parents were invited in to discuss a particular behavioural problem. On the whole, however, contact was slight and of a fairly general nature.

Summary

This is a good example of how a special provision can be gradually absorbed into the life of a school. Initially the department functioned in a relatively separate way for many of its pupils, though academically able pupils did join the main school classes from the outset. As time went on, increasing numbers of physically handicapped pupils began to attend main school lessons and currently very few experience no integration. This assimilation has been helped by a policy of staff integration: staff attached to the department have main school commitments and some are attached to other departments as well, while some main school staff teach in the department. The process has been deliberately gradual, and the limits of assimilation have by no means been reached. Development is set on the right lines, however, and augurs well for the future.

In the meantime, the physically handicapped pupils – and their parents – are wholeheartedly in favour of being in this school. They have access to a good range of curriculum opportunities and specialist teaching for those with learning difficulties. They particularly endorsed the opportunities to mix with able-bodied peers in a natural way; though there are relatively few close friendships with the latter, physically handicapped pupils have become an accepted part of the school and derive considerable social benefit from being there.

Questions for the future include the following:
1. Would pupils benefit if preparation for adult life was extended to include, eg careers education and sex education, and provided on

a more systematic basis? Would this be possible in fact in view of the many different timetables followed by physically handicapped pupils? If not, can alternative arrangements be made to meet their undoubted needs in this regard?
2. Will the extension of the integration programme to less able pupils be accompanied by the requisite changes in the academic organisation of the main school? How will this extension affect the curriculum offerings of the department? Will it in fact continue to offer a teaching base?
3. If more thought was given to facilitating opportunities for socialising and removing some of the obstacles, would this enhance the nature and level of social interaction between physically handicapped pupils and their peers?
4. Given the success of this integration programme, are the reasons for delaying entry to ordinary school till 13+ still valid, or could an earlier transfer, eg at 9+, be entertained?

7
Links between a special school and an ordinary school

This programme of integration involves campus-sharing arrangements between an all-age school for the physically handicapped and an adjacent comprehensive school. Some 31 physically handicapped pupils – a majority of those at secondary level – spend varying amounts of time at the comprehensive.

Historical résumé

The example of integration that we discuss here is based on a special school and operates by splitting pupils' time in a flexible way between two different institutions. The special school, Wiseacres, is an all-age school accepting pupils from five years upwards and retaining them until 17, as necessary. It serves the southern half of a mixed urban–rural authority. It is purpose-built, dating from 1976, and was deliberately located on the campus of two existing ordinary schools (primary and secondary). The intention from the outset was to seek to realise the potential for integration implicit in such a location. Before the school opened, pupils had attended other special schools – either within or out of the county – where there were minimal opportunities for integration. The decision was taken at authority level to move toward integrated provision for physically handicapped pupils, more particularly those of secondary age, along with building a new special school. The authority considered the sites of all existing secondary schools, turning down several possibilities because of various practical difficulties. The location eventually selected was chosen because space was available, conveniently between existing primary and secondary schools, and because the head teacher of Oakley comprehensive was extremely enthusiastic about the proposed venture. In addition, he had had some prior experience of mainstreaming physically handicapped pupils.

It may be noted that the northern part of the authority was served by a special school of long standing which had become run-down and was due for renewal. Plans to relocate it were drawn up prior to local government reorganisation when it was part of a smaller separate authority. It was eventually relocated under the aegis of the newly formed authority some 12 months after Wiseacres opened. It offered something of a parallel to the Wiseacres situation in that it was located near an existing secondary school. However, the distance between the two schools was slightly greater; the schools were not actually linked, and though the separation was not great it did constitute a barrier. Also there was not a primary school on the campus. In the event, integration took off more slowly on this site and remained less extensive.

Aims and organisation

Wiseacres opened in 1976 with 63 pupils on roll, 34 of primary age, 29 of secondary age. The majority came from an existing school for physically handicapped and delicate pupils, with a small number transferring from other special provisions and ordinary primary schools. The number on roll quickly increased to over 100 with more pupils being accepted from the educational mainstream and from a special centre providing for primary age children with cerebral palsy. Given the wide age range, the school is conventionally divided into infant, junior and secondary departments. Our concern here is with the secondary department since this is where the main developments regarding integration have taken place. Secondary age pupils were considered the most suitable group to seek to integrate first. LEA officials and the head of Wiseacres were agreed that therapeutic and medical interventions were at their maximum during infant and junior schooling, and would tend to disrupt any extensive programme of integration. (This was not to say that integration should not be attempted at this younger age level.) In addition, the adjacent primary school was overcrowded at the time and was considered unsuitable for children who would inevitably take up more than the average amount of space and would have difficulty in their movements.

Oakley is a group 10 comprehensive with 915 pupils on roll and 55 staff. The school is divided into Lower (Years 1, 2, 3) and Upper (Years

4, 5) school, each under a deputy head. Within each year group there is one remedial class, the remaining pupils being organised as follows:

Year 1 — Mixed ability teaching throughout, but maths and English are timetabled in parallel to facilitate setting and remedial withdrawal. Six forms in all (including remedial).

Year 2 — Two broad bands with parallel timetabling of English, science and French. Seven forms in all.

Year 3 — More complex because of double language situation. Two forms studying both French and German constitute top band, two forms studying only French are next, then three mixed ability groups. Eight forms in all.

Years 4 & 5 — All children study mathematics and English in sets according to their ability. In addition to the core subjects each pupil chooses five optional subjects. The school offers GCE, CSE and City and Guilds Foundation Courses, as well as non-examination courses.

The pastoral organisation comprises eight tutor groups within each year group. Superimposed on the tutor groups is a house system; there are four houses so that in each year two tutor groups belong to each house. The tutor is the main link with the individual pupil and communicates directly with the relevant deputy head. He or she also collates reports and information on pupils from subject teachers.

From the beginning integration was the *raison d'être* for the choice of location for Wiseacres. Considerable deliberation on the precise form integration should take preceded the inception of this practice. A joint policy document laid down a number of principles governing integration:

1. Children integrated should be within the normal intellectual range of the school (receiving them).
2. Children should not make *significantly* greater demands on the class teacher than the pupils of that school.
3. Pupils from Wiseacres would be evenly distributed across each year group (in so far as this was compatible with their academic achievements) so that no class in ordinary school should become the 'handicapped class'.
4. Pupils from Wiseacres would not generally be placed in the remedial department of the comprehensive school.
5. In the case of pupils integrated for part of their time, their commitment to the ordinary school would, for those specific times, take priority over any special school commitment.

6. Integration into the educational mainstream for a part of a pupil's time would be regarded as part of the normal special school curriculum. The decision on this would rest with the various school staffs, and in accepting a placement at Wiseacres parents would be assumed to be in agreement with this decision.
7. Physically handicapped pupils spending over 80 per cent of their time in the ordinary school would normally be transferred to the roll of that school. Before any transfer took place, however, parents would be consulted and transfer would not take place against their wishes.

Pupils

Wiseacres caters for physically handicapped, delicate and epileptic pupils within its catchment area. (It also houses two special classes for communication disordered children, and a class for partially sighted children. We are not concerned with either of these groups here.) When it first opened a considerable number of older pupils were officially designated as 'delicate', eg asthmatics, epileptics, bronchitics. Over the past four years the proportion of the school population with more substantial disabling conditions has been steadily increasing. A wide range of ability is represented. Entry to Wiseacres is formally determined at a 'needs meeting' attended by senior representatives of Area Health, Social Services and the school psychological service, with LEA officials and head teachers of special schools also present. However, the meeting serves largely an administrative purpose, the effective decisions having frequently been taken beforehand when the papers (SE forms) on a given pupil are routed through to a particular school and the pupil in question seen by the head teacher and other members of staff.

Children under the age of five are not put up for entry to Wiseacres. This is largely because a specialist centre nearby, set up originally to provide for children with cerebral palsy, now functions as a pre-school assessment centre. In addition, pressure on places has tended to push up the age of entry. Although the majority of children are accepted as infants there is a further batch of entrants at the time of secondary transfer when pupils who have been satisfactorily placed in primary schools find that their local secondary school is physically unsuitable or that they cannot cope with the greater work rate and demands of mainstream secondary education. Placement at Wiseacres does not mean that a pupil is necessarily retained there throughout his or her school career. In the first two years of operation the school transferred 32 pupils to other schools. Of these 13 went to ordinary schools; these suffered from curable conditions such as Perthe's disease or were classed as 'delicate' – none was seriously disabled. A further 15 pupils transferred to the roll of Oakley school. Many of these latter did not come from the catchment area of Oakley school but were nevertheless retained there as the extent of their integration gradually built up.

Before the integration programme started an assessment was made of all pupils of the appropriate, ie secondary age who were likely to benefit. As a general rule those of low ability were retained within Wiseacres. This comprised approximately half of the initial intake. Otherwise, each case was examined on its own merits and an individual decision taken on each pupil. Various criteria were used. Apart from the requirement that pupils be within the "normal range of intelligence", a principal consideration was physical stamina and how much a pupil could cope with physically. Other factors included: communication ability; mobility – wheelchairs presented little problem, and certainly "less of a problem than a child who is unsteady" who might be at risk in narrow corridors; standard of recording and legibility in written work; possible need for modified facilities or resources – "an electric typewriter really isn't feasible"; personality factors and social ability – "how he forms relationships with other kids... reacts to new situations"; level of attainment in basic subjects; speed of work and rate of handwriting; and the extent to which the need of specialist medical treatment or therapies might impinge on the time available for integration.

The pupils eventually selected to attend Oakley are, broadly speaking, those of average intelligence with a variety of physical impairments. Of 31 pupils attending in 1979, six had cerebral palsy, three muscular dystrophy, two spina bifida, while others suffered from a wide range of handicapping conditions – brain tumour, asthma, diabetes, epilepsy, talipes and so on. Nine pupils had moderate to severe mobility problems, thus making their handicap quite visible; all nine use wheelchairs though only six are actually confined to them. Only two pupils were judged to have a significant communication problem. Measured intelligence when available ranged between 80 and 110 for most of the group, though the distribution was skewed toward the lower end with few having IQ above 100. There were some who fell outside this including a boy with IQ of 66 – though he in fact attended Oakley for only a small proportion of his time.

Staffing

The teaching complement of Wiseacres is 19 teachers including the head, with nine classroom auxiliaries. The secondary department comprises six teachers; some have commitments in the infant and junior departments of the school so that there is the full-time equivalent of $4\frac{3}{4}$ teachers. They include a maths specialist and an English teacher, with others offering science, art, home economics and physical education. These teachers are involved primarily with the pupils who are not integrated or who integrate only minimally. These pupils are grouped into three classes: Year I; Years II/III; Years IV/V. Within the framework established to teach these pupils they may also provide a degree of support for those pupils attending Oakley.

It may be noted that staffing at Oakley has been augmented to take account of the integration programme. This is on the basis of one extra teacher for each eight Wiseacres pupils who attend for at least 80 per cent of their time plus a further teacher in respect of the partial integration programme. These extra appointments are not tied to the integration programme but serve rather to improve the school's staffing establishment and enhance its capacity to deal with educational problems.

As a special school for the physically handicapped Wiseacres has the usual complement of physiotherapy, nursing and care staff that one would expect: two physiotherapists and an aide, an occupational therapist, three part-time speech therapists, two qualified nurses and a health visitor. These staff are employed by Area Health and do not report directly to the head teacher. This fact is reflected in the degree of separation between educational and paramedical provision within the school. Both sets of professionals operate independently of each other. Teachers (at Wiseacres) receive information on the medical and physiotherapeutic implications of given physical conditions, but there is little evidence of physiotherapists making direct contribution to classroom practice or of other collaborative working.

This is perhaps no great problem as far as teachers at Wiseacres are concerned since a good many are experienced teachers of the physically handicapped and, in any case, the necessary specialist expertise is readily to hand. In an integration context, however, none of this is the case. Oakley staff do not have a background in physical handicap and can be presumed to be ignorant of many matters that bear on handling and educating the disabled pupil. While the pupils who integrate tend to be the less problematic cases and are less likely to make undue demands on ordinary teachers' time, there is clear need of a general introduction to physical handicap and the educational consequences. In an effort to provide this the head teacher of Wiseacres organised an 11-week in-service course in autumn 1978. This covered the main physical and sensory handicapping conditions. It was well attended by Wiseacres staff but poorly attended by Oakley staff. Those who did attend were senior staff. Otherwise, the only information that Oakley teachers receive concerning the physically handicapped is a list which is circulated at the start of each school year giving the names of all integrating pupils, a description of their handicapping condition(s), and information which may assist them in the classroom.

The involvement of outside specialist agencies in the programme of integration has been fairly slight. Contact with LEA officers and advisers is on an ad hoc and infrequent basis and would be in the context of, for example, solving problems, dealing with unusual situations or showing visitors around. The specific contribution of the careers service is discussed later. The school psychological service has tended to be involved in individual assessments, usually as a result of crisis referrals. More recently, a psychologist has begun visiting Wiseacres on a regular basis, talking to members of staff, sitting in on staff meetings and generally becoming familiar with work of the school. The aim is to move beyond the individual assessment role, "to consult much more with schools and get them to develop the skills...themselves". We note that the same psychologist does not cover Wiseacres and Oakley schools, which is a cause for some regret in the case of integrating pupils.

Accommodation and resources

The two schools are physically connected by means of a short, completely enclosed link corridor. Wiseacres, as a purpose-built school, does not present major difficulties as regards access, physical movement about the premises, accommodation or inappropriate facilities. The same cannot be said of Oakley. Parts of the building are two-storey. Most practical rooms, eg science laboratories, are on the ground floor though home economics and art/craft areas, are on the first floor – as is some classroom accommodation. A lift was installed to allow access to the first floor. One section of this floor is still inaccessible to the physically handicapped, although since these four rooms are used for geography and remedial work, it has been possible to arrange alternative locations for groups which contain physically handicapped pupils. The school also contains a number of mobile rooms, two of which are inaccessible to pupils in wheelchairs, as is a laboratory which is housed in a mobile classroom. Considerable modification to both the physical premises and facilities has taken place. For example, benches, lathes and other machinery in the technology department have been modified to fit the needs of disabled pupils, while more recently the home economics department has been adapted.

A serious problem in the past has been overcrowding in the corridors. A slow-moving wheelchair can cause considerable disruption at change of lessons, while an ambulant pupil on splints can cause an even greater hold-up as well as being physically at risk. (For this reason some pupils have taken to wheelchairs while on Oakley premises.) The problem has been also tackled by introducing a one-way flow within the central part of the school, and by allowing pupils whose movement presents difficulties to leave lessons a few minutes early. Although this has alleviated the problem, it has by no means overcome it, especially as the number of physically handicapped pupils in Oakley has increased.

There is also the matter of fire regulations. This proved quite difficult to resolve satisfactorily; it was 18 months before it was possible to establish satisfactory precautions in the event of fire. There is no means of escape from the first floor other than by pupils being physically carried down the stairs (in the event of fire the lift would be out of action). It has been stipulated that no more than six pupils with wheelchairs should be on the first floor at any one time. Also, fire-retardant doors which offer an hour's protection have been installed.

As regards educational (and other) resources, Wiseacres is well equipped with curriculum and other materials needed in the education of physically handicapped pupils and, as such, represents a major resource for pupils attending Oakley. Specialised items not available in the latter can be acquired from Wiseacres, and there is in fact a degree of transfer of resources for educational purposes. Thus, typewriters and other recording devices from Wiseacres are used in Oakley by a number of pupils who have difficulty with manual writing or notetaking. The main constraints seem to be practical ones – it has not been possible, for example, to arrange for the use of electric or adapted typewriters in Oakley.

Curriculum

As we have seen, a range of options is open, from little or no integration through to spending 80 per cent of the school week within Oakley – at which stage the pupil will generally transfer onto the roll of that school, though still continuing to receive specialist attention from Wiseacres (medication, therapy, etc) as necessary. The extent of the special school's contribution to a pupil's curriculum is therefore directly related to the amount of time spent integrated. While only eight pupils were integrated for 70 per cent or more of their time in autumn 1979, equally only five pupils were spending less than a third of their time in the comprehensive. So, for the majority of pupils who are integrated the educational contribution from Wiseacres is secondary to that from Oakley.

In the early days of this scheme pupils who were spending time at Oakley tended to receive more educational attention than their more seriously handicapped peers, in that Wiseacres staff sought to provide extra maths and English for them, to follow up aspects of the Oakley curriculum that were causing difficulties, and generally to supplement their educational programme by laying on those activities that could not easily be followed at Oakley (PE is a good example of the latter). This additional attention was justified on various grounds: the newness of the venture; the fact that staff were exploring novel ways of working; and, above all, because some pupils were joining the comprehensive a year late, going directly into the second or third year classes well under way where they might have missed out on essential groundwork.

Wiseacres staff became increasingly concerned at the potential imbalance in the treatment of the two groups, and this led to a reorganisation of its secondary department at the end of the second full year of the scheme's operation. This was in the direction of emphasising rather more the needs of the seriously handicapped pupils who spent little or no time at Oakley: "The kids in the home school must be catered for first... those integrating have to fit in with whatever is available" upon returning. In support of this it was claimed that the need of integrating pupils for specialist follow-up or supplementary work was now less than it had been for their predecessors since all were now commencing in the first year. Finding the right balance between the needs of two groups and meeting both sets of needs adequately within the limited resources of a small secondary department has posed considerable problems for Wiseacres staff.

Under the present arrangements, staff naturally seek to provide gainful use of time for integrating pupils on their return to Wiseacres. (Note that all pupils when not timetabled at Oakley are timetabled in the special school. This is because supervision cannot be arranged within the comprehensive when they do not have lesson commitments.) If their timetabled commitments at Oakley allow, all pupils receive a period of each of PE, music/drama and home economics. In addition, a supplementary period of maths and English is provided each week for those pupils judged to need it. There is some follow-up work in individual cases, organised on an ad hoc basis, and determined by the deployment of the staff of Wiseacres' secondary department. Some pupils will of course continue to receive specialised therapy or other medical treatment.

How is a pupil's timetable actually developed? As pupils approach the age of secondary transfer they are assessed in terms of academic ability. General tests of maths and English are used for this purpose, allied to the knowledge of individuals that the staff have. In the case of new entrants to the school, joining at the end of primary schooling, they are usually retained within the secondary department of Wiseacres for the first term while staff assess their capacities and attainments. There is also consideration of the personal characteristics of pupils mentioned earlier – physical stamina, communication ability and so on. Decisions are then taken about the extent of integration, which subjects an individual will take, how much support is likely to be needed and so on. These decisions are taken within Wiseacres and involve the head teacher, deputies and relevant class teachers. The educational psychologist may offer an opinion, and nursing and therapy staff are consulted to see if there are any overriding medical or physical reasons against integration. Having decided that a given pupil will attend Oakley and for how much of the school week, the decision on actual placement (the particular teaching group) is made by Oakley staff on the basis of information fed through to them and consultation between the respective liaison teachers.

Of course, decisions concerning the amount and nature of subjects taken are not arrived at simply by looking at the pupil's general ability and personal characteristics. There are various other factors to consider and staff stated or implied a number of working principles they had recourse to. In many subjects knowledge and understanding build up cumulatively and if integration is to come at all it must come early in the pupils' secondary career. Then there is the intention of stretching pupils' academically: "You know what they are capable of... you try to stretch them to their absolute limit." Another important concern is to avail of the superior resources – in terms of both subject specialism and learning resources and equipment – of the comprehensive school. Accordingly, there is a predisposition toward such subject areas as languages, sciences, history and geography. There is somewhat less of an emphasis on subjects such as PE and home economics where the circumstances of the special school can be more favourably tailored to meet pupils' special needs. In certain subjects, notably craft, specialist teachers have pointed to the difficulty of teaching the physically handicapped in classes approaching 30 or more pupils.

Preparation for adult living

A major difficulty of the integration programmes has been the making of adequate preparation for post-school living. Wiseacres staff were aware of this problem but felt hampered by various factors. Both schools ran leavers' courses. Some Wiseacres' pupils follow the course at Oakley, but in general it was considered not to be suited to the needs of physically handicapped pupils: its starting points were too removed from their experience, and there was no effort to make up for deficiencies in their experience. In any case, Oakley staff had assumed that preparation for adult life was the responsibility of the special school. Wiseacres' own secondary department was, as noted, directed primarily to meeting the needs of non-integrating pupils. In fact, the course offered was based on the Stara Leavers Programme developed for the slow learner. Moreover, those attending Oakley do so on an individual basis, and it is quite impossible to lay on a leavers' course at Wiseacres to fit in with so many different timetables. It may be noted that sex education is provided for girls within Wiseacres but not for boys.

Opprtunities for work experience have been limited. There has been a shortage of suitable openings for Oakley pupils in general, partly due to the employment situation in the area, and priority has been given to the able-bodied on the grounds that they will profit more from opportunity. In any case, it is careers service policy not to have physically handicapped pupils in the work experience programme organised at Oakley. Wiseacres has sought to develop its own work experience programme, but this is as yet extremely limited. A difficulty is the small number of leavers involved in any given year, allied to the range of special needs to be covered.

A specialist careers officer is scheduled to visit Wiseacres for an hour each week to provide a course described as "a personal programme of identification". This seeks to cover: the self; the self and employment; commonalities within different forms of work and so on. Due to irregular attendance and limited contact between the careers officer and the school's career teacher, this was more a matter of prospect than achievement. It should be noted that the irregular attendance on the part of the careers officer was attributed to the fact that Wiseacres, following Oakley, worked to a six-day timetable whereas the other special schools on his beat had five-day timetables, and as a consequence it was not possible for him to schedule regular visits.

Academic integration

In the academic year 1979/80 there were 31 Wiseacres pupils attending Oakley. The number of periods they spent there is summarised in the Table below. (Oakley works to a six-day, 48-period week.)

Number of periods spent at Oakley by Wiseacres pupils

Number of periods	Frequency
4–6	5
16	3
20–24	8
26–28	4
32–34	5
36–38	5
43	1
	31

It may be noted that pupils attending four to six periods do so for art only. Also, those first year pupils who are felt to be physically or emotionally capable of spending only limited time at Oakley will concentrate on subjects which it would be difficult to take up at a later stage – eg French. They would not take maths or English there since the same syllabus in these is available at Wiseacres.

Once a decision has been taken to place a given pupil in Oakley for a greater or lesser period of time and an appropriate class selected for him or her, the intention is to make a minimum of interventions. In each school a senior member of staff (deputy head from Wiseacres, senior mistress from Oakley) has formal responsibility for liaising on all practical matters involving the physically handicapped on a day-to-day basis. From the comprehensive side this role was defined as follows:

'The senior mistress... must keep them [Wiseacres] informed on administration procedures in Oakley which directly affect Wiseacres and on the welfare of partially integrated pupils. She is heavily reliant for information of this type on feedback from [heads of upper and lower school], as well as from heads of academic departments and individual teaching staff.'

In addition, there is a termly formal review of all integrating pupils attended by senior staff from both schools. This is discussed more fully later.

With regard to pupils' academic progress, three quite different sets of perspectives may be noted: those of the staffs of the two schools, and those of the pupils. Wiseacres staff were highly satisfied with the way the programme of integration had developed. They were aware of problems, but none was insurmountable and pupils were deriving a great deal of benefit. In four years of operation only two pupils had given cause for real concern. One teacher, however, observed that some pupils became diffident and lost confidence as a result of attending Oakley: "They lose their independence a lot... lack confidence in the practical subjects." It was felt that this might be due to pupils being brought up sharply against their inadequacies within the context of the comprehensive school, compounded by the fact that it was often impossible to allow every pupil practical experience of a task or activity in the time available.

Staff of Oakley school were less sanguine and expressed more doubts about the overall educational value of integration. They drew attention to numerous difficulties. One senior member of staff echoed remarks made by other teachers when he said that "he was not happy about what they are achieving academically". A number of pupils were seen to be struggling to cope with the demands made of them. Various possible reasons were advanced for this. First, the pace of work was faster than pupils were used to, the more so as Oakley was in the process of raising its academic standards. Secondly, pupils' lack of background, coupled with the tendency to look immediately to an adult to solve any difficulty encountered, held them back: "They're used to a 1:3 [ordinary teacher's perception] situation... I have seen staff giving more time [to] them – it's not fair on the class as a whole." One teacher spoke for several colleagues when he said, "They're lovely kids, but if I've got to spend 15 minutes with each child, it's not on...." (It is policy to spread integrating pupils across the various teaching groups with a usual maximum of two pupils per class.) Thirdly, there was a feeling that some pupils were taking too many subjects at Oakley; they worked at a slower pace and encountered numerous difficulties, not all of which could immediately be attended to by a member of staff. Fourthly, it was sometimes difficult to determine which ability band they were best placed in. Where there is doubt about a pupil's placement, Wiseacres' policy is to push for placement in a lower band so that the individual has the chance of moving up if he or she demonstrates the necessary ability, rather than risking demotion by demanding too much of the pupil from the start. Fifthly, there were comments which touch upon the immaturity of many integrating pupils – "not being used to formal education", "craving for individual attention", "completely different set of social values" (eg expecting members of staff to be friends and in some cases surrogate parents, as is possible within the special school).

Further difficulties – which both sets of teachers drew attention to – stemmed from organisational aspects of mainstream education: large classes (frequently 25 + pupils); the disadvantage of mixed ability grouping under certain circumstances; pressure of the examination system; and pressure on a pupil's time to get from one part of the school to another at change of lesson. In the case of fourth and fifth year pupils, for whom an option system exists over and above the core subjects, these difficulties were considered to be particularly acute where pupils were following examination subjects. It is possible that at this stage some pupils may be in teaching groups higher than their ability would warrant. For example, some pupils take the City and Guilds Foundation course even though it is highly unlikely that they will actually sit the exam at the end of it.

To return to the discrepancy in the perspectives of the respective staff, part of the reason seems to lie in the different aims and expectations teachers held of the integration scheme. Staff at Oakley seemed to expect that physically handicapped pupils attending their classes would achieve comparable standards to other pupils, and that while they might need some extra help, they would not require inordinate amounts of individual attention. When these expectations on occasion failed to be met, teachers regarded it as failure. Wiseacres staff, on the other hand, attached importance to other goals beside academic achievement. They did not disregard it, but they also sought the opportunity for their pupils to participate in the life of an ordinary school – a goal whose achievement was distinct from academic targets, though of course overlapping with them. This meant that success or failure was measured along different dimensions for them.

One particular factor related to what pupils are or are not achieving academically has to do with the nature and extent of support available from the special school. In point of fact this was relatively limited particularly in relation to the expectations of some Oakley staff: "We are carrying the load"... "It has got to be a two-way thing". The major difficulty here lay in the lack of direct contact between classroom teachers from the respective schools. This is partly the result of pressure on teachers' time, partly because the formal system of liaison in operation does not particularly encourage such contact. If a member of either staff wanted to make contact with his or her counterpart, the procedure was to get in touch with the liaison teacher who would make the necessary arrangements. The purpose of this was to ensure that the liaison teachers were kept fully informed on what was going on. The formality of the procedure, however, perhaps resulted in its being little used, since there was little direct communication between teachers.

There were other difficulties too. Oakley staff questioned whether Wiseacres staff were capable of supplementing pupils' work across the secondary curriculum, "when they don't know what we are doing". In any case, most are primary trained and acknowledged doubts themselves. While most felt capable of supporting in their particular subject up to CSE level, providing support in certain subjects (eg languages, science, history and geography) was particularly problematic. A further problem is the considerable difference between the nature and the level of curriculum of the two schools.

A further perspective is provided by the pupils themselves. We discussed with 15 of them what it was like to attend Oakley on a part-time basis. They were divided in their attitudes. The majority were highly enthusiastic; they were well aware of the greater competitiveness and demands of the ordinary school, but appreciative of the chance to be seen to hold their own, educationally at least, with the able-bodied. Attending Oakley brought with it various benefits: there was much greater breadth to a subject – "the teacher explains more over here"; more was demanded of them – "teachers expect you to do homework and to keep up with the lessons"... "you've got to think for yourself"; and for many it increased their confidence – one boy having successfully coped with the subjects he had been started on was now demanding more... "there is no reason why I shouldn't do art over there".

However, it was recognised by all that the benefits were not without their costs. The lack of general experience was considered particularly disadvantaging – "Their kids [comprehensive pupils] have got all the basics"... "They [special schools] slow you down, you miss so much". They had also found it difficult to come to terms with receiving less individual attention in the comprehensive. Having been used to small classes and a high level of support they sometimes construed it as abruptness and unwillingness to help when ordinary teachers treated them just like any other pupil. Some found this hard to take and hankered after the secure and familiar regime of Wiseacres.

Monitoring of progress

For the first two years of the programme the main check on how pupils were coping with attending Oakley was through a system of personal liaison between the two liaison officers from the respective schools. The intention was that any teacher who was having difficulties in teaching physically handicapped pupils or was aware of problems pupils faced would communicate this to the liaison officer, who would convey the message to his or her counterpart in Wiseacres. This apart, individual subject specialists completed a very brief termly report on the handicapped pupil(s) they taught, giving a test mark, an overall grade and a general (subjective) judgment.

There were two main limitations with this system of monitoring. First, too much was left to the initiative of individual teachers who, however well disposed, had many other demands on their time. The physically handicapped were a small minority, and any undue amount of time spent on their behalf would inevitably reduce the time available for spending with other pupils. Secondly, there is no substitute for *direct* contact between two teachers covering similar lesson content or at least working within a common subject area. Even if the subject specialist is sufficiently aware of the signals which indicate that a pupil is experiencing difficulties or not achieving his or her potential it is a considerable jump to this being effectively communicated to special education personnel, and their being able to put into operation the necessary remediation (eg reinforcement of lesson content, or additional supplementary work).

Fears expressed by certain members of staff, more particularly from the comprehensive school, that pupils' limitations were not being sufficiently closely noted and acted on, were instrumental in prompting the adoption of a new monitoring system midway through our study. This comprised an assessment of each pupil along five criteria: ability; attainment; integration with classmates (ie social assimilation); behaviour; and attendance. A five-point assessment scale was used. This was to be undertaken annually, overseen by the relevant deputy head. Discussion of the information thus elicited occurs at one of the termly review meetings attended by the head teacher and deputy from Wiseacres, the head, senior mistress and heads of upper and lower schools from Oakley.

The social context

Data on the nature and extent of social integration between the integrating pupils and the main pupil body at Oakley reveal contrasting perceptions. A social/emotional adjustment scale was completed on integrating pupils by Wiseacres' staff, using the following categories:
1. Well accepted, popular, has many friends in both Oakley/Wiseacres.
2. Accepted, popular in Wiseacres, has one or two friends at Oakley.
3. Accepted with small circle of friends at Wiseacres, somewhat isolated in Oakley.
4. Not a popular child – has one or two friends in Wiseacres, tends to be rejected at Oakley.
5. Rejected at both schools – avoided by other children.

The following distribution of scores was obtained:

Distribution of scores on social/emotional adjustment scale

Score	Frequency
1	0
1/2	6
2	14
2/3	2
3	8
4	1
5	0
	31

It was emphasised that isolation at Oakley was to some extent a consequence of spending relatively little time there. Lack of contact time more generally was considered a significant factor behind many pupils' lack of friendships with able-bodied pupils. Speaking of the wider group of pupils who have spent time in Oakley since the scheme began, staff estimated that 49 out of the 67 had derived social and/or emotional benefit. The head teacher of Wiseacres pointed to greater maturity, independence and social competence – 'They become more like normal secondary age children, less like the handicapped sub-culture in their attitudes and aspirations.'

A less favourable picture emerged from talking to members of Oakley staff, and in some cases pupils themselves. The rather immature behaviour that some displayed, and their general lack of worldliness, were quite widely commented on. 'Some over-react because of self-consciousness'... 'Many children bear grudges from their inabilities', were two teachers' comments. A third, describing one pupil in particular, noted how she was "very quiet... not sure of herself... afraid to ask". Having made friends with one able-bodied girl in particular, she was considered by this teacher to be "very happy in that little world of the girl next to her". More generally, there was a feeling that many pupils had failed to make the necessary mental switch outward to their new situation and remained psychologically part of Wiseacres. A senior teacher from Oakley noted a tendency among "the wheelchair cases to high-tail it back [to Wiseacres]" once a lesson was over. (Of course in some instances this might be because the lesson following was at the special school.) We ourselves did notice a reluctance to remain on Oakley premises if no lesson was scheduled. Further confirmation came from a Wiseacres teachers who remarked that even those pupils who had transferred onto the Oakley roll "still very much hang around this school... you're always chasing them back".

We discussed the general issue of social assimilation with some of the pupils themselves, 15 in all. Only two admitted to a desire to be back within the special school full-time, and – significantly – these were both adolescent girls who were severely physically disabled. The social reasons they advanced for this (there were also educational reasons) were interesting. One spoke of how able-bodied pupils would stare at her and jostle her in the corridors (she used a wheelchair). The other referred to the considerable teasing she had had to put up with and suggested that Oakley pupils only picked upon the negative aspects – "Some people can't see well on me."

As a group the pupils were unanimous that one of the two major difficulties they all had encountered was teasing (the other was to do with work rate and the more academic approach to education in Oakley). It seemed that teasing had been a problem in the early days of the programme and could still cause difficulties for a newcomer joining it. There was widespread agreement that in order to survive one had to be determined to do battle to deflect the taunts and jibes and to win the acceptance of the able-bodied. One older boy expressed this succinctly: "They all think they are harder than you are, you have to prove yourself. Once you've done that then you're made."

These pupils left us in no doubt that in their eyes attending an ordinary school – however demanding it could be, at times even distressing – was nevertheless preferable to special schooling. Just how demanding the experience could be did not seem to be fully appreciated by the staffs of the schools concerned. There was no indication from talking to Oakley teachers of the pressure from peers that many pupils undoubtedly experienced. Wiseacres staff, although they did not doubt that a degree of teasing occurred, were satisfied that this was nothing very serious, otherwise it would have come to their notice. This is not necessarily the case, however, since pupils had learned that one did not tell tales except in the most extreme circumstances. As one pupil put it, "You don't feel right going and telling the teacher [at Wiseacres] on someone." Keeping quiet had been internalised as another of the lessons of life.

Oakley teachers did recognise social benefits accruing to the physically handicapped from the integration programme. Particular mention was made of growth in confidence, improved social adjustment, enhanced understanding across a broader spectrum of life, and ease of interaction with able-bodied pupils. Understandably perhaps, there was more frequent mention from these teachers of the social benefits for able-bodied pupils: notably, the increased awareness of the difficulties that the physically handicapped faced, allied to a more sympathetic and humane response toward them.

A number of points need to be made to put the picture in perspective. First, the degree of assimilation of the physically handicapped depends in part on the amount of time spent in Oakley and on the nature of the subjects taken. Some spend relatively little time there, while many integrate for the more academic subjects where there is likely to be less informal contact. Secondly, integrating pupils returned to Wiseacres to maintain long-standing friendships with those who were not integrated. Thirdly, opportunities for social interaction within Oakley are limited. As one teacher commented: "It's what we have to offer at lunchtime as to whether they stay or not." In fact, there was very little and what there was was not particularly appropriate (eg sports). This was made worse by Wiseacres providing an extensive range of clubs and activities. (It should be noted that whereas clubs and societies have to be held at Wiseacres over the lunch period because the school is vacated at around 15.30, the majority of clubs and societies at Oakley take place after school.)

Fourthly, throughout much of the period of our fieldwork the school meals system worked against social interactions in that physically handicapped pupils could eat more cheaply at Wiseacres. Later, with the introduction of a cash cafeteria system at Oakley this anomaly was removed. However, those integrating pupils for whom movement was awkward or who perhaps were slow eaters were considered to face considerable pressures if they chose to take lunch in the comprehensive. Fifthly, for some pupils who spend most of their time in Oakley, lunchtime is the only period of the day when specialist therapy and other medical treatment can be carried out without disrupting their timetable. Further, the lack of specially adapted toileting in the comprehensive means that some pupils have to use breaktimes to use the facilities in Wiseacres. Sixthly, few of those who are integrated actually live within the catchment area of Oakley and therefore lack any natural affinity toward it. Also, there are no opportunities to meet Oakley pupils out of school hours, other than what individual sets of parents might arrange, because pupils are tied to the special transportation system of taxis and minibuses which leave school promptly at 15.30 daily.

In summary, our overall impression is one of tolerance by the able-bodied and some friendships. Most of the pupils we talked to claimed to have at least one friend at Oakley, in corroboration of the Table presented at the beginning of the section. The degree of assimilation was limited, however, and the physically handicapped remained a distinct group within the comprehensive school. One of the critical factors would clearly seem to be the lack of familiarity with physically handicapped pupils. Some of the first pupils entered in this scheme spoke of the ignorance and misperceptions among the able-bodied: "They treated you like you were robots"... "They didn't realise we were physically handicapped, they thought we were mentally handicapped". Had there been an explicit attempt to prepare Oakley pupils for the arrival of Wiseacres pupils, it is possible that some of the caution and misperceptions that arose subsequently could have been avoided. As things stand, it seems as if time and the increasing familiarity this brings, together with the greater numbers of pupils involved, are leading to a gradual improvement.

Parents

Contact between home and school tends to be fairly formalised. Opportunities for contact are the well-established ones – parent evenings, meetings with the specialist careers officer, school fêtes and so on. The fact that the integrating pupils attend two schools makes for a slight complication. This has been resolved by maintaining the special school as the point of contact even when a pupil is integrated for most of his or her timetable, so that Wiseacres mediates between parents and Oakley teachers.

We interviewed six sets of parents, four of whose children were integrated quite extensively. In a fifth case the girl in question, having reached the point where over 80 per cent of her schooling was provided within Oakley, had transferred onto its roll. In the sixth case the amount of integration was minimal (five out of 40 periods per week). With one exception, parents voiced considerable satisfaction with the arrangement. Three made mention of the fact that their son or daughter now had to work much harder, and that this was paying dividends with regard to school achievement. Two sets of parents spoke critically of what they perceived as over-lax special schooling earlier in their child's educational career: "He was left too long to do what he liked"..."The best thing that ever happened". Comment from a third set of parents disclosed raised aspirations for their daughter: "At first we thought she wouldn't do anything", but her last report had suggested considerable potential, "more than [we] expected".

The second main cause for parental satisfaction was the fact that their child was part of the mainstream, surrounded by and benefiting from 'normal' modes of behaviour. One mother who had been alarmed at the abnormal mannerisms that her daughter had picked up from special school – "being with handicapped bairns all the time makes her more handicapped" – had found considerable improvement since she began attending Oakley. "Mixing with others is bringing her on...She can now do ordinary things." In a second case, that of a girl who throughout her primary education had attended ordinary school but had had to transfer to Wiseacres at secondary stage, her father observed, "It [returning to the ordinary sector via the integrated placement] has changed her attitude, she's not so snappy and defensive...she has seen that there are other people in worse predicaments." A third parent remarked in very forthright fashion, "Handicapped people should be treated as normal wherever possible." In common with others, she saw special schools as very sheltered confines.

Despite the favourable reaction overall, parents did voice some concerns. One was the teasing that their son or daughter had experienced. (Most parents in fact made mention of this.) Whereas some spoke very matter-of-factly about this – "something she'll have to get used to" – others clearly were very worried about the effect this might be having – "she doesn't like being called 'spastic'". A second recurring theme was the absence of close friends. Even where a friendship had been struck up with an able-bodied pupil – this was mentioned spontaneously by three of the five sets of parents – the fact that all the pupils concerned lived outside of Oakley's catchment area made it very difficult to further the friendship outside of school hours. A third feature was the anxiety of many of the parents about the future. There was an underlying fear that integration with its attendant raising of aspirations might lead to greater disappointments later in life. As one parent put it, "It's OK teaching them, but what are they going to do in the community after that?" Parents appreciated the benefits of integration and were in no doubt about wanting them for their children, but they were also aware – perhaps in a keener way because of the integration programme – of the difficulties and potential disappointments that lay ahead.

Summary

This integration programme involves the sharing of pupils between different schools. A new special school for physically handicapped pupils sited on the same campus as existing primary and comprehensive schools has developed an extensive programme of integration with the comprehensive. Physically handicapped pupils join classes there, full-time or part-time as appropriate, transferring to the roll of the comprehensive when they spend most of their time there. The secondary department of the special school offers an appropriate programme for those retained within it, as well as providing some limited support for integrating pupils. The strength of the arrangement is the flexibility it offers; physically handicapped pupils have access to a full comprehensive curriculum, or to whatever selection from it that is judged likely to be beneficial, while retaining access to the resources and expertise of a special school. There have been many problems in working between two separate institutions with different systems and priorities, developing liaison between the respective staffs and so on, but much has been achieved: pupils' educational opportunities have been expanded greatly; social contact between the two groups, though limited, has led to more normal behaviour patterns, and greater tolerance on the part of the able-bodied; and the programme has won endorsement from pupils, parents and both staffs.

Questions for future development including the following:
1. While staff at the comprehensive school welcome the programme and are prepared to support it, many expressed diffidence or uncertainty about handling physically handicapped pupils or voiced concern about particular aspects of the programme. Will it be possible to meet these concerns by building on the liaison arrangements, through further in-service training or by other means?
2. Various difficulties have been encountered in seeking to prepare integrating pupils for adult life. Will it be possible to use the comprehensive school as a resource in tackling these problems, or is formal preparation best provided separately?
3. To date, there has been virtually no integration of staff. Would a measure of exchange be beneficial in, for example, strengthening the secondary curriculum of the special school or resolving the problems experienced by teachers in the comprehensive?
4. In view of the success achieved at secondary level, what steps will be taken to further integration at primary level, taking care to learn from experience to date? What will be the implications for the special school of a thoroughgoing programme of integration throughout the whole school?

Part Three
Provision for Pupils with Impaired Hearing

Alternatives to special schooling have been available for some time for pupils with partial hearing losses, either through units for partially hearing pupils or peripatetic services. The first units were opened in London and Salford in 1947/48 (DES, 1967). After this there was no development until the mid-1950s when further units were started. A period of slow growth was followed by rapid expansion in the 1960s. The number of units in England and Wales increased from 66 in 1962 to 348 in 1976 (NCTD, 1976). In many areas there was a parallel expansion in peripatetic provision for pupils with mild hearing losses. This development occurred slightly later, but there was rapid growth from the mid-1960s onwards. The number of teachers in post increased from 41 in 1962 to 363 in 1976.

Both of these forms of provision were developed for pupils with no more than partial hearing losses. These are pupils with impaired hearing 'whose development of speech and language, even if retarded, is following a normal pattern, and who require for their education special arrangements or facilities though not necessarily all the educational methods used for deaf pupils' (DES, 1962). This was in contrast with the profoundly deaf pupil who requires 'education by methods suitable for pupils with little or no naturally acquired speech and language'. These latter for the most part remained in special schools.

A number of developments led to a weakening of the former hard-and-fast distinction between partial hearing and profound deafness. Advances in hearing aid technology increased the capacity to make use of residual hearing, while the introduction and subsequent refinement of early auditory training (from upwards of six months) led to levels of linguistic competence hitherto considered unlikely. As far as education was concerned, there was a growing realisation that hearing loss was only one factor in determining the need for special provision and on its own was a limited guide to educational functioning. As a result some professionals working within the field of deaf education came to question schools for the deaf as the automatic placement for the deaf child. Pressure for change came from families as well, with parents urging that their children should at least be able to commence their education within a playgroup, nursery or infant school along with hearing children.

Both forms of provision described here fit into this general context. The first takes in three special centres – infant, junior and secondary – for pupils with a full range of hearing loss. Unlike the traditional unit for partially hearing pupils these cater for both profoundly deaf and partially hearing pupils. The second is an innovative project whereby pupils, again with a range of hearing losses, attend ordinary schools on an individual basis.

8
Special centres for the hearing impaired

This provision comprises three special centres for hearing impaired pupils located at three different schools (infant, junior and secondary) in a small urban authority. Each centre is designed to cater for up to 30 pupils.

Historical résumé

Historically, the authority in question had relied upon neighbouring authorities for a good deal of its special educational provision. This was the more feasible given the densely populated nature of the area and the wide range of good provision within easy reach, though some residential placement was necessary. However, in the early 1960s this practice was increasingly questioned and challenged. This was due to the shift both within educational circles and society at large away from special schooling; to changes in personnel within the authority; and to signs of impending financial stringency. A policy decision was taken to develop 'home' facilities wherever possible for pupils with special educational needs. The hearing impaired population was one of the main beneficiaries. Three special centres with some 90 places and a team of three peripatetic teachers have been created in the years since 1967. (The first centre was in fact situated within a neighbouring authority, becoming part of this authority as a result of boundary changes.) By this means the authority is providing for practically all of its hearing impaired pupils across the full age range as well indeed as for a number of pupils from other authorities – about one third of the total intake. The principal exceptions are the multiply handicapped hearing impaired and those few secondary age pupils who have remained in the out-county special schools they have long attended.

There was a phased opening of these special centres as the initial cohort of hearing impaired pupils moved through the school system. When the first – infant age – centre was opened integrated provision was still relatively uncommon and, not surprisingly perhaps, its early history was unsettled. It seems not to have been clear to all concerned that the provision for the hearing impaired was to be an integral part of the school and not an independent domain falling entirely under the jurisdiction of the teacher in charge. Some six years later, with a group of pupils ready to transfer to junior school, a second centre was opened at a separate junior school within the same vicinity. Secondary provision did not come into existence until autumn 1976.

Aims and organisation

The authority did not set down specific guidelines on policy for the centres, leaving it to individual teachers in charge and head teachers to develop their own working practice within an overall framework of integration as and when possible. It is considered important to retain flexibility, something that a tight and formal policy would not permit. In the absence of a head of service with overall responsibility for the three centres, however, common policy and working practice were slow in developing. Staff currently attach importance to liaison and are building links between the centres, but for much of their existence the three have tended to operate quite autonomously. It is only recently that the respective teachers in charge have been meeting regularly to discuss matters of policy and to try to co-ordinate their respective approaches.

The primary aim of this provision has been to provide special education for pupils with varying degrees of hearing loss. With few exceptions staff did not see the active pursuit of integration as a major target. The central goal of developing pupils' ability to communicate, preferably in an oral way, is no different from that of deaf education in general; the fact of being in an ordinary school made little material difference to the educational objectives. Teachers in all three centres would claim to be seeking to provide their pupils with the means to communicate linguistically with hearing people in a predominantly hearing society – a task that entails consciously supplying a good deal of the everyday knowledge and understandings that a hearing person will pick up incidentally.

Within this general consensus there are significant differences, depending upon the stage of development of the individual pupil. At infant level the emphasis is on developing the rudiments of language. Language reinforcement underpins every aspect of the curriculum, with the teaching of reading, writing and number woven in as and when appropriate. At the junior level it is principally a matter of language consolidation for the majority of pupils, together with the introduction of a somewhat rigorous approach to teaching the basics of reading, writing and number. For the small minority who have failed to make any noticeable progress in acquiring oral language, the critical issue became one of determining whether to persevere with the existing oral approach or to have recourse to manual techniques. At secondary level the initial effort was to place pupils in regular classes as extensively as possible. However, this has been found not to work – "A lot of time [should be] spent doing basic skills. As they get older, I feel you can be a little more adventurous with their integration... but it has got to be monitored... they have got to achieve something [from it]." In other words, if little benefit is seen to derive from integration it should not continue simply because it is perceived as a social 'good'. In secondary school then the prime orientation became one of seeking to develop basic knowledge, skills and understanding, with integration – when feasible – regarded as bonus.

Each special centre is under the control of a teacher in charge who has responsibility for most of the issues associated with daily running, though ultimately the centre falls under the jurisdiction of the head teacher of the school to which it is attached. Because of their size (each has places for around 30 pupils, though in November 1979 the number of pupils on roll was, respectively, 15, 23 and 28) each centre consists of three or more classes, each with its own class teacher. This is true even at secondary level – which represents a marked contrast with the main school where pupils move from class to class and have contact with a range of different teachers.

Pupils

This provision is intended to cater for all pupils in the authority whose special educational needs arising from hearing loss are such as to require more extended specialist provision than can be provided by the peripatetic service. (This service was only one teacher strong for much of the period under study.) The concern to build toward self-sufficiency, allied to the restricted role that such a small peripatetic service can play, must influence the nature of the intake. Also, having provided a structure – on a generous scale – the authority sought to use it in the most cost-effective way. Accordingly, severely and profoundly deaf pupils came to be placed in this provision, though not those with major additional handicaps. A further factor was the requests for placements from neighbouring authorities with limited provision of their own. These requests tended to be for pupils with more severe hearing losses and added to the high proportion of such pupils within these centres.

There would appear to be general agreement in the world of deaf education that having profoundly deaf pupils alongside the partially hearing makes for difficulties as regard educational practice. This was especially so in one case where the special centre served essentially as full-time base for the majority of pupils on roll. Even apart from their failure to achieve some form of oral capacity, staff were concerned that such pupils, though in the minority, were having a disproportionate – unfortunately negative – effect on the functioning of the centre. Although their number was limited they were "the most dominant type of child in the unit". The teacher in charge claimed that there were at least nine children who "linguistically could be good partials" but not one was attaining anything like his or her true linguistic potential. The presence of profoundly deaf children – even though by that stage provided for in their own fairly self-contained class – was held responsible to a considerable degree.

A moderate or severe hearing impairment is readily identifiable, so that the difficulties of identification and assessment apparent at other special centres (eg for the communication disordered) do not feature to the same extent here. Those admitted will all have a primary hearing loss. Some, in addition, may have secondary handicapping conditions, eg slight physical handicap or learning difficulty. Only the occasional child presents as a problem case. The infant centre has been used as an assessment unit for such children. One instance cited was of a completely non-oral immigrant girl of eight years who vocalised but was entirely unintelligible. In addition, she had a slight vision defect, was microcephalic, and was suspected of being moderately retarded. Alternative provision outside the hearing impaired sector would normally be provided for such children well before the time of transfer up through the system.

Admission policies, although largely informal in the past, have now been formalised and are the same as for all children in the authority entering special education. Initially, a child will be referred to the relevant area educational psychologist who will decide whether or not to initiate the SE procedure. In the past many referrals came from medical sources, but nowadays referral from a peripatetic teacher of the deaf is more likely. Under the SE procedure, the child's school (or pre-school peripatetic teacher) completes SE1; a medical officer and a psychologist complete SE forms 2 and 3. The psychologist then completes the summary SE4 recommending a particular placement and the forms are forwarded to the Director of Education. Nowadays, before a decision on placement is taken, both the child and his or her parents will visit the recommended provision. This permits the views of the teacher in charge to be taken into account. This has not always happened in the past.

Children can be accepted in this provision from as early as two and a half years, more especially those from immigrant families. Here severe hearing loss, allied to a different linguistic background to that of the school, was considered by one head teacher a serious added complication – she spoke of it as "a double deprivation". The majority of pupils are admitted between their fourth and sixth birthdays. The occasional older pupil is admitted. Once in the system, transfer upwards is fairly automatic. In the past there was no formal review system prior to transfer, though recently (January 1980) a multi-disciplinary 'hearing' team was established with the purpose – among other things – of reviewing all pupils in this provision prior to their normal transfer on to the next stage. The team comprises: specialist medical officer; social worker for the deaf; an educational psychologist who has oversight of the three centres; audiometrician; the relevant teachers in charge (and possibly head teachers); and a specialist careers officer (as appropriate).

Staffing

Staff turnover has been a prominent feature in two of the centres, and there have been few occasions when a full and settled complement of staff has prevailed. The infant centre has perhaps been the most stable, maintaining a favourable teacher:pupil ratio throughout the period and with very little turnover of staff. (Indeed, its complement of five qualified teachers of the deaf plus three NNEBs was retained for a considerable period even after the number on roll had dropped from 23 to 16, eventually settling at four teachers.) In contrast, the junior centre has struggled to attain a favourable ratio, being one teacher under establishment for long periods (four teachers to 23 pupils). There were also two NNEBs working full-time. The secondary department suffered more from not having a teacher in charge for several months rather than from any shortage of teachers per se. The present staffing ratio is six teachers to 28 pupils. The appointment of two ancillaries – an unusual development at secondary level but very welcome none the less – should be noted.

There are a number of general points to make about staffing. First, the authority has a commitment to formal qualifications. Teachers of the deaf are obliged to take a course of training recognised by the DES within three years of commencing teaching. In this authority, however, many are in fact seconded after only one year because of the urgent need to have qualified teachers of the deaf working in these centres. Secondly, there is generous provision of classroom ancillaries. Schools are free to deploy them as they see fit and this has led to some imaginative working, something that is widely recognised by the teachers of the deaf as a valuable contribution. In the secondary school, for example, they help out across the special centre generally, accompany teachers of the deaf on outside visits, and are responsible for cataloguing library books, putting up displays of work and so forth. In the junior provision, one of the two ancillaries, apart from the preparation of lesson materials and her general caring role, was also involved directly in the children's education. A teacher of the deaf would split the class into groups and while he or she would concentrate on, for example, specialised language work with individual children the ancillary would oversee the work of the rest of the children – perhaps checking story writing or number work. In addition, she undertook cookery with a mixed group of hearing and hearing impaired pupils once a week, and similarly for a period of art and craft with a further group.

Thirdly, there is the involvement of outside agencies. Again, historically there has been limited involvement. For example, there was little direct contact between teachers and ENT consultants. Obtaining medical details on children referred had proved particularly difficult for some considerable time prior to the introduction of the SE procedure. Contact with representatives of Social Services also seemed to have left much to be desired. The teacher in charge of one of the centres outlines how she felt obliged to attend to matters that ought properly to be undertaken by persons with the appropriate training. Reasoning that "if we didn't do it it wouldn't get done", she regretted the fact that although her job was to educate hearing impaired children, "very often teaching comes near the bottom of the list". She described how she did "speech, audiology, psychology ... I do things a parent ought to do like taking a child to the dentist ... [I'm a] social worker, a welfare officer, taxi service, school nurse, substitute parent..."

Circumstances changed quite dramatically for the better with the development of the multi-disciplinary 'hearing' team mentioned previously. Besides reviewing pupils' progress, the team meet fairly regularly to discuss any relevant topics concerning the education of hearing impaired pupils.

The main involvement of the educational psychologist who had oversight of this provision over the period of our study was in a research capacity – applying a battery of tests in order to ascertain the level of communication skills being achieved. This was with the express objective of gathering evidence in relation to the need for adopting a 'total communication' approach, at least for some pupils. Teachers were referring various pupils to him because of concern over their limited linguistic progress. It seemed as if there might be need for something other than the existing oral approach for such pupils, but a decision to introduce total communication could not be taken without firm evidence. In the event, teachers were unhappy about this on a number of scores: they questioned the relevance of the tests used and the way in which the testing had been carried out; and they felt that there was more need of the customary psychologist roles such as providing advice based on psychological knowledge, making practical suggestions and so on. One teacher remarked, "I can't get answers to the question I wanted to ask. All I want very often is a little bit of advice ... [when you're] with a child for a long time ... you only see a narrow channel." More recently, the working pattern has altered and the psychologist now spends a morning at each centre every three weeks, discussing any matters of concern that have arisen and doing individual assessments as necessary.

Accommodation and resources

All three special departments are purpose-built, occupying spacious, well-equipped premises highly suited to the task at hand. While the infant and junior centres feature both open-plan areas – which can be used for a wide variety of activities and by groups of different sizes – and a suite of rooms used for specific language or basic skills teaching, the secondary department is more conventional, consisting of a series of classrooms. Each teacher in charge has an office, and there is at least one other room where visiting professionals (eg educational psychologists, advisory staff) may carry out assessments or other work with pupils. Each department is very well equipped with regard to the basic physical fabric: all rooms have been acoustically treated (in part this involves carpeting throughout which makes the premises look attractive); there is abundant natural lighting which can be easily controlled; and the standard of artificial lighting has been uprated above the norm.

All the centres share a common problem of being located at the periphery of their parent schools – in each case occupying the only site considered to be available on the campus. There is little sense of isolation in the infant centre partly because immediately outside it lies a general activity area used by many children from the school. This physical separation is more of a barrier – both physically and psychologically – at the junior and secondary schools where the centres are quite separate from the body of the main school. At the junior school there is a covered way connecting school and centre which gives one the sense of traversing a divide. At the comprehensive the hearing impaired occupy their own self-contained suite of rooms which is well appointed and compares favourably in terms of space and fittings with the parent school.

The centres are well supplied with equipment and material resources, having a plentiful stock of items such as cookers and cooking utensils, tape-recorders, television and so forth. There is no shortage of audiometric equipment and hearing aids. Where there have been limitations in the past is in terms of learning resources. For example, the teacher in charge of the secondary department pointed to the fact that for the first three years of its existence there were no formal reading resources. When it came to establishing reading schemes she found she was having to start from scratch.

Curriculum

As noted, most teachers are trained teachers of the deaf and follow established practices in British deaf education, with an extensive concentration on the oral–aural educational approach. It should be pointed out, however, that during the course of our study the question of introducing an element of manualism as a supplement to oralism in the case of certain pupils was actively debated. In consequence a decision was taken to establish an additional special class whose working basis would be 'total communication'.

The particular curriculum content varies according to the age and special needs of the pupils. Broadly speaking, the overriding emphasis at infant level is upon developing language. Good infant practice is closely followed. Apart from the area of reading, specialist teachers adhere to the curriculum of the parent school, allowing for any necessary simplification of linguistic content and so forth. Plans of work are presented half-termly to the teacher in charge or head teacher. A particular theme is followed for a whole term with basic number and written work arising from it. The centre has its own reading scheme (Link Up), grounded in the everyday lives of the hearing impaired. Deliberate teaching of speech, based upon work carried out by Ling (1978), was introduced into the curriculum midway through our study.

At junior level the emphasis is on language consolidation, together with introducing a rather more rigorous approach to teaching basic literacy and numeracy. For much of our study there was limited contact with the parent school and in consequence few links with its curriculum. Some members of staff, for instance, felt that the maths scheme used by main school could easily have been adapted for the hearing impaired. Very recently the school's academic organisation has changed considerably under a new head teacher. Team teaching has been introduced within each group. It is intended that the hearing impaired and their teachers will be gradually absorbed into this arrangement, with of course considerable curriculum implications for them.

At secondary level the concern to develop further and consolidate basic skills is maintained. Contact with the main school curriculum is limited and is confined to art, drama, PE and games. In the first three years hearing impaired pupils spend about 20 per cent of their time taking these subjects in main school alongside hearing peers. For the older pupil specific preparation for adult life becomes important; this is detailed below.

A particular problem in the past has been the limited contact between the three centres. Among other things this led to a lack of continuity between the work carried out in the different centres, and pupils could find themselves being dealt with quite differently when they transferred from one centre to another. In some instances a lack of continuity was apparent even within a single centre, stemming perhaps from the failure of the teacher in charge and/or head teacher to ensure that all members of staff were operating within a common framework.

A gradual but fundamental revision of practice was put into effect by the present teachers in charge during the final year of our study. This was in the context of revising the basis of the curriculum, an activity carried out with guidance and practical assistance from specialists in curriculum development employed by the authority. Reading was given pre-eminence in both junior and secondary departments. (The infant centre had its own reading scheme.) Staff of a reading resource centre had developed an experimental literacy scheme based upon 100 common words. This was the starting point, the objective being to build toward a sight vocabulary of 60 words so that pupils could then use of commercial reading schemes. Reading for meaning was to be specifically emphasised. One teacher of the deaf explained, in reference to the fact that some of her pupils already had a vocabulary of perhaps 20 words, that "they have no idea of sentence construction, either spoken or written, they have no idea what to do with them". As well as being a source of advice and expertise in assessing pupils' specific reading problems and capabilities, the reading centre also served as a material resource. With regard to number work, a maths adviser worked with staff in all three centres in an effort to determine the mathematical needs of the pupils, and thence devise appropriate learning materials. In the event, a scheme originally intended for junior age hearing children was chosen and adapted. Language content was simplified, and the teaching was based on workcards. Older pupils in the secondary department pursued what was termed 'social maths', ie number work closely oriented toward post-school life. The one major area that awaited revision (late 1979) was spoken language. The intention here was to develop materials based upon development work carried out by Crystal at the University of Reading.

In all three centres there is a close association between teaching approach and curriculum content. The level of comprehension of many hearing impaired pupils fails to match what conventional indicators such as intelligence level might predict. This results in a need to modify the curriculum and present materials in a variety of different ways. As one teacher of the deaf explained: "We must limit our language at times in order for them to learn something. We use a lot more visual material ... When you read a story you can't just tell the story, you have got to have back-up visual material, you may even have your own sequence of pictures, you have got to have thought about what you're going to act out afterwards. You need to break the stages down into a lot more detail. You also have to feed what you give the children into what background knowledge they already have." Considerable thought then has to be given to how the particular content can be taught effectively.

Preparation for adult life

A particular aspect of the curriculum for the older hearing impaired pupil is specific preparation for post-school life. Some such preparation is necessary to a degree for all school leavers but is the more important for the hearing impaired leaver since his or her understanding of the world will be restricted through having missed so much incidental learning. It only applied to the secondary centre and was still in its infancy there as the need for post-school preparation had only recently arisen. It comprises two elements each running for two years: a school leavers' programme; and a Design for Living course. The former was devised within the school. The latter is a programme devised jointly by three special schools (catering for pupils other than the hearing impaired) and leads to a CSE qualification.

The leavers' programme was developed within the special centre, with some assistance from main school careers staff. It comprises general presentations and discussion on work-related issues and a work experience component, whereby pupils will be able to experience one or more work settings. The objectives identified by the teacher of the deaf responsible included: "trying to get [pupils] thinking about jobs ... work [to them] is something very vague"; "to get them thinking about how they see themselves in the job"; deliberately working on their social skills (these are notoriously poor in the hearing impaired); "getting them to come to terms with deafness"; providing the experience of different kinds of jobs and different sorts of work-places; and encouraging the gainful use of leisure time. It is hoped to impart the skills that bear on apprenticeships, getting jobs, wages, money management and so on. The Design for Living course covers such topics as home management, health, and initiating and maintaining social relationships.

As is often the case with a developing area of practice, initial difficulties were being experienced with both elements. The main problem with the Design for Living course was its language content, which was too advanced for the hearing impaired. (The course had been developed with a different target group in mind – the blind and physically handicapped.) The course comprises a series of assignments – eg preparing a meal for two – the intention being for one assignment to be completed each week. However, the linguistic and conceptual difficulties it presented the hearing impaired were such that a given assignment could take as long as three weeks. The teacher responsible noted that she was giving over twice the normal amount of time to the course and pupils were still getting only a limited benefit from it.

As regards the leavers' programme, a particular difficulty has been found in obtaining work experience placements. So far all placements have been in sheltered environments (eg school or college offices). The teacher organising it pointed out that, although many employers claimed to be willing, the stipulations of the Health and Safety at Work Act were regularly cited as a reason why a placement could not be offered to hearing impaired pupils. An added complication is the presence of considerable numbers of out-county placements in the centre. This presents various potential difficulties: location of work placements (in the pupil's home neighbourhood or within the host authority?); liaising with specialist agencies (eg careers service) employed by another authority; crossing local authority boundaries; and the considerable additional travelling involved.

Monitoring progress

In the past there has been considerable variation across the three centres in terms of what records were maintained and how effectively pupils' progress was monitored. Our impression was that satisfactory practice had only obtained at the infant centre. More recently, there have been attempts to improve recording procedures in the two other centres, and also to develop a more uniform way of maintaining records.

The infant centre had at one time maintained the Stoke Record System which covered both personal details and educational development. This was later abandoned as inadequate for educational planning, although it continued in use for personal background and medical details. It became a supplement to the detailed planning and recording carried out by individual teachers. These include: 'child studies', which are updated on a half-termly basis, and incorporate academic progress, social attitudes, and any specific problems or successes; reading and number records; an outline of work done in relation to the aims of the topic pursued, with a (subjective) assessment of its success or failure; and teachers' appraisals of out-of-school visits.

At the junior centre, there was little evidence of any detailed monitoring of pupils' progress in a systematic way. The record files we saw were thin, in some cases containing little more than basic audiometric information and details on family background. The Stoke Record System in use for a time in the infant centre had been allowed to lapse. One teacher of the deaf noted that upon her appointment there was nothing to go on that would directly assist her in planning schemes of work for her pupils: "I had no indication whatsoever of what they could do ... You've no idea what a child has read, or with what degree of help." She had simply been given a record book – "no use whatsoever". Nor was there any indication of a parallel set of records being maintained by individual members of staff, as was evident in the infant centre. At the close of our study steps were being taken to improve this situation.

At secondary level, both formal and informal measures were in evidence. Of the former, when we began our research, subject specialists used to report annually on the progress achieved by hearing impaired pupils in their teaching groups. However, the teacher in charge felt that these needed to be completed termly and, rather than addressing particular subjects, should be directed toward general areas of development, eg speech and language, social development and so on. Subsequently, a revised record form was developed for these pupils. It contained details on reading ability, a check on progress with phonics, a check-off system recording other achievements, and teachers' general comments. Subject specialists could still comment using the customary record form, but this now tended to be used in a supplementary capacity. This would be updated annually.

However, greater emphasis appeared to be accorded to the more informal channels which the teacher in charge, in particular, employed. Enjoying good relations with the various subject specialists involved with the hearing impaired, she felt that any problems pupils did experience would be picked up and communicated as necessary to specialist teachers of the deaf. An important safeguard was the fact that they exercised great care in selecting main school classes. Wherever possible they seek to work with those teachers who are most willing to have hearing impaired pupils in their class and who appear most capable of dealing adequately with them. Additionally, while each pupil's circumstances are reviewed annually, should any member of staff raise a specific problem, a special review can be initiated.

Academic integration

Academic or classroom integration was most apparent in the infant centre, where the age of the pupil, allied to certain organisational factors, made achieving this much more straightforward than later on. At this age level integration is largely social, but this serves important educational ends. Teachers were well disposed – "I haven't had to work on teachers' attitudes ... they've wanted to have a deaf child in their class" (head). Also relevant is the fact that infant education is less formalised and structured than secondary schooling, so that a child can be fed in and out of the ordinary classroom quite flexibly without causing disruption. There has in fact been a fair degree of exchange within the infant school. Children integrate for activities such as play time and assembly ("when a lot of good social integration goes on") and for those activities where there is not a high premium on language, eg PE, art and craft. Both head teacher and teacher in charge are in agreement that any integration must allow a reasonable chance of success and positive interaction. "I would rather err on the side of letting their learning be done in [the centre] than pretend they are getting a lot out of integration" (head teacher). "There is no use sending them in to the regular classroom to flounder" (teacher in charge). The extent of integration is tailored to the individual child's oral potential – to a point indeed where a very small number of children might spend much of their school day in the regular classroom and be withdrawn only for an hour or so of specialist support.

Later on in our study, we found that both children and members of staff were being brought together in a more purposeful way than previously, when the social benefit of integration had perhaps been too readily assumed. Teachers from main school had suggested that instead of hearing impaired infants coming into the ordinary class once a week and joining in with whatever was going on – this was described as more of a "play situation" – that perhaps these opportunities should have a more specific purpose. Subsequently, the intention behind integration was to be spelled out. Thus, one boy was integrated for language work based on a commercial language scheme. Words that he had difficulty with were entered in a book and later reinforced by his teacher of the deaf. Another example cited was of two middle infants who spent about half of their integration time engaged on number work within a group of hearing children. One other child was receiving weekly sessions on handwriting and reading.

This reappraisal of practice was to be carried even further subsequently, as the favourable staffing ratio caused by a marked fall in the number of pupils on roll continued to prevail. This allowed of considerable flexibility of practice. Not only did pupils continue to feed out into main school for quite specific purposes, but they were often accompanied by their teacher (or in some instances a nursery nurse) who would combine with the ordinary teacher to form a teaching team. Thus, three top infants and their teacher of the deaf were based in an ordinary class; similarly for a fourth top infant and a middle infant with a second teacher of the deaf. In a third instance, a teacher of the deaf worked for part of the time with two hearing impaired children plus groups of pupils from main school who needed extra help with language. A further two children with hearing loss, this time of nursery age, were based in the school's nursery with a nursery nurse from the special centre.

At the junior school there was very little integration throughout the period of our study. There had, apparently, been an early attempt to integrate on a large scale with some rather ambitious placements. This had failed and had "left a lot of antagonism" among main school staff which effectively impeded further attempts to integrate. "The climate isn't right for there to be more integration. We like the teachers to show the interest first . . ." was the belief held by one of the teachers in charge during the course of our study. Whether this was primarily due to ignorance or apprehension on the part of ordinary teachers, lack of leadership or simple disinclination is difficult to say. However, when compounded with specialist staff who stressed caution and the importance of the specifics of deaf education the outcome was strongly separatist tendencies: "It's all very well to say more integration but we feel that the time is so precious . . . We are so well qualified [but] is it fair on the children to put them with teachers who either cannot or will not give them very much attention, who don't understand their problems . . . ?" The severity of the hearing loss and the poor ability of many of the pupils at the time did not help matters: "You've got to be able to have enough hearing to pick up . . . from the teacher." Other contributing factors included high staff turnover in the centre, which militated against building good relationships with ordinary teachers; difficulties in obtaining staff, which meant that at any time there was often a number of relatively inexperienced teachers who did not have the confidence or competence to provide active support for an integration programme; and the physical separateness of the special centre mentioned earlier.

Nevertheless, there was some integration in evidence, with emphasis on the social benefits. It was fairly common practice for a group of hearing impaired pupils to combine with age peers from main school for weekly sessions of art, craft and PE/movement. A notable feature here was the three-way division of all the pupils involved between the respective class teachers and a nursery nurse. On the occasion of our final visit there was more integration taking place, with better planning and forethought. Rather than whole classes being integrated, the focus was on individual pupils joining particular classes where it was thought they might benefit. For example, three older pupils were integrating for three periods of language work each week, in addition to craft and PE/games. Two first year pupils were spending four and six periods respectively in main school, in addition to the customary art and craft which they did in common anyway.

It should be noted that the new academic organisation recently introduced at this school has altered the position very considerably. Hearing impaired pupils are already spending more time in ordinary classes. It is envisaged that they will shortly be attached to registration groups in main school and receive all their teaching alongside their hearing peers, being withdrawn only for highly specialised individual or small group work (eg specialist language work). The new head teacher outlined the situation as follows:

'The children integrated in main school will be supported by specialist teachers and NNEBs working in close conjunction with the year team. One specialist teacher is attached to each year group and supports all the hearing impaired within that year *and* also teaches hearing children as well. The specialist teacher is a full-time member of the team with a full teaching commitment within the team.

'"The Unit" is now a Resource Area for the whole school and the classrooms within the Resource Area are used as an extension to the main school . . . .'

An aspect of integration practice illustrated in this new development but evident all along in both infant and junior centres is the importance of being seen to provide a service for the parent school. This can take various forms, eg providing additional help for children who are experiencing educational or other difficulties not occasioned by hearing loss, or teaching hearing pupils. There were various examples of this: two hearing impaired five-year-olds playing in the activity area of the special centre along with reception children from the parent school and in the company of an NNEB from the centre; two hearing impaired children joining a group of hearing children in need of extra help with their language development, under the control of a teacher of the deaf; another teacher of the deaf sending all but one of his group into regular classes and receiving in return five pupils from these classes for remedial number work.

The initial policy at the secondary department was one of maximum integration under the then teacher in charge. This was considered to have been a failure by staff who joined subsequently: pupils were missing out on basic teaching and anyway needed the structure of the department – "they found a variety of teachers absolutely bewildering". The alternative adopted was for all pupils to be withdrawn to the special department "for a grounding in the basics", being released onto "the house roundabout" – art, music, drama, PE/games – for around 20 per cent of the timetable. Individual pupils may be integrated for additional activities but only after careful consideration of their needs and capabilities and whether they are likely to benefit.

We did not have the opportunity to collect detailed information on how the remodelled practice was actually working out, though some points can be noted. As regards information and support for the ordinary teacher, the preference of the specialist staff was for a low-key approach: "Tell them very generally what they are going to need to know ... don't inundate them with details." One teacher put this very forcibly: "Teachers of the deaf have to be very careful about making themselves too special ... We have always got to appear a bit ignorant [so as to] elevate the classroom teacher." The point was not that one should deny or conceal one's expertise but rather should refrain from parading it and emphasise instead the contribution that class teachers can make from their background and expertise. Over-emphasis on the specialist aspects of deaf education tended to create a mystique, making some teachers feel inadequate and reluctant to receive hearing impaired pupils into their classes.

Clearly, tact and sensitivity are essential in this role that teachers of the deaf occupy, but there is a danger too in excessive delicacy. There were signs of basic lessons not having been learned: some subject teachers were extremely reluctant to continue wearing radio microphones after introducing the subject matter of a lesson, while others were perceived to lack the confidence to allow teachers of the deaf into their classes while teaching. One teacher of the deaf who had gained access to a lesson felt that insufficient effort had been paid to involving those hearing impaired pupils present – possibly because the teacher had not realised how little could safely be assumed about what they had understood. This teacher firmly believed that as teachers of the deaf they ought to be actively seeking to support within the regular classroom. The feeling among a large number of teachers of the deaf was in fact that the present practice of subject teachers coming across to the special centre, outlining an area of difficulty and asking for it to be covered in a separate lesson, was not particularly efficient. At one time a teacher of the deaf had joined pupils in science lessons in main school. A science teacher who had been involved spoke extremely favourably of this, but the practice had not continued.

The social context

At infant level there was widespread agreement among both ordinary and specialist teachers (and parents too) that the opportunities for integrating had brought with them definite social benefits. Through shared PE/movement, creative work and other classroom-based interactions, and from the increasingly structured out-of-school visits, which may involve pupils from main school, many hearing impaired infants were considered to have developed more normal modes of behaviour and to have struck up lasting associations with hearing children.

In the junior and secondary centres, by contrast, many staff were less sanguine. One junior teacher pinpointed the lack of contact: "How many of them can name hearing children that they have contact with? How many hearing children would be able to name hearing impaired children? You sometimes wonder how vulnerable are they – you see them making a fool of themselves in the playground." A classroom assistant from the same centre who had been in a position to observe the interactions between the two groups pointed to the naiveté and lack of social awareness on the part of the hearing impaired and suggested that this interfered with establishing good relations: "Hearing pupils give an awful lot of friendly approaches . . . but it doesn't seem to float the other way. The deaf are given so much . . . they don't think they have [ever] got to give anything back." Another teacher of the deaf questioned the value of the contact since the only interaction she had observed was her pupils "associating with trouble-makers". Our own observation would suggest that there was indeed little contact. For example, we watched six hearing impaired junior girls have lunch together. At no time were they approached by any other pupils. Out in the playground, although there was some mixing, most pupils were hanging around the passageway between main school and special centre. The teacher in charge stated this was quite typical. It was a cause for some regret that relationships between hearing and hearing impaired children which developed were interrupted at age seven when the two groups of pupils transferred to different junior schools. Locating the infant and junior units in different schools with quite separate catchment areas was widely acknowledged to have been a mistake.

The situation at the secondary school was less encouraging: there was no indication of anything more than the occasional friendship; the hearing impaired as a group were rather negatively perceived; and they frequently displayed marked immaturity in behaviour and conduct. Some extracts from our fieldnotes exemplify this:

i) Two boys in an art lesson. '[They] initially presented some problems, splashing other pupils' work and pushing their chairs into people.'

ii) A group of four hearing impaired pupils in a home economics lesson. 'The teacher said that the children were "playing up" [because of the observer's presence] and that normally they were good. My presence may have been a contributory factor but from my observations the children could be cheeky, stubborn, naughty and immature. Their relationship with the teacher was not always one of respect . . . They were often silly and giggly – or shouted at the teacher when they didn't want to do things.'

iii) In the playground at lunchtime. 'When they have all finished [eating] they . . . go outside into the playground. They go to a corner of the gym and huddle together and poke and tease one another. They stay in this grouping (which, incidentally, had been in evidence the previous day) until it's time for the bell.'

This picture was amplified by remarks from teachers, who observed that the hearing impaired were "quite dependent on the Unit". "There is a fair amount of teasing." "They definitely don't integrate in the playground . . . communication generally is aggressive . . . warding people off, threatening." "They were conscious that they are deaf and different. Given half a chance they won't wear their hearing aid because this brings attention to their deafness." "A lot of our children are ashamed to communicate." At breaktimes their preference was to remain with their own group in the non-threatening environment of the special centre: "They see themselves as separate . . . . at times you have to drive them over to main school."

Observations carried out in both lessons and playground suggest that hearing impaired pupils were at best tolerated. In the classroom they invariably were seated slightly apart from the main body of pupils or remained with hearing impaired peers. We observed two groups taking lunch, five hearing impaired boys and a smaller group of girls. There was no interaction with any hearing pupil. After lunch the five boys remained together in a group, while the girls met up with another bunch of girls also from the special centre. They came together forming a single group of eight, walking rather aimlessly about, with many interruptions to stand around talking. Occasionally, a hearing pupil would briefly approach them, but in general there was minimal interaction and then often of a teasing nature.

Various reasons can be advanced for the restricted nature of the interactions. First, there is the limited oral capacity of so many of these pupils. This inhibits communication in fairly obvious ways. Moreover, the limited capacity to verbalise meaning, emotion and so on, when allied to poor social skills, leads to their getting into fights more often. Language can frequently serve to defuse tense social situations; in its absence physical conflict is more likely to result. Ignorance of the basic principles of socialising can lead to the tendency described by one teacher of the deaf of being "quick to jump the gun", bringing trouble upon themselves with hasty and ill-judged reactions. Dinner ladies on playground duty noted that the hearing impaired could be very aggressive and were often involved in fights: when they saw or heard other pupils laughing they seemed to assume they were laughing *at them* and so lashed out.

Secondly, there is the effect that adolescence has. As pupils grow older and become increasingly aware of their difference from others, in particular their verbal deficiencies, it is hardly surprising that in the words of one experienced teacher they become almost "ashamed to communicate". Thirdly, this is exacerbated by the fact that most pupils do not spend time in the company of hearing peers. They have relatively limited opportunity to get to know them better or to seek to make themselves known. Under these circumstances any individual who is only too aware of his or her poor speech will be inhibited from striking up relationships where spoken language is at root. Fourthly, a natural consequence of this is to turn inward, back to territory which is non-threatening. The size of the special centre does not help in this respect, in that there are enough pupils to offer a range of friendships. There was considered to have been more interaction between the two groups when there were fewer hearing impaired pupils at the school; the smaller numbers and age range covered had meant that they had to be more outward-looking in order to develop friendships.

Parents

In the case of children with impaired hearing the earliest possible involvement of the parents in their overall development has become recognised practice in recent years. The need for this support for parents, which is usually the responsibility of the peripatetic service, does not disappear when the children start school and indeed can become important in new ways then. Unless the peripatetic service is in a position to maintain this support for parents of children attending specialist provision, the support must be provided by the children's teachers.

Staff at the infant centre have traditionally had a good deal of contact with parents, though this has fluctuated over time. Initial contact was through occasional social visits, which brought to light problems and anxieties parents felt or circumstances behind the parent/child relationship. Staff agreed that they should seek to develop a more definitely interventionist strategy. They began by inviting parents in for afternoon tea. Although the socialising element was still to the fore, it was felt that some parents derived considerable support from being put in contact with others who also had a deaf child. The next stage was to invite up to four parents into school for a whole morning. They were spread across the centre, one per class, and sat in on the various activities involving their child. At some point each teacher ensured that she would spend some time working individually with the child concerned, watched by the parent. This was followed by structured conversation with the parent, with teachers seeking to impart knowledge and ideas through demonstration and discussion. Parents visited on a rota basis, each coming into school roughly every six weeks. They were expected to attend and the majority did so willingly.

This seemed a valuable activity, that was highly rated by teachers and parents alike. By retaining the child as the focal point throughout, the parent was shown through demonstration how to communicate with the child, how to reinforce school work, when to give in to the child's demands and when to insist on her own demands being met, and so on. Teachers commented that it "can help parents find ways of helping their child outside school". Two mothers we spoke with were also enthusiastic. "You can go and see how much she has progressed from term to term ... It is good for Sarah, she can show me herself what she has been doing [items of work, books, etc are on hand]. At home she can try and tell you ... [but] you don't always understand." For the other it had been an even more salutary experience: "I hear him talk ... they told us he did things, how well he read – he just didn't do it with us [at home]." This mother implied that had she not had this opportunity to see for herself what her child was capable of, she would have remained convinced that not only was he profoundly deaf but mentally retarded as well. What she witnessed at school "gave us hope".

With this second mother an even more specific intervention occurred. Her natural tendency had been to smother Johnny with love and affection in an effort to compensate for the guilt she felt at his being handicapped. She had become quite over-protective and Johnny, sensing that he could always get his way, was extremely spoilt. When the mother sought to encourage responsible behaviour she was rewarded with tantrums, made worse by the lack of any verbal communication. She herself had been on the verge of a breakdown. Staff at the school were at pains to point out that her handling of the situation was not in Johnny's best interests. She knew they were right but could not bring herself to accept it. However, eventually she was both persuaded and obliged (because of her health) to "literally pass him over to the school". Through paying regular visits to school, seeing Johnny handled both individually and as part of a group, being given practical tips (for example, not to make everything so fraught with tension but rather to make things more light-hearted), all combined to give her "more confidence to say '*you're* going to have to do it now' ".

Contact with parents was much less in evidence at both of the other centres, and tended in any case to be of a general nature. This reflected in part the fact that pupils were now older. Staff at the junior centre did not make home visits – indeed the teacher in charge questioned whether staff had the necessary skills and sensitivity. At the secondary centre home visits were encouraged and two members of staff visit on a regular basis. Since many pupils were from neighbouring authorities this makes considerable demands on teachers' time. Also, it was pointed out that the authority does not pay teachers' expenses for home visiting.

In both schools parents are encouraged to visit whenever they feel it necessary. In addition, there are the customary open evenings. At secondary level these were not well attended and in an effort to compensate the school devised a system of year-group open evenings for pupils in the first, fourth and fifth years. These were very well attended – in part, it was felt, because the smaller numbers of parents involved meant that each set of parents was likely to be able to spend more time talking with members of staff.

Apart from open evenings, a further source of contact was the home-school book, maintained for each pupil, into which messages are entered, eg items of news, particular achievements, specific teaching points that the teacher would like the parent to practise, and so forth. This was maintained on a daily basis at the two primary age centres, and weekly at the comprehensive school.

Despite the various efforts being made, some parents were nevertheless dissatisfied about the nature and extent of contact and made a number of critical comments. One set of parents, for example, perceived staff as having shown little concern at their calls for homework, or at their requests for "more attempt to involve us in projects they are doing". The mother of an older pupil spoke bitterly about what she perceived as disinterest on the part of the school. She was concerned at the considerable teasing her son was experiencing and at the poor educational progress she perceived was being made. While there was perhaps an element of over-concern in this parent and possibly some misperceptions, there did seem to be an unfortunate breakdown in communication. For example, she clearly did not understand the reasoning behind the programme her son was following. Over a seven month period no reports on the boy's progress had been received, and little effort seemed to have been made to harness the parent's concern in a constructive way. Although the mother had visited once and had communicated her worries on several occasions, her concerns had by no means been laid to rest or even diminished.

Summary

This provision serves virtually all the hearing impaired pupils in the authority apart from those covered by the peripatetic service. As a result it caters for a mixture of profoundly deaf and partially hearing pupils. Many of the professionals involved have not seen it particularly in integration terms, viewing it rather as a means of providing education for pupils with severe hearing loss which happens to be in ordinary schools. The infant centre has been the exception here, with a good deal of casual exchange with its parent school from the early days and carefully planned functional integration in recent years. The other centres have operated fairly autonomously within their parent schools, though changes are in train, particularly at junior level where the school's academic organisation has been transformed and it is the deliberate intention to incorporate the hearing impaired into this in an integral way. One of the main achievements over the period of our study was the increasing collaboration between the teachers in charge, with a view to determining common approaches, rationalising curricula to ensure continuity and so on.

This provision enjoys a favourable staffing ratio, good premises and resources, and the active co-operation of the three head teachers involved. While it can face the future with every confidence, there are a number of pressing issues to which the closest attention must be paid:

1. Plans are now well advanced to open a small specialist unit based on total communication for those pupils who have failed to make satisfactory progress in developing oral language. This will be located in a classroom on the campus of the comprehensive school. There are various questions to be resolved here. At what stage, and by what means, will it be determined which pupils shall enter this provision? How will it relate to the existing special centre in the school? Will junior age pupils be considered for placement there?

2. Considerable effort has gone into curriculum development and revision in recent years. Can the momentum behind this be maintained? Will it lead to greater continuity in the educational programmes followed by pupils as they move from one centre to the next?

3. In view of the limited social interaction between hearing impaired and hearing pupils at the junior and secondary schools, is there a case for deliberate intervention in social relationships on the part of staff? For example, could social situations be structured by teachers of the deaf to facilitate more meaningful exchanges between the two groups?

4. Would hearing impaired pupils have greater access to the mainstream if teachers of the deaf were in a position to join mainstream lessons and offer support to hearing impaired pupils *during* a lesson, or if they developed more detailed strategies for following up and reinforcing the content of lessons at a later stage?

5. Staff have experienced various difficulties in preparing pupils for adult life, eg language content of course adopted too complex, work experience placements very difficult to obtain. As the number of leavers increases, will it be possible to resolve these difficulties?

9
Individual integration of hearing impaired pupils

Twelve pupils whose hearing losses range from partial to profound deafness attend, on an individual basis, ordinary schools within their home neighbourhood. They follow normal lessons in these schools, supported by a combination of teachers of the deaf and 'support' teachers.

Historical résumé

The authority in question has been noted for its pioneering work in the field of deaf education. By the late 1960s it offered a fully integrated service comprising a school for the deaf, units for the partially hearing and peripatetic provision, with easy transfer of pupils from one to the other as judged necessary. There was also an audiology clinic under the control of an audiological physician. A further notable development occurred when the future of the special school which was old and overcrowded came up for consideration. The Department of Education and Science proposed that a new school for the deaf be built on the campus of an ordinary school. However, the head teacher, with the authority's backing, argued that the special school should be dispersed, its pupils being relocated in special departments within ordinary schools and the former special school premises retained as a resource centre and headquarters of the service overall.

For the origins of individual integration we must go back to the early 1970s. The head of the school for the deaf had become increasingly convinced that all but a small minority of the hearing impaired could benefit from being exposed to a normal speaking environment. Commenting on the basic dilemma of deaf education – seeking to help those with little or no language by gathering them together with others who shared the same problem – he said: "It is a negative situation when a child with communication problems is put with children also with communication problems ... The level of linguistic development should be related to the linguistic environment." Although special schools placed great emphasis upon language training, delivered by specially trained teachers, the *natural* use of the developing linguistic patterns, particularly among pupils themselves, was often missing.

Apart from the head teacher's own convictions, based upon extensive experience in deaf education, support for his stance came from a thesis prepared by a former colleague of his. This presented evidence showing that hearing impaired school leavers made rapid gains in language and communication skills in the two years after leaving special schooling (Follwell, 1943). Further confirmation from more general sources led the head teacher to believe that they might anticipate these gains by giving pupils the opportunity to experience normal language models much earlier: "Put them out in the mainstream with the layman and they should rapidly improve in language and communication." At about this time he met an academic who shared his views and who had also been active in introducing severely hearing handicapped infants into the mainstream of education abroad. The latter had the "technical know-how" of how to go about integrating. The head teacher was familiar with the workings of the local education authority and had a detailed knowledge of the pupils concerned. The two formed a loose working partnership and set about developing a plan for the individual integration of hearing impaired pupils.

They presented a proposal to the Education Committee that a small number of hearing impaired pupils, some of them suffering from severe or profound hearing loss, should be placed, with support, in ordinary schools on an individual basis. An extensive and at times heated debate ensued. There was widespread opposition to the proposal, both from fellow teachers of the deaf and other colleagues. Some maintained that it was "cruel to isolate the severely deaf child" while others criticised the proponents for "seeking nebulous social gains at the cost of an educational loss". Convinced that these criticisms were not based on sound evidence and indeed probably owed much to rhetoric, they pressed ahead with their proposal – which would at least lead to some evidence on the matter. They argued that it would "stand on its educational merit". In the event, their case was carried and they were given the go-ahead for "a pilot project".

The programme began in May 1973 when five third-year juniors and one second-year junior were placed in their neighbourhood schools. Two were profoundly deaf, the other four partially hearing. Numbers eventually built up to 12. Gradual development was envisaged from the very beginning. This was justified on the grounds that the selection and preparation of schools could not be done hastily. In its seven years of operation the programme has developed to the point where it is now a full option when it comes to taking a decision on the educational placement of a hearing impaired pupil. The other placement options available are three special departments for the severely and profoundly deaf (two at secondary school level); two other departments, one primary and one secondary, essentially for the partially hearing of average and below average ability; and placement in the local school with support from the peripatetic service, currently four teachers strong.

Considerable care is given to selecting schools to take part in the programme. When a given pupil is being considered, the head of the special school first seeks the opinion of advisory staff as to the suitability of the local school. If there is no encouragement to go ahead then the matter will not be pursued further. Assuming a favourable response, the LEA's permission is sought in order to make a formal approach to the school. The head meets with his opposite number to find out how he or she is disposed to integration and, more specifically, whether he or she would be willing to take on a pupil with hearing impairment: "At this stage [all I'm looking for is] a sympathetic hearing." An opportunity for the head to see the pupil concerned is arranged. Next the teachers are informed. The head of the school for the deaf cautioned against enthusiasm that did not extend to staff or was for the wrong reasons such as the prestige value. He stressed that all staff should have a say, not just the head and prospective class teacher. So he seeks an opportunity to address staff of the school, outlining what is entailed and answering any questions.

Assuming everything is favourable thus far, staff of the school are invited to visit the pupil in his or her current provision, meet with teachers, examine records and voice any worries or concerns. The full procedure may take up to six months or more. With secondary schooling, parents have the right to choose from any one of the 14 comprehensive schools in the authority. A similar procedure to that outlined above is still likely to be followed, however. "There is theoretically a free choice although there is an element of guiding the parent – we do try to guide parents towards schools where we have had successful experiences" (head of school for the deaf).

Once a definite school has been settled on attention turns toward encouraging a receptive attitude among staff of the school, together with communicating a basic understanding of hearing impairment and its educational consequences. At primary school level, the teacher who will be responsible for the hearing impaired pupil is chosen very carefully. Ideally, "I'm looking for sympathy without emotionalism ... [someone] well organised – [knows] where she's going and how she's going to get there." There is also the question of continuity of staffing. Staff of the school are addressed as a whole – it is very important that they should all have some understanding of "the problems of communication and amplification." In addition, booklets are distributed which briefly explain the educational consequences of hearing impairment. There is also an annual series of three evening presentations open to any interested party from a school containing hearing impaired pupils.

Late in our fieldwork the head of the school for the deaf was paying return visits to schools, seeking to provide information and guidance to school staffs which had changed considerably since this action was first undertaken. It is intended to repeat this exercise annually. Also, a series of 22 slides have been made illustrating various aspects of working practice: a pupil working unsupported in an ordinary class; a pupil receiving support within the ordinary classroom; a pupil withdrawn from class and receiving assistance from a support teacher; and children at play. The slide presentation spans the age range and at secondary level an attempt has been made to cover a variety of subjects. This presentation, lasting around 35 minutes, has already been made to parents with children in the programme and to head teachers whose schools contain a hearing impaired pupil. Plans are in hand to extend it to teachers in the schools concerned.

Organisation and aims

This particular practice started off very much as an experiment since no other authority in this country had attempted anything similar and there were no existing models to guide practice. The assumption was that through being educated in this way hearing impaired pupils would be better able to take their place in the mainstream of society. The aim then was to discover *which* hearing impaired pupils, with *what* degree of hearing loss and possibly other handicapping conditions, were likely to benefit. The enhanced linguistic development expected of integration carried out on an individual basis has already been noted. It was also the aim to avoid the 'cloistered' effect often found within segregated institutions: special schooling "tended to make them 'deafer' than they needed to be ... out of phase with community and behaviour patterns" (head of school for the deaf).

Furthermore, there was the question of educational benefit: it was believed that the pupils with impaired hearing would be stimulated by the "more businesslike, more brisk" working environment of the mainstream, would be initially "shocked by the work rate". Also ordinary teachers would not hold "too low a goal" for deaf pupils, unlike some of their special school colleagues who were perceived as "conditioned" by their experiences within the special school. The head teacher himself acknowledged that he had had to revise upwards his expectations of what hearing impaired pupils could achieve as a result of the progress made by those in the individual integration programme; some were successfully tackling work that he would never have thought of setting for them.

It was intended that pupils participating in the programme should play a full part in the normal life of the school. There was no illusion that the very real disadvantages – primarily in regard of communication – stemming from hearing loss could be ignored or willed away. The organisational implication was that pupils would need considerable assistance if they were to compete academically with hearing peers and be assimilated socially into the wider peer group. An extensive corps of overseeing and supporting staff (teachers of the deaf and support teachers) was available to provide this.

Pupils

'We now know from experience that this alternative pattern of education is suitable for children of a much wider range of abilities than was first thought. We are, we believe, successfully educating some children in the scheme who are of less than average intellectual ability and whose communication skills are not of a high standard' (from a publication by the head of the school for the deaf).

Ideally, suitable candidates should meet the following criteria: "be emotionally stable ... [able] to take the knocks of the outside world"; be of at least average intellectual ability; have good communication skills; not have any significant secondary handicap; be of an outgoing nature; have supportive parents; and come from an English-speaking background. However, these criteria are employed flexibly and none of the 12 pupils in the programme satisfies all these requirements – in fact, some only satisfy a few. What is considered most crucial is the need for emotional stability and the absence of any significant secondary handicap.

Of the 12, three are partially hearing, three severely deaf and six profoundly deaf (hearing loss in excess of 90 db). The extent of hearing loss ranges from an average of 65 db to an average of 107 db. On a five-point ability rating scale (A–E), teachers' estimates of potential show that the majority are of average or slightly above average ability (six rated B, four rated C). Two boys were considered to be of below average ability. At first, low ability pupils were not considered – a pupil was only considered for entry if the head and his staff felt fairly confident of his or her capacity to succeed. Once the programme had proved educationally viable they were prepared to be more flexible with regard to the admission criteria. Encouragement in this came from the academic partner who maintained that "the greater the handicap of the child, the greater his need to be exposed to normality". Reading ages are from one year to as much as six years behind chronological age, although for two pupils reading age matches chronological age. (One is a profoundly deaf boy whose reading has improved greatly.) The majority of pupils are considered well adjusted socially, though in two cases an element of immaturity was detectable on occasion, and one girl was considered to have a very naive outlook on life.

Likely candidates for the programme were initially identified by the head of the school for the deaf, in conjunction with senior members of his staff. There is a continuing, mostly informal involvement with the audiological physician, who will have known pupils from the age of six months and can comment on the physical and audiological background. Other professional agencies are involved as and when necessary. Informal interaction is the preferred mode of working.

To date two pupils have had to be withdrawn from the programme, one for reasons of frequent and persistent truancy and one because of failure to make educational progress. This would seem to endorse the admission criteria that those involved seek to apply. However, this is not to say that there have not been problems – not all of the opportunities presented by integration are desirable. For instance, one boy fell in with the 'wrong crowd' at one stage and was suspected of minor theft. Where a participant meets with serious educational difficulties, the flexibility of practice offers the possibility of providing a considerable amount of help on a tailor-made basis. Thus, one boy of secondary age who faced marked difficulty with a particular subject received twice the amount of his previous support from two teachers of the deaf. When educational (or other) difficulties persist a pupil can and will be transferred out of the programme.

Staffing

One of the key features of this integration programme is its generous staffing level. While all pupils join normal classes with their peers they receive additional assistance from two sources: teachers of the deaf; and 'support' teachers. Three teachers of the deaf are now involved, though for most of the seven years or so of operating – when there were fewer pupils – there were only two. The support teachers – four in all, equivalent to 3.1 persons as some work part-time – are qualified and experienced teachers who do not possess a specialist qualification in hearing impairment but have received some specific training for the programme.

The head teacher of the school for the deaf is in overall charge, but the operational responsibility is in the hands of a teacher of the deaf who is designated teacher in charge. The head remains closely involved with the programme through the teacher in charge, visiting the schools and organising in-service training for both class and support teachers. He is also responsible for selecting pupils to take part in the programme and liaises with schools over prospective placements. The teacher in charge is responsible for leading the support team, arranging pupils' and staff's timetables, guiding the work of support staff and generally overseeing the programme on a day-to-day basis.

Each teacher of the deaf is responsible for a small number of pupils and their respective support teachers. There is a basic division of labour between the teacher of the deaf and support teacher. The teacher of the deaf is responsible for providing auditory training, the teaching of speech and other specialist language work, for liaising with the school, and for supporting and supervising the work of the support teacher. The support teacher's role has to do in a general way with assisting hearing impaired pupils in the classroom and reinforcing their lesson work. This is discussed in more detail below. (More recently, these roles are often combined as support teachers have acquired specialist training and become qualified teachers of the deaf.)

The programme is largely self-contained in that no other professional agency has any significant involvement. Most auditory problems can be resolved either by the support teacher or through the teacher of the deaf who seeks to visit each pupil daily. When necessary, a pupil can be readily referred to the audiology clinic where he or she will be seen by the audiological physician. Regular audiological checks do of course involve audiology clinic staff. Pupils' progress is monitored jointly by class teachers, the support teacher and the teacher of the deaf. To date there has been only slight involvement of the school psychological service – though at the time of writing there are plans to involve a newly appointed psychologist who has displayed an interest in the education of the hearing impaired.

The role of the support teacher

The support teacher is a key figure in the programme. Employing qualified teachers specifically to *support* the work of other teachers is unusual in special education in this country. So we examine their work in some detail.

They were all trained and experienced teachers though without prior training in deaf education. One of the initiators of the programme believed that it was not necessary to recruit teachers for this work, claiming that suitable ancillary staff could with a little training and guidance from a teacher of the deaf do the job quite adequately. He argued that too high a level of support could be educationally undesirable as well as hindering a pupil's assimilation into the class. This view was not generally held, however, and did not prevail. In fact, the tendency was toward greater training as the programme developed. A number of support teachers trained as teachers of the deaf and by the end of our study only two support teachers were not qualified teachers of the deaf. For those who were not qualified in-service training was provided. This took various forms at the different stages of development of the programme – formal lectures, seminars and apprenticeship arrangements.

The support teacher's primary role was to provide back-up for the work of the class teacher, by helping the hearing impaired pupil to understand lesson content and carrying out appropriate preparatory and follow-up work. Discussion with support teachers elicited the following detailed role components:

　i) providing assistance in the classroom by, for example, ensuring pupils understand announcements and instructions and grasp information provided;

ii) reinforcing lesson content by going over it outside the classroom and providing additional explanation and practice;
iii) reinforcing the specialist language work carried out by teachers of the deaf by spending time in conversation and helping pupils with their reading;
iv) facilitating and promoting the pupil's assimilation into the particular class and into school life generally by encouraging hearing pupils to include him or her in classroom activities, explaining some of the things that caused difficulty and intervening over misunderstandings or instances of minor aggression.

In conjunction with the teacher in charge and the teachers of the deaf, they are also concerned with
v) establishing and maintaining sound professional links with class or subject teachers;
vi) maintaining contact with the home.

While broad guidelines on supporting were laid down at the outset, the way in which teachers apportioned their time between these different activities and carried them out in detail depended on the individual pupil they were supporting, the subjects being supported and the particular class teacher. Generally, they sought to support *within* the classroom, withdrawing pupils as little as possible. This entailed gauging when to intervene with explanation or reinforcement and when to stay in the background. Teachers were conscious of the danger of directing pupils' attention away from the class teacher to an excessive degree and creating a lesson within a lesson. Sometimes work was unfinished at the end of a lesson and this might be taken up in a withdrawal period subsequently. In individual cases, pupils were withdrawn from music and radio broadcasts with specific speech and language work substituted. Another pupil was withdrawn from a subject where the teacher spoke very unclearly and seemed to have difficulty in coping with having a hearing impaired pupil in class. (Pupils are not withdrawn automatically in this kind of situation. The teacher in charge first seeks to improve on the situation by providing guidance to the class teacher or the support teacher or arranges for the pupil to be transferred to a different teaching group for that subject.)

There were particular difficulties at secondary level. Priority was given to supporting lesson content, as opposed to reinforcing the work of the teacher of the deaf. The amount of support possible was necessarily restricted: "You pick up the essence of the lesson and [decide] what you can leave out." It would be impossible to cover all lesson content satisfactorily so teachers must set priorities. The aim was to convey the essential content of the lesson while maximising the pupil's understanding of it. Various strategies were described. One teacher sought to cover one lesson of every subject each week. A colleague tried "to cover half the lessons during the week ... I support not only for that particular lesson but to get the drift of the rest of the week". In her view it was "a waste of time to support completely". (While true in the case of the two pupils she supported, it cannot be assumed that this will necessarily be so in every case.) There is also the danger of over-supporting, leading to a situation where the pupil becomes over-dependent on the support teacher; this also runs the risk of "isolating ... rather than integrating [him]". This particular support teacher described how when a pupil first took up a subject she would support totally but pull out as quickly and as far as possible consonant with the pupil's needs being met. Thus, for one of her two pupils, a fifth former, she was present within the classroom for three out of four periods of social studies; all four periods of geography; and three from five periods of mathematics (the boy was of average ability, at best). She withdrew him for four periods of English each week; and a further period was taken with a small group for whom she provided remedial English.

At a comprehensive school which had two support teachers for four hearing impaired pupils at the time, with a fifth due shortly, each teacher allocated her time across all four pupils on the basis of the subjects she felt most able to deal with. Thus, for Marisa one of the teachers was present for two double periods of biology and one double period of maths. Her colleague 'supported' a further two double periods of maths in as much as she was present at the beginning and end of any lesson where new content was being introduced, specific tasks set or some form of test taking place, and approximately 60 per cent of Marisa's English, something which the subject teacher felt was "absolutely essential". Here, support took a number of forms: the class might work as a single unit with the support teacher acting as interpreter, taking notes of the key elements and reinforcing these at a later stage; it might be split into smaller groups with the support teacher taking her own group of pupils including Marisa; or it might be an oral lesson where the teacher asks questions and pupils respond, or where pupils read out passages from books or from something they have written. It was acknowledged that Marisa's presence limited to some extent the amount of oral work that was done.

The support teacher's crucial role as a mediator may be noted, primarily between the hearing impaired pupil and the class teacher but also between the pupil and the teacher of the deaf and between the pupil and other pupils. This meant that tact and flexibility were required – "You've got to make yourself acceptable" – in addition to teaching competence. It also meant that while their work was crucial it was secondary to that of the class teacher. One noted that it was "a passive role for most of the time", while another commented that "you are never in control of the situation ... you're just backing up somebody else's work, never really teaching them anything [of your choosing]". The support teacher did not have her own class and did not determine what was to be taught. This did not mean of course that the job was passive in itself. The task of selecting what should be reinforced from a lesson or set of lessons and presenting it in a form appropriate to the needs of a hearing impaired pupil within the constraints of a conventional lesson was a continually demanding one that required a high level of resourcefulness and professional competence.

Accommodation and resources

The primary accommodation requirements for hearing impaired pupils are quiet areas for auditory training, acoustic treatment for the benefit of hearing-aid users and adequate lighting for lip-reading purposes. In the early days small open-topped booths were constructed within classrooms in the primary schools that the first children attended. These were acoustically treated in order to cut down the level of ambient noise. It was also thought that they would reduce the visual distraction for the hearing impaired. However, they were only availed of for a limited period. All the schools currently involved have sufficient spare space outside the classroom to facilitate any withdrawal that proves necessary. Acoustic treatment has been more problematic, for the simple reason of cost. As pupils move from room to room within a school and from one school to another, it would not be feasible to provide full acoustic treatment for the large number of rooms that would be involved. This is particularly so at secondary level. In some cases partial treatment has been provided by means of carpeting and curtaining. This has not been done, however, in all of the withdrawal areas, a factor which must be regarded as a drawback since these areas are used for auditory training, speech improvement and so on. It should be noted, however, that the widespread use of radio aids greatly reduces the effect of poor acoustic conditions.

Apart from the high level of staffing, the other major resource is personal aids to hearing. When the programme began every pupil was provided with a radio hearing aid. A transmitter and battery charger were also included. Apart from this no other expensive equipment is required. Teachers of the deaf have their own auditory trainers which they take around from school to school. If there is need of a tape-recorder or other technical apparatus then in the past these have been acquired from the school for the deaf which has functioned as a back-up resource. Being fully a part of their respective schools, pupils naturally make use of all relevant school resources. The organiser pays over a yearly capitation allowance to each school which is intended to cover the cost of classroom consumables.

Curriculum

All participants in the programme follow the normal school timetable of their classmates. There will, however, be some modification to this, on two main grounds: first, the need for some form of specialist teaching (eg auditory training, speech improvement) or for additional back-up work where some part of the curriculum is causing difficulty; secondly, when it is felt that a pupil is unlikely to derive much benefit from a particular subject or activity and that his or her time might be better spent on other activities. Thus, Jimmy was placed at one point into a lower band English group. He was withdrawn for one English lesson each week and supported within the classroom during other English periods. Jimmy did not appear to be making much progress, however, so his support teacher withdrew him altogether from these lessons, providing content that she felt would be more relevant to his everyday experience. Jimmy received one-to-one tuition except for one period a week when he joined a small group of remedial pupils.

The content of the specialist teaching and reinforcement work can be illustrated with a few examples. Alexis is a partially hearing boy attending a junior school. He was visited three times weekly by the teacher of the deaf for a half-hour speech and language session. She described how she would spend time on speech improvement; hold a conversation, requiring that he listen, lip-read, comprehend and respond; and finish with some reading. Over and above this he received some five hours of his support teacher's time each week. The latter described what she sought to do with Alexis: "I have to back up what the class is doing but I have [also] to see he has a much wider understanding of things." This can sometimes mean "doing a lot of the things that aren't on the curriculum or [are] not what the class is doing". (Support teachers have to diverge from the timetable at their discretion.) Marisa is profoundly deaf and attends a comprehensive school. She began her third year by taking seven subjects. However, during the autumn term more and more of the support teacher's time was taken up with going over new vocabulary, mostly from her humanities lessons, to the detriment of her other work. Eventually it was decided that the only sensible thing to do would be to withdraw her from this subject at the end of term.

The amount and extent of support that a pupil receives can be quite finely tuned according to need. Thus, the generous adult:pupil ratio allows for every pupil, upon transferring to secondary school, to receive up to twice the amount of support that he or she was previously getting. This is in recognition of the fact that this transition is a major step. Such a level of support may continue for as little as a week or for much longer if need be. Wayne had recently made this transition on the occasion of one of our four visits. A teacher of the deaf was spending 60 per cent of his working time with him. In Wayne's case he was fulfilling not so much a specialist teacher of the deaf role – he was not at the time providing specific speech and language sessions because he felt that Wayne would derive more lasting benefit from following the normal timetable closely – but rather offering basic support across most of the curriculum. After the first month or so he tried to determine which subjects Wayne might be withdrawn from, but found this very difficult. He had thought that music and RE could be dispensed with, but Wayne was enthusiastic about both and, according to the staff concerned, doing very well in them. Here are reports presented by Wayne's support teacher, having consulted with subject teachers at the close of the first month:

Music – '[Wayne] has done very well ... has fully followed the basic scores and can work them out independently. His auditory response to rhythm and beat has been astonishingly good ...'

RE – 'With very simplified explanations [Wayne] has kept up to date with his class ...'

Other subjects which might have been expected to present difficulties seemed, at the time, not to be doing so. Take English, for example – 'his total participation in his present class has been encouraging ... [Wayne] volunteers naturally to participate and respond to learning situations ...'; or science – '[Wayne] is finding this new subject fascinating. He is unlikely to achieve the standard of written work required ... but he is fully with the subject taught in the class as it is very visual and practical. His involvement in practical work, understanding, recapitulation and enjoyment of this subject is excellent ...' Admittedly these were early days; and there was the very extensive support that Wayne was receiving (eg three and a half out of five maths periods, all four science periods).

In general, pupils drop one or more subjects as they move through the school, particularly where they are considered to be deriving little benefit. This is partly to enable adequate support to be provided. Thus, Jimmy had also followed a full timetable upon entering the school. However, history quickly proved problematic and was dropped at the end of the first year. All other subjects, including science, were retained until the end of his third year, although despite being quite extensively supported some had to be taken with lower ability pupils. In the fourth and fifth year an 'options' system is introduced. Jimmy retained his strong subjects, generally the more practical ones (technical drawing, engineering, geography, social studies – which he dropped midway through his final year – and mathematics), with specific remediation/speech and language work in addition. His command of language was very poor. Accordingly, one seventh of his timetable was taken up with language work provided by the teacher of the deaf. His support teacher, even when supporting in specific subjects, also put considerable emphasis upon general language work.

Preparation for adult life

The programme commenced with junior age pupils and it was some time before specific preparation for adult life became necessary. Initially, the lack of clear guidelines led to some unco-ordinated efforts which, though effective in terms of securing some job opportunities, did not fit into the system of careers guidance being planned. A support teacher was given responsibility for careers guidance for all pupils in the programme.

Pupils follow the 'design for living' and other courses that seek to prepare their hearing peers for adult life in the comprehensive schools they attend. These courses can be supplemented by support teachers who elaborate on work arising in the courses – explaining the nature of particular jobs in more detail, teaching pupils how to write letters of application, giving advice on dealing with banks, post-offices and so on. Particular attention is paid to coping with interviews. Visits to workplaces are made and to date the locations visited include a public library, offices, dress and furniture factories. Several pupils have had a week's work experience doing clerical tasks.

Monitoring progress

The two chief means of recording pupils' progress on a regular basis are: a profile maintained by the teacher of the deaf in conjunction with a pupil's support teacher; and a weekly diary maintained by the support teacher. The profile is updated twice yearly. Entries are made on the pupil's general academic attainment, commenting on such aspects as reading, writing and number in the case of a primary age child, and under various subject headings for the older pupil; together with an indication of social and emotional development (relationship with peers, attitude to school and work). There is also detailed comment from audiological and linguistic standpoints. The use of hearing aids and progress in auditory and lip-reading skills are noted. There are detailed comments on speech, broken down under: airflow, voice quality, resonance, fluency and rate of utterance, intonation pattern, pure vowels and diphthongs, consonants and blends. The weekly diaries contain more general entries – for example, where a pupil has shown a notable leap forward, is experiencing extreme difficulty or is under undue pressure, or if there has been prolonged illness or a crisis of some kind. Support teachers draw on this more subjective documentation when collaborating with the teacher of the deaf on the updating of the profile.

There is also informal discussion among the various parties involved – which simultaneously serves a basic accountability function. The head of the school for the deaf maintains a watching brief, mainly through his daily contact with the teacher in charge. In addition, he holds semi-formal meetings with support teachers roughly once a term, essentially for the purpose of seeing how individual pupils are faring, but also to discuss the programme in a general way. These meetings have tended to stay at a relatively formal level. The organiser does have the opportunity when visiting schools to talk more informally with support teachers about the particular pupils they are responsible for and any difficulties they face. Support teachers in turn are in daily contact with the teachers of the deaf – though pressure of work, more particularly as regards the teachers of the deaf, made for less direct interaction than was intended. Support teachers pointed out that visits from the teacher of the deaf did not always coincide with the time they worked with a pupil. Nevertheless, there was the intention that these visits should coincide; also that support teachers should be free of other demands on their time to enable them to sit in on sessions of speech and language work held by the teacher of the deaf. This was partly to facilitate instruction of the support teacher by direct example, and partly to provide an opportunity to discuss how pupils were progressing.

A further level of monitoring was carried out by the academic involved with the programme from the early days. This was part of an effort to provide objective assessment of pupils' progress and relate it to progress made by similar pupils in other forms of provision. (The latter enterprise was made difficult by the lack of comparable controls and the small size of the sample – longitudinal data were available on only five pupils.) This involved measuring pupils' reading attainment, by means of the Hamp (1976) Test, and speech production, by means of the Test of Speech Production: Consonant Articulation (Dale, in press, adapted from Dale, 1972) and an unpublished test of mean rate of utterance. Reading ages were collated annually, other test scores slightly less frequently. These provided useful longitudinal data, in some cases extending over five years, though as noted by the head of the school for the deaf they did not cover important aspects such as pupils' growth in receptive language or social competence.

What benefits are pupils deriving?

i) *Educational progress*

With the exception of one profoundly deaf pupil, who was eventually withdrawn from the programme, there was widespread agreement among those closely involved that pupils were benefiting: the generally higher standards and expectations prevailing in the mainstream had been to their advantage; and they had been exposed to a much broader curriculum, especially at secondary level, than a special school could of itself provide. Profiles drawn up by the teacher in charge of the pupils give an indication of their educational progress. Take the following profoundly deaf girl of above average ability: 'Maths is her favourite subject and she does well in a class of middle stream girls. Her written language is of a very creditable standard – almost normal.' Another profoundly deaf girl of only average ability was doing less well but making progress none the less: 'Struggles with maths. She has difficulty in remembering new concepts and needs constant practice. [However, her] word order is generally accurate and she appears to enjoy writing.'

The importance of intellectual capacity is evident in the following extracts. A partially hearing boy of below average ability: mathematically, he 'holds his place within a low stream class'; his written language 'is not good'. Wayne, mentioned earlier, was considered in the area of number to be 'similar to those in the lowest third of the class. [His] written language is very poor. He can remember some very limited structures.' Jimmy gives a more mixed picture: while mathematically he was average, his written language was 'poor [although] he has quite a good vocabulary. He finds word ordering difficult as he has acquired very little in the way of language rules.' By contrast, Marisa was considered to have 'a good number sense and works methodically through assignments. [Her] written language has improved a lot ... There has been an increase in the length of sentences, more variety in her use of adjectives.' Marisa's academic progress is underlined by the fact that she will be entered for CSE examinations in four of her six subjects, and for the RSA exam in a fifth (office practice/typing).

Despite these undoubted successes, the programme has by no means been free of problems. Apart from the basic – and inescapable – dilemma of attending an ordinary school to win 'normality' while simultaneously being dependent upon very intensive support in order to survive there, some concern was expressed about the content and teaching approach of some lessons. The head of the school for the deaf sat in on a number of lessons. While many were appropriate and even excellent, some were not and occasioned grave concern. He described a science group containing John, a partially hearing boy of above average ability. The class had been working largely alone. For much of the lesson John had been uninvolved and no particular attention was paid to him. Another area of difficulty related to providing the necessary support across the curriculum at secondary level. Thus, one severely deaf girl of average ability was withdrawn for slightly over two hours a week, but this was considered by the head teacher to be far too little to cover lesson content – let alone to provide any specific speech and language work considered necessary.

With regard to linguistic development, pupils' achievement appears to have been less than what some of the staff working in the scheme had hoped for. Rate of utterance very often remained quite low, while both vocabulary and structures employed were still limited. This was particularly worrying given the intensive speech and language work undertaken by the teachers of the deaf. It should be noted, however, that of the severely and profoundly deaf only three had been in the programme for the majority of their school careers. Most of the others had attended special schools for several years. Another factor that may have a bearing was the reluctance of many of the pupils to speak in the ordinary classroom. Classroom observation which we carried out disclosed frequent recourse to exaggerated 'mouthing' and gesture among both hearing peers and teachers when communicating with hearing impaired pupils.

With just one exception the speech of all the severely and profoundly deaf pupils was considered unintelligible to strangers. The exception was a profoundly deaf girl of average ability whose 'oral expression is good ... uses many colloquial phrases ... pupils and teachers understand her quite well'. At least three other pupils were considered 'oral in outlook', which gave some cause for satisfaction. Although their speech might be unintelligible to the unsophisticated listener, they had the necessary determination to make themselves understood. In one girl's case her sentence construction was considered to let her down; another was considered too concerned with the subject matter rather than how she went about communicating this. There were many mentions of pupils having picked up colloquial phrases, something perhaps less likely to happen in a special school. Finally, it should be noted that despite lacking intelligible speech all concerned were able to make themselves understood by their classmates and generally make sense of what the latter said to them.

ii) Social development
Considerable success was reported on this second main objective of the programme. Comments on general social development were particularly positive: 'completely normal' ... 'quite confident socially' ... 'has a tremendous determination and perseverance which are beginnig to bring rewards' ... 'confidently tackles most things in a serene, unflappable way' ... 'completely assimilated'. This was borne out by the evidence from our case studies. Jimmy was considered to be 'growing up to be quite a confident young man'. He was "extremely outgoing ... very personable – very much a personality about school", according to his support teacher. If anything, Wayne's social success was even greater – in fact, this was a major reason for retaining him in the scheme for so long since academically he was achieving very little: 'completely accepted by other children in the class [who] have a great affection for him' ... 'participates in most school sporting activities and is one of the best

swimmers in the school', something that has brought him great prestige. Support teachers considered that every participant had progressed in social and emotional terms.

It should be noted, however – and was regularly commented on – that many of them failed to form close friendships. Even "outgoing", "personable" Jimmy was considered to be tolerated rather than to have developed firm friendships. It was noted that 'the boys sometimes tease him but [he] takes it in good part'. Another boy who was generally accepted also lacked a special friend and was at times treated 'as a bit of a baby', because of his rather immature behaviour. The girls seemed more fortunate and there were various mentions of having at least one close friend, if not being part of a tight-knit friendship circle. As to the reasons for pupils' difficulties here, a number of factors beside hearing impairment were implicated. Chief among these were personality factors – immaturity as mentioned above, a spiteful streak perhaps, and so on. As regards the hearing impairment, a critical aspect seemed to be inadequacies with regard to speech. Even Jimmy and Wayne were relatively disadvantaged in this respect. As Jimmy's support teacher pointed out, not only could he not communicate on any meaningful level with his peers, but his very poor communication necessitated placement in a low ability band where he came up against others with less ability and often considerable emotional problems. In Wayne's case, although 'he continues to communicate with gestures, mime, words and phrases – other children manage to communicate equally well with him – there has been no stress on either side' (support teacher), the fairly rudimentary nature of the interaction was quite apparent. While at first year level this perhaps was not too serious, "each year the gap is getting wider between [Wayne] and the rest of the class" (support teacher). (He was in fact transferred to a special department after some 18 months or so in the programme.)

Parental involvement

One of the responsibilities of the support teacher is maintaining contact with the home. In point of fact support teachers varied with regard to the priority they gave this and the amount of time they devoted to it. One, for example, had not visited the home of either of her two pupils. A colleague stated that she sought to visit twice a term at most. By contrast, a third said she would visit three to four times a term, more often where necessary. The mother of one of her two pupils had been under considerable stress and this teacher had become very involved in the boy's home life. Other sources of contact with the home included teachers of the deaf and class teachers. We acquired little information on the latter, though teachers in one primary school noted the difficulty of getting any parent to visit school, partly because many children were from immigrant families where little English was spoken.

The knowledge teachers of the deaf had of pupils' home environments seemed quite extensive. Various comments in the pupil profiles testify to this: '[Anna] is encouraged to work hard at school. The parents can be too strict on occasions...'; 'family support is excellent. They attend all parent evenings'; 'Greek-Cypriot family. Greek and broken English spoken at home. A warm loving family who unfortunately don't see the need for extra help from them for their children's development.' Contact remained at this informal level and did not extend to formal involvement of parents in educational support programmes, something that had been hoped for at the programme's inception.

Summary

This highly innovative approach to deaf education has developed from tentative beginnings to a point where it is now an established part of the authority's provision for hearing impaired pupils. Conspicuous features have been the commitment of the head teacher of the existing school for the deaf – the programme was an integral part of his overall plan to disperse his (well-regarded) school into provision based in ordinary schools – and the high level of staffing support. This has necessitated provided training and developing new forms of collaborative working with class teachers. Pupils have progressed academically and there is a general consensus that they have benefited socially and emotionally. In short, the programme is providing a satisfactory education for a sizeable number of hearing impaired pupils, the majority of them severely or profoundly deaf; and in doing so demonstrates the possibility of educating far more hearing impaired pupils in ordinary schools on an individual basis than is currently thought possible – provided resources are available.

Part Four
Provision for pupils with impaired vision

Opportunities for educating pupils with impaired vision in ordinary schools have expanded relatively slowly – despite the encouragement forthcoming from the Vernon Committee (DES, 1972) which urged cautious experimentation with integrated provision for these pupils. Research by Jamieson et al (1977) disclosed that while peripatetic services for the visually impaired were steadily expanding special class provision was extremely limited. The majority of visually impaired pupils assessed and requiring special educational treatment in 1980 were still in special schools, as the accompanying table shows.

Educational provision for visually impaired (England, 1980)

	Special School	Special class
Blind	1033	1
Partially sighted	1825	145
Total	2858	146

Most pupils with moderate and severe loss of vision are educated in special schools, except perhaps very young children (pre-school and infants) who are increasingly likely at least to commence their educational career within ordinary schooling. Historically, special schools for the visually impaired have been fairly isolated from the educational mainstream. Throughout the 1970s there were indications that this isolation was beginning to break down – most notably, in the 'Open Education' experiments of Tapton Mount and St Vincents (Jamieson et al, op cit) where some pupils from these schools receive their secondary education in adjacent comprehensive schools. Although the schools concerned were highly selective about which pupils took part in these co-operative ventures, the development was a pioneering one. Although no other scheme has since been initiated on such a comprehensive scale, there are some indications that special schools for the blind and partially sighted are seeking to establish links with ordinary schools so that curriculum opportunities for their pupils may be enhanced and social isolation reduced.

Another route is to develop provision in ordinary schools. Aside from peripatetic support, which is primarily for those with less severe vision impairment, this takes the form of some kind of special centre attached to an ordinary school. This can be anything from a self-contained unit to a resource area which is an integral part of its school. We discuss here an example of the latter form of provision, catering for pupils at primary stage.

10
Resource area for the visually impaired*

This provision is a specialist resource centre for primary age pupils with impaired vision located within an ordinary primary school (nursery to age 11). There are 14 visually impaired pupils on roll.

Historical résumé

The authority in question, in common with many other small metropolitan boroughs, traditionally had very little in the way of specialist provision for pupils with special needs. As far as the visually impaired were concerned, those with mild loss of vision remained within the mainstream, while the special school provision of neighbouring LEAs was made use of in those cases where specialist provision was judged necessary. The shift toward developing provision locally came about for several reasons. Starting in the 1960s and running on into the '70s there was a shift within the broader society toward greater assimilation of the handicapped and other minority groups into the mainstream. The then assistant education officer (special education) was keen that his authority should be active on this front. Aided by a like-minded senior educational psychologist and the prevailing buoyancy of the economy, there was a positive explosion of special education provision, some of which had opportunities for integration built in.

Encouraged in particular by publication of the Report of the Vernon Committee (DES, 1972) which urged cautious experimentation with integrated provision for the visually handicapped, the authority pressed ahead with its plans. "An embryonic unit", attached to a new school for the physically handicapped, opened with three children of primary age. It was envisaged that up to 24 blind and partially sighted pupils would

---

* Chapter 10 is based on 'Resource area for the visually impaired' in *The Practice of Special Education* (1982), edited by Will Swann.
We are grateful to the publishers, Basil Blackwell, for their permission to include this chapter.

eventually be educated together from nursery age through to the end of junior schooling. Each child's circumstances would be thoroughly reviewed at around age seven and, if it was considered to be in his or her best interests, he or she would then transfer to a special school. Along with this unit, the authority appointed its first peripatetic teacher of the visually handicapped early in 1977. Her responsibility was to support pupils with visual difficulties who were already attending ordinary school.

A new appointee at senior administrative level was strongly in favour of integrated provision, and one of his earliest actions was to seek to change the location of the planned provision for the visually impaired. He went in search of a suitable ordinary school, one that had the necessary resources and "the right sort of staffing". The school eventually alighted on was chosen because it was considered a good school, run by a head who was held in high regard within educational circles. It extended across the full primary age range – a nursery department was being planned at that particular time – and there was sufficient space to enable the nursery extension to be modified in order to incorporate a specialist resource for the visually impaired within a single new building. The head was happy to accept this as "a new challenge", and thereafter her enthusiasm and commitment have always been to the fore. She immediately called a meeting of her staff at which she described what was proposed, expressed her own enthusiasm and enlisted their support.

The next consideration was the need to "foresee problems that might arise and forestall them". The head worked at fostering sound attitudes among staff toward pupils with special needs: allowing plenty of opportunities for anxieties and concerns to be talked out; obtaining relevant reading material; communicating information and insights she herself had gained, and so forth. Staff arranged visits to a range of special education establishments – schools for the visually impaired and for pupils with moderate and severe learning disorders, and provision within the authority for the hearing impaired. In addition, some attended a DES course on future developments within the education of the visually handicapped.

Advance preparation was not restricted to the teaching staff; the school's own pupils and their parents were also involved. The pupils were prepared mainly through assemblies – "I told them stories about handicapped people, about the kind of problems they have, about the ways in which they will need help" (head teacher). With regard to their parents the head called a meeting where she and the principal educational psychologist spoke to parents about the planned development and showed them relevant slides. Time was put aside for answering parents' questions. The head considered this action had been particularly well rewarded: "Parents can do a great deal of harm through ignorance ... [the fear that handicapped] children will take up valuable teaching time and [our] children will suffer... If you can answer their fears then they are always ready to support."

The specialist facility – termed the Resource Area – opened at the beginning of 1978 with the transfer of three children plus their two members of staff from a temporary location in a special school. A gradual build-up of numbers was envisaged. This has perhaps been even more gradual than was anticipated. A week after opening four more children began. A period of 16 months then elapsed before the next batch of four pupils arrived. Currently there are 14 pupils on roll. Staff consider that the maximum number that could be catered for is about 20.

Aims and organisation

There was no existing provision within the authority that would provide a working model for the resource area. There were units for the hearing impaired that operated along traditional lines, and a visit was made to a unit for the visually impaired in another authority. These visits and other preparations had sensitised the head to possible problems that could arise with regard to integrating both special education staff *and* pupils with special needs into the mainstream. For the staff concerned, however, it was essentially a new venture and the early stages were exploratory – trying something out, appraising it, making any necessary modifications, and so forth.

There were certain broad principles that the head teacher was anxious to incorporate. The most outstanding of these was a determination that both pupils and their specialist teachers should be fully assimilated into the school. She did not "want them to be isolated" and was quite prepared to force integration as much as possible. The head's initial emphasis was placed on building more normal modes of behaviour and developing social relations with sighted children. This was in marked contrast to the teacher in charge of the resource area, whose attitude was that there would be plenty of time for social development later; what mattered most was developing sound educational foundations, especially for the educationally blind child who would be working within the medium of braille.

This related to a difference in perception as to how the provision should operate. The teacher in charge envisaged a relatively autonomous unit whereas the head intended that it would operate on a 'resource room' model, whereby pupils are withdrawn from the regular class for specialist assistance as and when necessary. Basic work in the '3 Rs' was seen as the province of special education staff with integration for all creative and practical work, for blind and partially sighted children alike. It quickly became apparent that the partially sighted children were capable of remaining in regular classes for the bulk of the day. The resource room model appeared perfect for them. The educationally blind, by contrast, had need of a greater amount of specialist attention. This had to be provided within the resource area. (A further reason was that the teacher in charge was himself physically handicapped and became increasingly wheelchair bound.)

A critical factor in the organisation of the new resource area has been the team-teaching approach adopted by the school, based upon vertical grouping. Before the addition of the nursery and provision for the visually impaired, the school was divided into three departments: infants – five to seven year olds; lower school – seven to nine; and upper school – nine to eleven. In each department there were three teachers, one of whom held a Scale 2 post and acted as co-ordinator of the team. The co-ordinator was responsible for writing schemes of work, organising the grouping of children (for mathematics, topic and reading), keeping records and monitoring the standard of display work. Each day the team met to discuss the following day's work and talk over any problems with individual children.

It was into this context that the resource area arrived. Little change was made in the existing organisation of the school. A member of each team was given responsibility for liaising between immediate colleagues and staff in the resource area. Time was set aside for co-ordination to discuss "what children are doing, how we can stretch them, problems encountered... whether [the educationally blind] can come in [to a lesson]", and so on. There were difficulties in the early days. The teacher in charge complained that teachers with little or no specialist knowledge were deciding when he as the specialist could deliver special education: "I don't agree that people who are non-specialists can assess whether a problem is there... Ordinary teachers put forward the programme they wish and... I have to accept it." The perception of main school staff was that "the person with the knowhow is not willing to pass this on", and they began to begrudge the extra effort that was demanded of them.

Some time later the teacher in charge retired. His replacement was a member of the school staff, a senior teacher who had been away on a year's secondment undertaking specialist training in visual handicap. On her return, the assistant in the resource area went on secondment, and was replaced by another teacher from main school whose interest in the visually impaired had grown progressively. This led to considerable changes in working practice and an improvement in attitudes. Although the educationally blind children still spent some time withdrawn from main school they were now based in regular classes. In addition, both the resource area staff were in a position to work out in main school and felt at ease doing so.

The present level of operations was reached in September 1979 when two new members of staff were appointed, making a resource *team* for the first time. This has permitted the 'resource room' model of working to be fully embraced, with pupils being withdrawn only for specific training or in case of serious difficulty with work. A member of the resource team was placed in each department, becoming a full member of the departmental team but having the additional responsibility of teaching and preparing work for the visually impaired. The teacher in charge concentrates on the educationally blind as well as co-ordinating practice overall.

Pupils

Pupils provided for are those within the normal range of intelligence whose primary handicapping condition is visual. Pupils on roll suffer from a variety of visual disorders – nystagmus, glaucoma, retrolental fibroplasia and so on. The pupil of markedly low ability who in addition has a vision problem is unlikely to be accepted on the grounds that the provision is intended for those whose primary handicapping condition is visual impairment. A visually impaired pupil with an additional physical problem is likely to be accepted as long as this does not necessitate constant nursing support. There is, in fact, a girl attending the school who has a severe arthritic condition.

The congenitally blind child is likely to be picked up at birth, or soon after; the partially sighted child, depending upon the severity of the vision loss, may be more difficult to spot. This is particularly the case where there is a very gradual deterioration in vision. Diagnosis and assessment in the more severe cases of vision loss is essentially a medical function whereas less severe visual deficits may well be first suspected by educators – a child's class teacher or the peripatetic teacher of the visually handicapped.

It is this latter group who have given most cause for concern. Their more severely impaired peers are generally quickly recognised and the appropriate course of action taken. For the partially sighted there are two main areas of difficulty. First, the vision loss is often much harder to detect. Secondly, the peripatetic service has operated very fitfully since its inauguration in 1977. Only one teacher strong, the first appointee was off work for considerable periods of time. It is only since September 1979 that the service has operated consistently. It is now administered by the teacher in charge of the resource area in this school – officially designated 'co-ordinating teacher for the visually impaired'. One of the strengths of this arrangement is that the peripatetic teacher is no longer working alone – she has colleagues and a professional base that she can draw on.

It was originally conceived that the resource area would acquire the majority of its intake through individual head teachers querying particular children's vision. In fact, of the first seven entrants this seems to have applied in only one case, a partially sighted girl who had been "coping quite well" in an ordinary infant school but who, it was felt, would experience mounting problems as schoolwork became more difficult and print smaller. The visual impairment of the remaining six pupils was readily identifiable: one was suffering from leukaemia and his sight was deteriorating rapidly; a second was educationally blind, and a third had limited vision in one eye only; three others had significant vision loss.

Head teachers raising questions about individual pupils' capacity really came into play only with the third batch of entrants, four in all. It quickly became apparent that there were serious difficulties here. In one of the four the visual deterioration ought to have been noted – though the head teacher of the school containing the specialist resource remarked that she had only heard about the boy "by accident". All four pupils were six years or over. One, a boy of eight, was unable to read. In every case their educational development was significantly retarded though none was considered to be of below average intelligence. In the opinion of the resource area staff, their class teachers had either failed to pick up their visual problems or had wrongly diagnosed this, classifying them perhaps as 'less able', 'lazy' and so forth.

An alternative perception was that teachers were raising questions about certain children but educational psychologists were not acting quickly enough – "psychologists are just not prepared to get these forms through". They were considered to be reluctant "to take the child out of the home and [local] school environment". Whatever the social and emotional gains, from an educational standpoint precious time was lost – "We are getting them when [they] are getting frustrated; they can't cope, they are falling behind" (head teacher). In fact, all four pupils have shown considerable improvement since joining the resource area, but there is concern within the school about the possibility of other children missing out in this way. Not surprisingly, the psychologists' viewpoint was somewhat different. They felt too much emphasis was being placed on *potential* difficulties and were unwilling to make referrals based on prediction as opposed to demonstrated difficulties. The decision should be a pragmatic one: the child should not be removed from his own school just because difficulties can be anticipated for him but only when he or she had started meeting the difficulties.

Over the last six months of our study the head teacher and teacher in charge of the resource area have sought to tackle this problem. Their solution has been to develop what they call "educational guidelines", practical guidelines to assist teachers in ordinary schools to determine for themselves whether a pupil has a visual deficit of sufficient severity to necessitate specialist *monitoring*, if not specialist assistance. Heads and teachers are being urged to call in the peripatetic teacher or even come direct to the resource centre if they have the slightest concern about a pupil's vision.

To date only one pupil has reached secondary stage, an educationally blind girl. She had been nearing the end of primary schooling when she transferred (from a special school) to the resource area. As she would have had only a few months there until the time of normal transfer, it had been decided that she would be retained for an additional year. Part way through this year the educational psychologist serving the school put forward two options, both residential special schools. After extensive debate, during which the educational issue was clouded by the girl's very sound social relationships within the home community, it was decided she should go to the more local of the two schools, even though academically she would probably not be 'stretched' there. However, the head teacher was still unhappy and proposed that the girl attend a comprehensive school close by. She visited the school and secured agreement for a two-week trial.

With intensive support from staff of the primary school the girl was fully integrated into the timetable over a two-week period. The only subject she was excused was French. At the end of this time the experiment was appraised, and there was unanimous agreement that it had been highly successful. It had worked "extremely well" from an educational standpoint. In addition, the girl herself had enjoyed "a very happy fortnight". The head of the comprehensive was ready for her to transfer immediately, but staff of the primary school urged caution in the belief that the girl's needs would be better met by a phased transfer. This was considered to be working quite well now after initial teething difficulties. However, all concerned are at pains to emphasise that this should not be regarded as an automatic transfer for all visually impaired pupils.

Staffing

This has increased as the number of pupils on roll has expanded. There were two members of staff – only one of whom had a specialist qualification – for the initial seven children. The present position is that three teachers – one of whom is qualified – form a resource *team*, attending in particular to the 14 children on roll. In addition, the specialist peripatetic teacher is available for consultation – working out, as she does, from the resource area, and undertakes occasional teaching of pupils as necessary. However one cannot compute a simple staff: pupil ratio from this because of the school's team teaching approach. Members of the resource team also teach sighted pupils, while their main school colleagues will naturally deal with any visually impaired pupils in their teaching area. Because of the head teacher's insistence that handicapped children should take part fully in the life of the school, no separate allocation of ancillaries was made to the resource area. The allocation of ancillaries to the school as a whole was increased by one.

Providing specialised training for the teachers involved has been accorded considerable importance. An unusual model of secondment operates: rather than advertise for teachers with an appropriate specialist qualification, the preference is to appoint someone – often from the existing school staff – with a good teaching record in ordinary education to work within one of the teaching teams, with a view to seconding them at a later date. This is a useful trial period, both for the school and the teacher concerned, prior to taking a decision on secondment. Also, the value of the on-the-job training made possible by the team-teaching arrangement should not be overlooked. Advice and guidance can be given quite naturally as and when necessary with specialist expertise always close at hand.

There is considerable involvement of specialist agencies in this particular scheme. At its inception both the school medical officer (SMO) and a senior medical colleague were particularly active. The latter – who was himself partially sighted – had visited the school and spoken to members of staff about the consequences of impaired vision for everyday living. The SMO has been extremely supportive throughout; as too has the educational psychologist. As the one outside specialist who makes a distinct educational contribution it is worth considering this latter person's involvement in more detail.

It is the preference of the individual concerned to play down the 'testing' role – "there is not a lot of [traditional] psychology going on at the moment". He visits roughly every three weeks during which time he seeks to question practitioners' assumptions and practices, feed in practical suggestions where a child is presenting particular difficulty, generally allowing and encouraging considerable teacher autonomy. For example, for several months a little girl in the school's nursery, suffering from "a combination of handicap – retrolental fibroplasia, a general slow learner, language is particularly difficult", had presented tremendous management difficulties, and consequently with regard to appropriate educational programming. The psychologist had sought to "sharpen up some of the programming and assessment they [teachers] might make in terms of criterion-referenced assessment". In practical terms he stressed the need for more extensive and more focussed individualised assistance, concentrating particularly upon attentional training and discrimination work.

A feature of the school's involvement with outside agencies is the assessment meetings held periodically (at first half-termly but now every six months). These were introduced by the head teacher because of concern at the poor working links with social services and with certain medical officials, notably ophthalmologists. There has been improvement subsequently in both cases: specialist social workers have been regular attenders from the second meeting on; closer contact with ophthalmologists has come more recently, partly as a result of the senior medical officer persuading the consultants concerned to visit school and see how their clients were coping outside of the clinical settings. The value of these meetings is threefold. First, their primary purpose is to appraise both the general circumstances and the educational progress made by all the pupils over the six month period. Secondly, it is a multi-disciplinary working group, with the majority of those present involved with the pupils in some way. Also, it is a forum within which the ordinary teacher has an active role when discussion turns to particular pupils that he or she teaches. Thirdly, these meetings have served as a means for disseminating information and concerns about a pupil across various professions and have led to various treatments and services being provided which would ordinarily have taken a great deal longer to organise, and possibly would not have materialised at all. An example of this was the senior medical officer arranging physiotherapy for a girl with severe arthritis. Hitherto she had not been receiving any therapy whatsoever. School staff made representations about this and as a result the senior medical officer arranged first for intensive treatment in a hospital setting and then for twice-weekly visits by a physiotherapist to the school.

Accommodation and resources

The resource area is purpose-built and reflects the considerable thought that was given to the sort of facility needed at the planning stage. It comprises: a suite of four rooms, two quite large and well-equipped, and two others appropriate for individual or small group work; a pottery kiln which is extensively used by main school pupils; offices for the head teacher and secretary (originally intended for the teacher in charge but taken over by the head as a means of promoting integration – the existence of the resource area was kept at the forefront of people's minds in this way); and toileting provision. Given that pupils are now all based in regular classes and use the resource area only for withdrawal work, either individually or in small groups, the premises are highly satisfactory. They are quite open, colourful and have adequate lighting.

Over time an extensive stock of physical and material resources has been built up, not merely for the 14 pupils on roll but for all pupils with visual problems within the authority. The original intention that it should serve as a resource centre for other schools is very much a reality. There is an extensive range of low vision aids which anyone can try out (under the supervision of the peripatetic teacher). Indeed, the local eye infirmary has referred children to the school in order that they may try out specialist aids. In addition, there are considerable large print resources, closed circuit television and video-recorder, and various large-scale play items. An additional allowance of £750 per year is made to finance classroom consumables (eg large print extracts of school texts), low vision aids, etc. Larger items of equipment (eg CCTV) have been financed out of the capital loan.

Two potential limitations are being increasingly realised, however: the amount of time and effort required by having to braille out school texts and all school work set for some of the pupils; and the shortage of suitable large print books for the partially sighted older juniors. Apart from the brailling that is done by the teacher in charge or the peripatetic teacher, staff receive considerable assistance from the RNIB and the Leeds Braille Book Club (subsequently renamed the Yorkshire Braille Service).

Curriculum

The curriculum followed by the visually impaired and the working philosophy on which it is based have evolved in the course of time. In the early days these pupils were taught largely by one teacher, joining regular classes only for the occasional creative or practical activity. They were receiving a rather traditional education, in marked contrast with the informal, individualised approach based upon projects and workcards that the main school adopted. The teacher in charge at the time considered this totally inappropriate for his pupils, particularly the educationally blind: "With this team-teaching, in an individual research [ie topic-based] situation, you can't ask a blind child to [do this] – they've got to use whatever braille material you have." His reservations extended to the partially sighted. He pointed to numerous problems – print size, poorly designed and reproduced handouts and worksheets, and the difficulties they faced from a learning approach which placed such strong emphasis upon writing skills.

Above all, the disadvantage of being with teachers who had little real understanding of the educational consequences of vision impairment was stressed: "The attitude is that the child can see, therefore we use formal methods... How much they can see is not apparent to them." Ordinary teachers were considered to be at a disadvantage in having very little specialised knowledge: "In a way they don't think there is anything wrong with them... they [don't] fully understand what [partial sight] means." In consequence pupils were considered to be missing out in certain respects; if they spent more time in the resource area, "they would be getting a lot more care, social talking, language, sitting up straight... that would be brought out consciously". However, as things stood, "once they've done their educational bit [teachers] think they have done their task... there is a lot of this social training they are not getting here".

As noted above, personnel changes and training have brought changes in philosophy and approach. All 14 pupils are now based in main school and receive individualised attention from the appropriate teaching team. The present working philosophy is one of sound infant and junior teaching, with close monitoring of individuals' progress – essentially by means of extensive working contact with the pupil – and delivering specific remediation and/or training in special skills (eg typing, brailling) as necessary. Wherever possible the visually impaired work on the same tasks and with the same materials as their sighted peers. The school seeks to provide 'a balanced curriculum of academic, creative and physical activities' for all its pupils. 'Each day is divided into four working sessions, one always catering for mathematics and another for topic... The remaining times may be spent doing art and craft work, music, language or one of the following, physical education, games or swimming. Reading is done incidentally throughout the day.' The school's team-teaching approach relies upon extensive use of workcards and other individualised assignments, with teachers providing individual or small-group tuition – "we work in small groups, each child... at his own level". The individualised approach was considered most appropriate for all pupils but was particularly advantageous for the visually impaired.

The close working relationship between the resource team and the rest of the staff has been a critical factor. One member of main school staff described how colleagues had always been "willing" but that they had not always been "aware of how much extra attention the visually handicapped child required". Liaison with the resource team had been necessary to overcome this problem. For example, the feasibility of working on the same tasks will have been discussed beforehand with the co-ordinator for the visually impaired. In many cases there is simply the need of closer supervision and a little extra attention. If the co-ordinator feels that a particular activity would not be to the pupil's benefit then she will arrange either for separate work or for the pupil to spend extra time on existing work where progress is slow or difficult.

Matters become considerably more complex when a pupil is working in the medium of braille. There are at present two braille users. In the past problems have arisen from the fact that there was only one member of staff with a knowledge of braille. If this person was already occupied or was otherwise not available, there was very little that main school staff could do except wait or send the child to the specialist teacher. There is in any case a time-consuming procedure of "double-handling": the resource teacher brailles out a task set by the teacher for the pupil to do; when the pupil has completed it the specialist has to overwrite the brailled response for the ordinary teacher to mark. This, and other difficulties, while they have not disappeared entirely, have been eased with the advent of a second person versed in braille, and with the resource team being dispersed among departmental teams and working out within main school. For example, the co-ordinating teacher spends up to 75 minutes each day in main school. For much of this time she takes a mixed group of pupils for number work. Among its number the group contains an educationally blind girl and two partially sighted pupils. Main school staff feel able to cope with the various craft and practical activities with the exception of PE. For PE a teacher will be available whenever apparatus is in use to supervise and assist as necessary. In one girl's case, where vision loss was compounded by arthritis, a welfare assistant was detailed to work with the child, for the most part separately from the rest of the group.

Any pupil can be – and is – withdrawn whenever remediation is difficult within the classroom setting. Thus, in the case of the boy learning braille, he is sometimes withdrawn by the co-ordinator for specific training. Similarly, another child is being taught to use a jumbo typewriter by the school secretary. Again, should a pupil experience difficulty with some aspect of the curriculum then he is likely to be withdrawn at some stage and one of the resource team will work over the material or through the problem in detail.

Of particular note is the contribution made by one of the welfare assistants. This person spends a considerable part of her working week with the visually impaired pupils, and with the educationally blind in particular, helping out generally and undertaking specific activities where necessary. The physical education work referred to above is a case in point. Another concerns artwork. She had helped one educationally blind child to make a replica of a Viking ship from balsa wood. A considerable amount of carving was involved in this, some of which the girl had done for herself. The welfare assistant fully recognised the danger – it was a "calculated risk...you blunt the edges" – but felt that it was justified in terms of the girl's sense of achievement.

Monitoring progress

Records are formally maintained on all pupils on a termly basis. Typically the co-ordinating teacher comments on the specialised aspects of the pupil's education and the various members of the teaching team remark on the more general features. The following areas are addressed:
- social and emotional development
- physical development
- educational development; sub-divided into the following categories: reading, spelling, grammar, creative writing, mathematics, topic, art, PE, music, braille and typing (where appropriate)
- general observations.

Entries are, for the most part, descriptive, though reading ages are given. Any significant developments that occur within the term (eg a particular outcome of an assessment meeting – the two week trial at the neighbouring comprehensive school for one pupil, for instance) are also formally recorded.

The major source of ongoing monitoring is the discussion that takes place on individual pupils at the termly assessment meetings which the head teacher inaugurated some 15 months ago. Concerned about the apparent lack of working contact between different disciplines she set about bringing together representatives from different professions. These meetings are held, quite deliberately, at the school. This allows individual members of staff to attend, coming in on discussion about particular children within their area of the school. Although the educational psychologist functions as chairperson, the meetings are quite informal.

The social context

The concern at one stage in the past that some pupils, the partially sighted in particular, were missing out on the deliberate teaching of social skills has already been noted. The head teacher also was worried at that time by the mannerisms – "baby voice, screaming, high pitched laughter" – that she noticed whenever the educationally blind children were in and around the resource area. "You don't get this when they are in the main school." However, as the working of the specialist resource has evolved, with both pupils and staff spending more and more time in the 'normal' environment of the main school, these negative aspects have been overcome. Various comments from teachers testified to this. "Participates well in a group" was the remark on one infant child. "She is talking about [being in] the juniors – socially it would be bad to keep her back" was said of a little girl in infants. "You should see him eating his dinner ... he doesn't like being helped – he's very independent", of a boy whose remaining sight is deteriorating. "More independent than the other children" was said of a fourth child, a partially sighted girl in lower juniors.

The only cause for concern with regard to their development as independent individuals was a comment made with a particular boy in mind but considered by staff to apply to at least three others: "Everybody loves him ... [his good personal relations] work a bit too much in his favour" – in the sense that sighted pupils were a little too eager to assist, thereby depriving him of some opportunities for independence. This was reinforced in the case of an educationally blind girl: "Many of them [friends] are tending to spoil her ... if you will do things for her she will let you." However, school staff have taken steps to curb the excessive enthusiasm of sighted children to do things for the visually impaired. While not prohibiting this, teachers pointed out that it was not in the children's best interests: "We're very grateful but if you carry on you're going to make Sarah very lazy.' It was felt that sighted children had modified their behaviour of their own accord once they had seen how their teachers responded.

The visually impaired pupils are an integral part of school life – registering with ordinary classes, attending and participating in assembly and school concerts, playing with sighted children at breaktimes, taking dinner with friends from their respective classes, and spending time with them in the same lessons. This underlines how completely they have been accepted, and that the various opportunities open to other pupils are open to them also. All have friends in the school; some are part of quite extensive friendship circles. One particular action taken in the early days may well have influenced this – loosely teaming each visually impaired pupil with a 'buddy', a sighted pupil from main school recognised for his or her sympathetic qualities. The school never made a big issue of this, and in fact it quickly lapsed, but it may have helped in winning early acceptance. The present situation was succinctly expressed by an ancillary – "We are even beginning to hear tales [about them]" – a sure sign of acceptance!

We conclude with an extract from our fieldnotes, an assembly which one of the research team sat in on:

'Clare, Sarah and Jane were all present with their respective classes.

Sarah and Clare both gave the impression of being close to at least one child and in Clare's case there were three or four girls who stuck close by her. [It was later affirmed that she was very independent and preferred to do things for herself.] I was struck by the fact that all of them took a full part in assembly and did not stand out in any way. Even more noticeable was the general lack of concern that the non-handicapped children paid them. This is not to say that they were ignored ... the point was that they just didn't stand out as anything exceptional ... they were a normal part of things.'

Pupils with impaired vision attend for the same length of day as any other pupil – something the head teacher had insisted on. Accordingly, they have every opportunity of taking part in the various clubs and activities that occur during school hours. When it comes to participating in extracurricular activities they are at a disadvantage in living beyond the school's catchment area. This is particularly true of the out-county pupils. However, on various special occasions school staff have ferried children to and from school outside school hours when parents were unwilling or unable to do so.

Parental involvement

The school makes a point of having good relations with parents though, inevitably, the fact that some (about one third) live outside the authority means that the extent of contact is not always ideal. There is an open-house policy whereby if a parent is concerned about some matter he or she is encouraged to visit school and talk it out. The reverse applies too. The head and/or co-ordinator of the resource team quite regularly invite in certain mothers to talk about specific – mainly management – issues.

There are the customary occasions when school and home come together – open evenings, fêtes, concerts, etc. There would appear to be many such occasions at this school. From discussion with two parents a high degree of parent–school involvement was evident – both parents, neither of whom we have any reason to believe was atypical, instancing six to eight contacts over a 12 month period. These included open evenings, school plays, the Christmas bazaar and so on. More significantly, both were able to recollect at least one occasion when a visit to school had been for the express purpose of discussing some aspect of their child's schooling. In one case the mother spoke of two separate visits, one to discuss her daughter's progress generally, the other when she had been concerned about the development and quality of her daughter's handwriting.

However, we did become aware of several instances of management problems that parents were experiencing. To some extent these may stem from the fairly tight, hard-working regime which operates at the school so that children, when they arrive home, tend to unwind in a rather extreme way. The mother of one child remarked upon the very different behaviour exhibited by her daughter at home and in school and admitted that she felt unable to deal adequately with this. In another case a child's mother had on several occasions been 'dressed down' for neglecting her son. The two cases outlined above are quite contrasting, one a very motivated mother actively seeking to co-operate, the other careless perhaps or possibly not taking in what she is told by teachers.

Where there have been extensive home visits this has tended to be when a child is presenting serious management problems at school and a marked discrepancy in handling between home and school is suspected to be at the root of this. This was certainly true of one little girl who began in the school's nursery and whose disturbed behaviour – screams and violent outbursts – used to frighten other children. She is now more balanced – although her parents had difficulty in coming to terms with the likelihood that she would have considerable learning difficulties even if she were not visually impaired.

Summary

This is a good example of a school's existing academic organisation, in this case team teaching, being extended to provide a highly effective example of resource model working. Visually impaired pupils have become an integral part of the school and their educational needs are met with very little separation from their peers. Key features have been the commitment and close involvement of the head teacher, and the seconding for specialist training of existing school staff who were teachers of proven quality and had developed an interest in teaching the visually impaired.

Provision for the visually impaired is still developing in this authority. Key questions for the future include the following:
1. What shape will the developments at secondary school level take? Will it be possible to replicate the successful integration achieved at primary level? What new forms of organisation/alternative kinds of

support will be necessary? What will be the relationships between primary and secondary provision?
2. In view of the unease expressed about identification procedures, what steps will be taken to ensure that no visually impaired child will remain in his own school without specific recognition of his impairment and appropriate specialist help?
3. Given the low staffing level of the peripatetic service, what steps will be taken to strengthen the service? How will the service relate to the primary resource area and the developing provision at secondary level?

Part Five
Provision for Pupils with Speech and Language Disorders

Specialist provision for pupils with speech and language disorders is of relatively recent origin, and is still quite limited in some areas. Until the early 1970s many of these pupils would have been inappropriately placed in other specialist provision (eg for partially hearing, ESN or maladjusted pupils) or would have remained in an ordinary class without support. Nationally, there is only a handful of schools that cater specifically for their needs; these deal in the main with quite severe cases and usually entail residential placement. At local level a number of language units have been established in recent years – a development that is continuing – but their coverage and modus operandi vary considerably.

An up-to-date list of educational provision for the speech and language disordered child is given in Lancaster (1981). This displays the great diversity of provision – language units attached to ordinary and special schools, other provision in schools, language schools, language units attached to Child Guidance Centres, language units run by Area Health Authorities, diagnostic and assessment units and classes, and pre-school provision. Language units attached to schools constitute the most common form of provision. Lancaster lists over 100 language units, with the majority attached to ordinary schools. Approximately half cater for infants only and half for the entire primary age range; very few cater for secondary age pupils.

In this section we present two examples of language class provision for pupils with communication disorders. The first comprises two classes at the same school, catering for infant and junior age pupils. The second consists of two classes attached to separate schools in the same authority, dealing with infant age children only.

11
Special class provision for pupils with communication disorders (1)

This is a provision for infant and junior age children with communication disorders, located within a small urban authority. It comprises two classes catering for 16–20 pupils. It is situated at a small infant school but is administratively independent of it.

Historical résumé

This authority like most others had no specialist provision for pupils with speech and language or communication disorders in the early 1970s. Pupils with very clear needs might be placed in one of the specialist language schools, but this was exceptional. The usual choice for young children with communication problems was between an inappropriate placement in a specialist provision – which could be for partially hearing, educationally subnormal or maladjusted – and making do without specialist support, other than what an understaffed speech therapy service might provide, in an ordinary class. This situation reflected in part the low level of awareness about specific language disorder and the absence of suitable provision.

The initial case for establishing this provision was made by staff at a Child Development Unit (CDU) operating in the city. This is a multi-disciplinary assessment facility where pre-school children are assessed over a period of a fortnight by a range of professionals. A group of children emerged who were judged not to be intellectually handicapped but retarded because of speech and language problems. Over a two-year period 34 such children were identified. A number of staff working with these children at the CDU, including in particular the speech therapist, became convinced of the need for specialist language provision for them.

A number of reasons for initiating new provision were advanced. First, these children's needs for specialist attention were not being met, and it was unlikely that they would be met under existing schooling arrangements, be they ordinary or special. A small number might manage in well-supported primary classes, but for many this would be grossly insufficient. If they went to ESN schools, it was felt that speech therapy services would be deployed inefficiently and spread too thinly, quite apart from the manifest problems of labelling and inappropriate environment. Secondly, residential placement was appropriate and available for only a very small number of these. Thirdly, given that speech therapy services were limited, it was felt that a unit or language class was the best way of providing the requisite specialist help and resources.

The various professionals concerned agreed with the case presented. Discussions involved mainly the speech therapist, principal medical officer, assistant director of education (special education) and principal educational psychologist. A proposal to set up an infant age speech and language class was put before the Education Committee and this was accepted. (The authority points to a history of generous special education and pre-school provision, with a wide range of purpose-built provision and more than the national average of special school places.) It was hoped to provide a junior class as well, but that decision was left pending at this stage. A school which had a spare demountable on the edge of its playground was offered for use and, despite many limitations, designated as the temporary home of the speech and language unit.

The class opened in June 1976 with five children and operated with its full complement of eight children from the following September. Development was gradual, and all parties testify to learning a great deal from experience. Some of these developments are described below. The most significant of these was setting up a junior class. A good many of those initially identified as needing specialist help were of junior age, but it was two years – September 1978 – before a junior class was established. This was in an adjacent demountable. The presence of the second language unit made the existing site thoroughly unsuitable. Both classes eventually moved to a new location in September 1980.

Aims and organisation

This special centre sees its primary function in relation to children with a specific speech and language problem (cf below, Admission Criteria).

Given this target group, the aim is one of eventual re-integration. The staff seek to work with pupils in such a way that they will return to the ordinary classroom full-time. The expressed aim is to "give children sufficient skills to cope with normal full-time education". This of course has implications for admissions policy, since children who were unlikely to return to full-time education would not be considered well placed.

A further aim implicit in the centre's work and in many statements made about it is to continue assessment and diagnosis. A ready and once-for-all diagnosis was not possible for many of the centre's clientele. Diagnostic information was available from the CDU which most children would have attended on a half-day basis over a two week period. Given the complex nature of language disorder, however, and the well-attested difficulties of diagnosis and in particular of devising suitable educational programmes, this information was only regarded as tentative and the starting point for more prolonged work. Consequently, a further focus of the work was to refine diagnosis on the basis of ongoing and varied interactions.

A unit model was adopted, as noted above, with first one class and then a second. These are in separate rooms and carry out their daily activities separately though with a good deal of contact and exchange between the two teachers. Their curriculum overlaps and they exchange teaching groups on a regular basis. The teacher in charge described "a flexible system of interaction" with frequent discussion of difficulties and teaching problems. They come together for daily assembly and for activities such as dance and games. They exchange groups for a morning once a week in order to keep in touch with each other's teaching. Also, the junior teacher takes the infants for music while the infant teacher has the junior for art.

Two unusual features of the centre's organisation are worth noting: its relative independence of its host school; and its links with children's own neighbourhood schools.

The centre comes under the immediate jurisdiction of an assistant director of education and the teacher in charge reports directly to him rather than to the head of the host school. This is interesting in the context of Warnock recommendation 7(6),[1] the more so as the situation arose in part out of a concern to keep children in touch with their own

---

[1] "Special classes and units should wherever possible be attached to and function as part of ordinary schools rather than be organised separately or attached to another kind of establishment such as a child guidance clinic.

schools and facilitate their eventual return to them. There were other considerations: it was never intended that this school would be more than a temporary base; the site was unsuitable and militated against seeking close links. All of this meant that the centre developed as an autonomous entity and functioned independently of the host school. There were some exhanges of course, both of pupils and staff. These are detailed below.

There are advantages and disadvantages in this arrangement. It does seem to have militated against ready acceptance of the unit and easy integration of the children. Staff have felt a certain pressure to 'sell' the centre, an activity that can take up time which could have been spent in the centre itself. There has also been a tendency to make sure that children from the centre do not make nuisances of themselves, and their sometimes unusual patterns of behaviour are subjected to tighter control than might otherwise be the case. As regards integration, both the teacher in charge and the adviser concerned with it acknowledged that the amount of integration going on was less than had been anticipated. A further consideration relates to the role of the head of the host school and the degree of support that can be expected. While in this case staff found they received the support and commitment they wanted and needed, it is reasonable to suppose that this support will not always be forthcoming. Heads will feel less involved with pupils who fall outside their domain and are not their responsibility.

On the positive side, the direct link with senior officer level has been very helpful. This is a relatively novel form of provision and one that is dependent on a wide range of professional co-operation. The close involvement of a senior administrator has helped considerably in establishing the centre and sorting out teething problems. Furthermore, given the commitment to maintaining links with the children's own neighbourhood schools, it was felt that too close a link with the host school would, as far as the children were concerned, be undesirable, since they would have to cope with a threefold identification – to the centre, to the host school and to their own school.

The nature of the link with the neighbourhood school is highly unusual. The children attend the centre for four days a week, and on Fridays go to their 'own' schools. Broadly speaking, the arrangement is that the specialist language work is done at the centre and the children fit in with whatever is going on at their own schools on Friday. Some heads were reluctant at the outset and questioned the wisdom of the idea – though they eventually came to welcome it. Also, as noted, it meant that the centre stayed relatively detached from its host school. Staff felt there were good reasons for the arrangement, however, and remained committed to it: it facilitated pupils' return to their own school since they stayed on its roll and could not be 'disowned' by it, and also they kept in touch with neighbourhood peers; school staff were kept up-to-date on a pupil's progress, were informed on the means used to overcome his or her difficulties and perhaps acquired some relevant skills themselves; and teachers at the language classes were helped to keep in touch with the curriculum and standards of the neighbourhood schools. Details on how the arrangement worked in practice are given below under the heading 'Integration'.

Pupils

While it was clear from the outset that the centre's concern was in general terms with children who had speech and language problems, some difficulty was experienced in formulating a clear-cut admissions policy. The difficulty arose from the range of speech and language problems and the uncertainty of diagnosis and partly from the fact that the different professionals involved had, because of their particular training emphasis and experience, different conceptions of what the classes might achieve. In the early days some speech therapists were reluctant to make referrals to the classes on the grounds that there were no explicit criteria governing admission. Psychologists, too, tended to have a different view from speech therapists as to who were suitable candidates, and this led to some disagreement. (In fact, most of the early referrals came from the speech therapist and educational psychologist assigned to the centre.)

The staff concerned were unhappy about the situation as they felt they were vulnerable in the absence of an explicit policy. After much meeting and consultation, a policy document was hammered out.

Admission criteria

1) *Early referral is important, and it is preferable that children be referred before the end of the first year in Junior School.*
2) *It is appropriate that no child shall be considered for admission until he has had 1 full term in normal school.*
3) *The Unit caters for those children who have failed to develop sufficient communication skills to cope with ordinary school placement. These may be described as children with retarded/ disordered receptive and expressive language and/or articulation disorders, plus associated difficulties in learning in the areas of reading, writing, etc.*

4) The aim of the Unit is to give children sufficient skills to cope with normal full-time education.
5) The Unit does not cater for those children who could best be described as being predominantly handicapped in one or more of the following ways such that they would require placement under the following headings.
  i) ESN (M&S)
  ii) Partially hearing
  iii) Maladjusted
  iv) Autistic
  v) Partially sighted
  vi) Physically handicapped
  vii) A child whose language impairment can be shown to be primarily related to cultural factors and whose needs would be best met by minority support services, etc.
  viii) A child whose language impairment can be shown to be the result of lack of stimulation or appropriate learning environment.

This was a working document and the intention was to develop more positive criteria based on what the centre can offer in the ways of curriculum, professional support and so on.

At the same time, an admissions procedure was formalised. The majority of candidates would have been known to the Child Development Unit, and some information should have been available on them. The formal procedure required 'clear recommendations from the speech therapy and school psychological services'. Parental permission should be sought, and the head of the school concerned should approve the recommendation. The medical officer attached to the unit is responsible for collating relevant information on children on the waiting list. The final decision about any child's admission is based on the recommendation agreed by those present at the admissions case conference. This comprises: assistant director of education (special education); teacher in charge or other teacher when appropriate; speech therapist; educational psychologist; and clinical medical officer.

In practice, admission conferences are held twice a year. They are held at the centre, and the personnel listed are usually in attendance. Reports are available from a speech therapist, psychologist and the school. (All the candidates will have been at school for at least a term before being put up for admission.) The effective power of decision seems to lie with the teacher in charge, the psychologist and the speech therapist. These will usually have visited the school and obtained information from the head or class teacher there. A difficulty in obtaining adequate hearing tests on some children was reported in the early days, but this was subsequently resolved.

A particular problem was experienced in communicating to colleagues not directly involved with the centre what sort of child it was catering for. Mention has been made of the uneven pattern of referral from speech therapy and psychology. The speech therapist and the psychologist assigned to the centre did arrange for their colleagues to visit in small groups for an informal teach-in. It was felt, however, that it would be unreasonable to expect all the speech therapists and psychologists to be equally aware of the sort of child best suited to it. Not only would referrals be less frequent from some, but they would in some cases not be as well documented. The notion of routing all referrals through a single speech therapist and psychologist was, however, rejected.

Most of the children who have been admitted to the centre have grossly defective articulation. Their oral difficulties generally have a marked effect on their ability to cope with such skills as reading and writing, even when comprehension is apparently within normal limits. They span a wide range of intellectual functioning with full-scale IQs on WISC or Stanford–Binet varying between 74 and 129. The severity of their disabilities varies and centres on specific areas not necessarily related to intelligence. For example, one pupil with IQ 128 at age 10 still had a marked articulation problem, described as 'developmental dyspraxia'; he continued making vowel distortions, had discrepancies in voicing consonants and disturbance in prosody which involved the inclusion of extra syllables and atypical use of stress.

Staff described their clientele in terms of three groups, defined in relation to specific developmental language disorder:
  i) children with a deficit in comprehension with 'near normal' sounding speech;
  ii) children with a deficit in both comprehension and expressive language;
  iii) children with seemingly adequate comprehension, but poor expressive language.

The great majority of children fell into the second category, with only three out of 36 falling into the first, comparatively rare group, and about six in the third group.

Staffing

There are two teachers, a full-time nursery nurse (later there were two), a part-time speech therapist, a secretary who comes one afternoon a week and on request, and a dinner assistant. Neither of the teachers had any formal background in language disorder. (Until 1979 no training was available for language unit teachers, other than the dual speech therapy/teaching qualification.) The teacher in charge had had a main subject option in educational subnormality in her basic teacher training and had experience of a range of pupils with special needs and ways of treating them. She had not taught in ordinary schools except on teaching practice. As she was in post for two terms before the centre opened she had the opportunity to go on courses and visit various specialist language provisions as well as providing peripatetic support for a large number of children designated as having speech and language problems. The other teacher was junior trained and taught for a year in primary school before spending two years in a delicate school where there were a number of children with speech and language problems. The ancillary was NNEB trained and had had a variety of experience, including a year at the Child Development Unit, where many of the children would have spent some time.

The speech therapist had worked in a language unit previously and also knew the local schools quite well. She was assigned two and a half days per week to the infant class initially, half a day of which was 'floating' to facilitate home and school visits. This was later increased to three and a half days when the junior class opened. The psychologist assigned had a generous allocation of time and visited at least weekly. As well as preparing reports for admissions and review case conferences, the psychologist was involved in curriculum development and in following up children when they returned full-time to their own school. It was considered advantageous for the speech therapy and psychological services to keep the same person assigned to the centre for as long as possible in order to maintain continuity. This happened in the case of speech therapy but was not possible for psychology.

The centre did not have a social worker attached to it. A considerable number of the children and their families seem likely to benefit from Social Services involvement, yet the latter commonly has not been available. On occasion, it has been judged necessary to involve the National Society for Prevention of Cruelty to Children to deal with crises. The situation was generally considered to be unsatisfactory. It was accepted that the job of running a language unit entailed a certain amount of contact between staff and children's families, but the absence of a Social Services involvement meant that teachers were on occasion taking on a social worker role – for which they had neither the time nor the training. Some unease was expressed about this.

Accommodation and resources

The initial accommodation, which has housed the centre on a temporary basis to date, consists of two demountables at the edge of an infant playground. There is plenty of space in these and they have been converted into attractive and stimulating environments. They suffer from a number of drawbacks, however. First, the facilities for individual speech therapy are inadequate: the infant classroom has only a noisy and cramped stockroom, while the junior classroom has no withdrawal area. Secondly, the buildings are prone to extremes of temperature, noisy and lacking in storage space; they require constant attention from building services. Thirdly, the toileting facilities are unsatisfactory, requiring as they do a long walk across an open playground, with no facilities for dealing with 'accidents'. Fourthly, there is no grassed play area for ball games, etc; this is considered quite a problem with a group which is hyperactive and clumsy on the whole. It was hoped that these problems would be resolved when the centre was rehoused in new premises.

Both classes are very well resourced, having an impressive array of toys, educational materials and equipment. This stems in part from an initial generous grant by the authority in setting them up and in part from money received from charities. There is, as would be expected, a particular strength in literacy materials. These include: Breakthrough to Literacy; Racing to Read; and DISTAR Language I. There are four language masters and two tape recorders shared between the two classes.

Curriculum

The working philosophy of the centre is based on normal infant and junior teaching practice plus specific remediation provided on an individual basis. It is intended that the pupils should return to normal full-time education, so the aim must be to provide them with sufficient skills to cope with this. These skills relate to the patterns of problems the children exhibit, which can be specific reading and writing disabilities, sequencing difficulties, poor short-term memory, laterality problems and so on. Remediation must be carried out in such a way as to enhance the possibility of returning to ordinary education. Children are kept in touch with the work their age peers are doing through the centre's own programme as well as through contact with their own schools.

The major part of the speech therapist's time is given over to working with individuals, mainly for treatment but also for assessment. Infant class children are withdrawn to a separate room for individual work. Treatment has a twofold focus: promoting language development where it has been lacking; and remedying inappropriate learning. As for assessment, tests such as the Reynell Developmental Language Scales are used, but the emphasis is on informal ongoing observation based on the child's patterns of language and interaction in the classroom.

Otherwise, the speech therapist works along with colleagues, especially the teachers but also the psychologist, and pays some visits to parents and the children's neighbourhood schools. Work with colleagues includes helping to clarify for individual children how their use of language impinges upon educational progress; working out individual programmes; and establishing a basic vocabulary and set of language structures which it would be appropriate to expect of these children. Home visits are used to establish rapport and gather information or supplement existing files. School visits are also for the purpose of gathering information and finding out how the pupil is coping, but they are for giving information as well: they can communicate to the class teacher a realistic view of the pupil's actual and likely progress, get over "an idea of where the child is at, what I think he might be doing". This exchange of information is of course essential to ensuring that the school and centre act in concert and that the different inputs the pupil receives complement each other.

The professionals involved with the centre attach considerable importance to interdisciplinary working. There is evidence of good working relationships with a great deal of informal contact focussed on children and their families. There has been much discussion of admission criteria in relation to the functions the centre should be fulfilling – a topic where views have differed considerably.

A particular joint activity has been the task of developing an assessment profile for the children. This is a set of categories, broken down in fine detail, for 'reading' a child in terms of educational possibilities. The intention is that it should lead to detailed individual programmes, with

objectives and means for attaining them spelt out precisely. The class teacher monitors the programme in action and reports back so that it can be modified and extended. It should be noted too that this can provide a very detailed record of a given child's educational progress. The categories finally arrived at were:
1. background information:
   (a) family developmental history
   (b) linguistic development
   (c) physical development
2. language comprehension/expression
3. learning skills
4. reading
5. writing
6. number
7. art/music
8. physical activities
9. science
10. social/emotional skills.

This profile took a great deal of time to develop, and it was subject to a number of limitations in practice. For some children a high degree of specificity was required; the breakdown had to be very fine for it to be of practical use. It was difficult to carry out for the older pupil since there was a wider range of development to take into account and establishing baselines was more problematic. It imposed tight constraints on teaching, and was in fact never implemented for the whole group. Nevertheless, the exercise was judged to be of use in sharpening perceptions of pupils' problems and ways of dealing with them; in monitoring their progress in a more accurate and relevant way; and in helping the teacher to communicate with colleagues more precisely.

Integration

The question of integration raises particular considerations in this centre, since it has links with a set of neighbourhood schools as well as its host school. As noted, the amount of contact with the host school turned out to be less than expected. Aside from playtime, the main contact was in PE lessons, music and movement, and occasional swimming. (This was only for the infant class since the school was infant age.) Pupils did not join the main school assembly since it was considered too long, and also they arrived in school too late. Lunch was taken in common at first, though at separate tables; lack of space made this impossible when the junior class started, and all the children took lunch in the special centre.

The centre has offered a form of integration in reverse for two children from the host school. One child would not have qualified for a formal placement, but his language development was slow and he was judged likely to benefit from the unit's expertise. They attended part-time, with considerable improvement reported. It is not intended to encourage the informal placement of children who have not been referred formally; if too many children were placed in this way it could deflect the centre from its proper purpose.

All pupils attend their own neighbourhood school on Friday. This idea met with some resistance from heads at first – one objected strenuously to the notion of "being a baby-minder on a Friday" – but most came to accept it and some were quite enthusiastic about it. Class teachers varied in their reactions. Some took it in their stride, while others were uncertain and apprehensive even. Much of the initial contact was with the head, and class teachers commonly had a child from the centre for several months before having direct contact with centre staff. This seems regrettable in view of the benefits – of clarification and reassurance – claimed for such contact. One class teacher said, " I felt I was working very much in the dark. X appeared on Friday and I didn't know what he was doing for the rest of the week." She then met one of the staff and her attitude changed dramatically; "the air was cleared" and she felt confident that she could "do the right sorts of thing with him".

Most parties concerned – centre staff, main school staff, parents – saw the benefits of this arrangement in terms of social rather than academic benefit, though some heads had queried it on the grounds that little academic work was done at their schools on Friday. A surprisingly common view was that no serious work could be done on a one-day-a-week basis. The children would do their basics for four days at the centre, with the Friday seen as providing general curriculum enrichment and the opportunity to hear normal speech patterns. No particular changes were made to accommodate them and they had to make whatever sense they could of what was going on. Some schools did take care to ensure that academically the time was not wasted. One school, for instance, had all pupils working individually or in very small groups on the Friday morning, so that the visiting pupil could have something tailored specifically to his or her needs. In the afternoon the class worked as a group on projects that were self-contained and did not refer back to work done in the week in the child's absence or forward to the next week.

One regular form of communication between centre and school is the work folder which accompanies the child each week. (This is also taken home.) It contains his or her timetable at the centre, an outline of current work, and workbooks. The latter might include a reading book, language master cards, speech therapy work and a homework book. Teachers used the folder to find out what work pupils had been doing during the week. It served as a guide in drawing up appropriate work for the Friday and also offered a means of communication with centre staff. Some teachers seemed to make little use of it, however, and in at least one instance claimed not to be able to make sense of it. This folder would seem to offer an excellent opportunity for ensuring continuity of curriculum, and it is unfortunate that it has not been used more widely – whether for lack of detail in the contents of the folder or for insufficient contact between the teachers.

The problem of continuity looms larger as pupils get older and are considered for full-time placement in their own school. A transfer is usually phased over a period of time, with the pupil attending for two days a week, and then three before eventually attending full-time. As yet, few children have gone through this process, but it is evident that close attention to the detail of a child's academic programme is necessary if the transition is not to be confusing and educationally weakening. It should be noted that a decision on transfer is based on factors such as improvement in speech to a point where the pupil can communicate fairly readily; independence of the teacher in classroom work; stability and emotional maturity; and ability to handle relationships with age peers at the host school. Information is also obtained on how he or she is fitting into the local school on the Fridays, and how the integration programme generally is going.

A main aim of the 'four plus one' arrangement was to enable children to maintain contact with their own schools. This seems to have been achieved in the main, with some very encouraging progress, in spite of the attendant problems. Many of the children found the experience difficult at first but in most cases settled down eventually. One boy suffered considerable anguish and on Fridays produced floods of tears. At the time of interview, however, he looked forward to going to his own school and without hesitation named three or four friends there. The class teacher did observe, however, after a visit to the centre that he seemed much more outgoing and confident there than at the school.

Another boy had been very withdrawn prior to going to the centre – "If we spoke to him he would weep ... there was no attempt to take part in anything." Now, by contrast "he will come and talk ... bring messages ... bring dinner money ..."

Parents acknowledged these difficulties too but felt that it had been worth persevering. One parent pointed to a particular problem at the beginning of the school year when the children have to adjust to a new teacher, new classroom, new place to hang coats; the other children take it in their stride, but a child from the centre has only one day a week to absorb it all. Parents likewise seemed unconcerned about teasing. Little had been reported, and the view that 'anyway they've got to get used to it'. One school sought to pre-empt any teasing by being very open about the situation: the class teacher prepared the class by discussing the new arrival with them and putting the boy's speech problem in the context of individual differences generally and the problems other people have. This approach was claimed to be very successful.

In two cases long-term difficulties were reported, where children were regularly absent, were not settling down, and did not seem to be benefiting from the experience. One child in particular was very immature for his age and had difficulty in moving from the warm and relatively free-wheeling atmosphere of the centre to a school where there was considerable emphasis on academic standards and correct behaviour. In both cases centre staff suspected parents of colluding in the children's absences. Both cases point up the need for close liaison between home, school and centre staff if this arrangement is to succeed.

One of the principal difficulties of this provision has been the establishing of adequate liaison between centre staff and school staff. The former acknowledged the importance of this: for breaking down opposition to the children's presence in their schools; for convincing colleagues that what they themselves have to offer is useful; and for transmitting the necessary skills for teaching and managing these children. They admitted that the situation was far from satisfactory: contact in many cases was insufficient; class teachers were not getting the support they needed; and the requisite skills were not being transmitted.

A number of reasons can be advanced for this. First, contact with the school was through the head, and sometimes stopped there. It was claimed that the effort of 'selling' the work of the centre and legitimating the need for direct contact with the class teacher took a disproportionate amount of time. If this happened, the absence of direct contact meant that class teachers and centre staff were unaware or uncertain of ways in which they could usefully work together. Two teachers who – eventually – visited the centre found it an eye-opening experience and one with considerable implications for their perceptions of the child and how they treated him. Both regretted not having made the visit much earlier. Thirdly, the absence of a systematic procedure for regular two-way visiting between centre and school made for sporadic and ad hoc contact. It would seem essential, for instance, that class teachers be released to visit the centre as early as possible in the school year. This would provide the basis for regular and direct contact between centre staff and the class teacher throughout the year.

It should be noted that staff were tackling this problem in a concerted way by the end of our study. A number of steps were being taken. All class teachers and head teachers were asked to visit the centre during the child's first week there. A programme of visits to neighbourhood schools was drawn up for the year, and letters were sent to head teachers explaining the purpose of the visits and requesting some time with the class teacher on her/his own. All visits to schools are written up and kept available in a central file so that other staff at the centre are aware of whatever contact there has been. A series of general meetings for teachers with pupils at the centre was also planned. The first such meeting, which attracted a total of 20 teachers, was given over to describing the nature of specific speech and language disorder and included the viewing of a videotape about speech handicaps.

Parents

Staff have good relations with parents. Open days are held where the work of the centre is explained. This is valued by parents for the sense it gives of being involved in the effort to remediate their child's problems. There is a general policy of open house, and parents are encouraged to make contact whenever they wished. Many of them do so, by telephone and visit. Some home visits are made. More recently these have been made at the same time as school visits to provide continuity; as with the latter, all visits are written up and details entered in a central file.

Much of this contact seems to be at the level of a befriending service on the part of the staff. Occasionally it is more than that. Some of the family backgrounds are excessively difficult and, as noted, social services involvement is not readily obtained. In these cases staff find themselves taking on social worker roles. In another case where a boy was suffering rejection because of difficult behaviour at home, the teacher drew on Portage ideas to devise a programme of behavioural objectives. Home-school books are used as a means of regular contact with parents and also to pursue didactic ends. With younger children they may just note items of interest, some from parents, some from teacher. As they get older and communication skills increase, the books become more structured. Children take them home at weekends with detailed work for them to do and sometimes a specific involvement on the part of parents. Parents sometimes respond with queries and comments on particular difficulties, suggesting alternative ways of doing things or even setting their own homework. It should be noted that these home–school books are used with all children whose parents are willing and able to co-operate – usually about three-quarters of the parent body.

Summary

This provision for pupils with speech and language problems has been running for four years. It started life as a single class for infants and expanded after two years to take in a junior class. Many problems have had to be solved: unsuitable location; lack of experience in running language classes – there were few models to draw on; difficulty in identifying target clientele; an unusual mode of integration; some resistance from staff in ordinary schools. On the plus side, there has been a committed staff, working with co-operation from Area Health and other Education staff.

There has been considerable progress and the centre has developed into an effective provision for a small group of pupils whose quite specialised needs were not being met prior to this. Of 16 pupils who have left, 11 have returned to normal education full-time, four are attending day ESN schools, and one has gone to a residential school for speech and language disordered children. A further three children are attending normal school for more than one day a week preparatory to returning full-time. The problems have not disappeared but much progress has been made: new premises have been acquired; staff have built up experience; the referring agencies have a clearer idea of the type of child that can benefit most; and many heads and teachers from the schools are well disposed toward the work of the centre.

The future shape of the centre will perhaps depend on its responses to five major questions:

1. How will it adjust to its new location? What response will it make to the opportunities for contact and exchange with its new host school?
2. Will the centre have a role for those pupils whose needs are not serious enough to warrant a place at the centre but who have a significant speech or language problem that could be ameliorated by the expertise of centre staff? How would this work out in practice?
3. Given the need for more effective contact with the neighbourhood schools, will it be possible to achieve this and support class teachers in a systematic way? Will the new arrangements resolve the difficulties found in the past?
4. What provision will be made for those pupils who reach secondary age without being in a position to return to full-time education?
5. In view of the difficulties experienced with some pupils after they returned to ordinary schooling, as reported in the appendix, will arrangements be made to monitor pupils' progress over the longer term and provide further help as necessary?

Appendix: follow-up study of ten leavers

The first teacher in charge carried out a follow-up study (Sinclair Taylor, 1980) of the first 10 pupils who returned to ordinary schooling full-time. At the time of the study they had been discharged from the centre and in their schools full-time for periods from two months to three years.

All 10 teachers affirmed that the ordinary school was the best place for these pupils. Seven teachers, however, felt that they needed extra help and personal attention, and four had definite reservations about their capacity to cope academically in the future, especially at secondary level. As regards current academic progress, five pupils were rated as average or above; the other five all had problems with the mechanics of reading and fluency and were judged the worst readers in their classes. Six were the worst spellers in their classes with sequencing and phonic work a particular problem. When asked about children's particular strengths, teachers described five as good at art and three at games.

Socially, the pupils seem to have done quite well. None was described as isolated socially, and three in fact were described as very popular. Eight had special friends. No teasing was reported. Most of them related well to staff, but four were described as shy – "Seems to have to rehearse things before she says them", "Still somewhat diffident" and so on. The ability to integrate socially was felt to be associated with personality factors rather than language skills.

Little or no support was available to teachers to assist them with dealing with these pupils. The report speaks of 'a singular lack of any regular help'. This is in the context of (a) none of the teachers having any relevant training and (b) eight teachers saying that they 'definitely felt unclear' about the pupils' problems. Moreover, the detailed information on each pupil passed to the schools did not reach the teacher in several instances.

12
Special class provision for pupils with communication disorders (2)

This is a provision for infant age children with communication disorders within a large metropolitan authority. It comprises two classes attached to separate schools and caters for up to 16 children.

Historical résumé

As with the previous example, this authority like most others had no specialist provision for pupils with communication disorders in the early 1970s. The particular needs of these pupils were frequently not recognised. Most were attending ordinary schools with whatever support an understaffed speech therapy service might provide, or were placed in special schools, usually for those categorised educationally subnormal. A few were placed in one of the specialist language schools.

The impetus for developing more appropriate educational provision for these children came from a group of professionals working out from a hospital-based Child Development Centre and involved in the diagnosis and assessment of children with communication difficulties. The three professionals concerned – the principal educational psychologist, a speech therapist and a paediatric neurologist – recognised the existence of a group of children "who, even with regular speech therapy and fair cognitive ability, were not going to succeed" in ordinary schooling and yet were not in need of the highly specialised approach of a special school. They felt it was their responsibility – and a challenge too – to develop some form of middle ground alternative.

Fuller consideration of the matter revealed that there were "no precedents to go on". Whatever form this provision took it would inevitably be a pioneering activity, "a shot in the dark", as one of those involved later was to describe it. They opted to establish two Language Development Units for infant age children with specific language disorders. Having presented this plan to the Education Committee and secured agreement for it, they set about putting it into practice. The psychologist drew upon his knowledge and experience of the authority's schools in order to determine suitable locations for the classes. In both instances he was able to capitalise upon his sound relations with the head teacher.

The classes, which opened in April and September 1974 respectively, were intended from the beginning to be quite small (a maximum of six – later increased slightly). Language disorder is less prevalent than many handicapping conditions. Those responsible obtained an indication of the likely incidence level from a study carried out in another urban authority in the 1960s. This suggested a prevalence rate of specific language disorder among school age children of normal intelligence of around 1 per 1000. Subsequent experience was to prove this figure a reliable working guide – roughly one per 1250 of the child population of primary school age and normal intelligence is in the language classes.

A notable feature of the planning and initiation of this provision was the very informal way in which it was handled – "nothing is written down". This informality was considered an asset on account of the flexibility it gave. Particularly in a new situation where there were few precedents or existing working models to draw on, it was felt that formal written procedures would have held up the development. Some staff did acknowledge, with the benefit of hindsight, that the absence of explicit agreements did have drawbacks. "We should have had a common plan" to guard against uncertainty and to "clarify the roles [of the school staff involved]". It was felt too that the provision was vulnerable to staff changes; it could be seriously affected, for example, by a new head teacher who had different priorities or was unsympathetic to the mode of working that had evolved.

It should be noted that these classes were part of a comprehensive attempt made through the 1970s to meet the needs of all pupils experiencing problems with their language development within the authority (and four or five neighbouring authorities which had little or no provision of their own). Thus, two more classes, located at an open-air school and a maladjusted school respectively, were opened to provide for junior age pupils who, in addition to language problems, also had slight physical or emotional problems. A fifth class was attached to a special school for children (aged 5–13) with moderate learning difficulties. The 'language team' based upon the Child Development Centre seeks to use the provision available in a flexible way.

Finally in this section, a brief mention of the particular schools chosen to house the two classes. One was a nursery/infant school with about 250 children, while the other was a small city-centre school with about 150 across the primary age range. We have already noted the good relations between the principal psychologist and the respective head teachers. Both readily welcomed the suggestion that their schools should house this specialist provision – indeed, one head's view was, "I don't see how you can treat them anywhere else." She spoke from personal experience, having a child of her own with a communication disorder. Having handicapped children attend ordinary schools was to her a means of "releasing a normal child into a normal world". Their handicap was such that "they might never have broken out of it" if placed in a special school where they might hear little normal language. There was also the perceived benefit of "peer competitivity" which they would experience in an ordinary school – "he probably wouldn't have been stretched in the same way that he is here by his peers" if attending special school. Additional factors in the choice of these schools included: availability of space; the fact that one of the schools had already taken children with language problems – "We've always had them before, it's just that they've been screened out"; and the presence on one of the school staffs of a teacher who had a general interest in language development and who, furthermore, was regarded by her head as "a well-organised infant teacher who had already proved herself in a large class setting".

There was no formal consultation or preparation of the school staffs, though one head made a point of discussing it with staff and emphasising that it was an honour for the school to be chosen for this development. The teachers in charge, upon being appointed, did a good deal of informal dissemination about what was proposed, what these children's difficulties were and so on. Each saw it as her responsibility to win an acceptance for her children in the school. It undoubtedly helped that in both instances the teacher appointed either was or had been a member of the school staff and was thus not a total stranger about the school. Both were appointed one term before their class took in its first pupils. This was deliberate – to facilitate their own preparation and to strengthen relations with the parent school. As one head observed, it meant that the teacher was not "an expert who suddenly appeared in the staffroom".

Aims and organisation

The two classes serve the parent authority together with a few neighbouring authorities which have little or no suitable provision of their own. Their primary function is in relation to children of infant age and normal intelligence who have a specific speech or language disorder. This is directly related to the goal of eventual integrating of a child back into his or her local school. (This includes placement in an 'opportunity class' for children who face general difficulty in their learning.) This goal directly influences the choice of pupils for the classes since those who were unlikely to be able to cope with ordinary schooling subsequently would not be considered well placed. When the classes first opened there was an idea in currency that the specialised intervention would only be for a short term (perhaps as little as six months). One head teacher had held out against this – "I insisted they must spend the whole of their infant career here." It was subsequently agreed that pupils would be attached to the language class for a considerable period of time, at least two years in the majority of cases.

Another important facet of the working philosophy behind these classes is the notion that specialist support should be provided within a context of 'normality'. A written account by a member of the speech therapy service explains further:

'The aim of the language units is to give the children the specialist help they needed while keeping them within the context of a normal school and home life ...

'We aim to enable the children to re-integrate into an ordinary school class; initially in the school where they attended a language unit but eventually, whenever possible, in a similar school in their own neighbourhood. We felt it to be a major disadvantage of the "unit" system that as children's language and communication skills improve, we are able gradually to "wean" them out of the unit and into an ordinary class, while keeping them "attached" as long as necessary to the unit, to which they return for special help'.

There is also a strong concern that any intervention should commence from as early an age as possible. This is contingent upon early referral – which in turn necessitates that the provision is known about by referring agencies and that criteria for admission exist and have been publicised. Considerable time and energy have been devoted to this end. Diagnosis and assessment are undertaken by a central language team based in the Child Development Centre. This team sees itself as co-ordinating the service overall – conducting assessments and co-ordinating assessments done by teachers, recommending particular placements to the authority's Placement Committee, providing the requisite specialist intervention in part, monitoring children's subsequent performance, and recommending discharge or further specialist attention at the close of infant schooling.

Both classes are subsumed under the parent schools, each teacher in charge being answerable to the head teacher – though at one school the organisational arrangements were not clear-cut. The head teacher, appointed after the class started, stated repeatedly that he was unsure of the precise relationship that the authority intended between school and language class – "I would like to have it in black and white where I stand with this unit" – and implied that this lack of clarification was a considerable drawback. Certainly there are unexpected differences between the two classes. For example, while both teachers in charge are paid out of special services, only in one case is the teacher regarded as a full member of staff (with position guaranteed in the event of the class closing or moving). Again in one school the teacher has a formal responsibility for language development across the school as a whole (this is intended as justification for paying the special schools allowance); in the other the teacher while also involved with colleagues does so from her own initiative rather than through a formal appointment by the school. Both teachers have a good deal of autonomy in their working, though again the two locations differ in regard to how this has come about. In the one it seems to reflect the fact that the teacher is the language expert in the school; in the other it is a function rather of the distancing of the class from the main school consequent on the lack of clarity as to who has formal responsibility for it. Some of these differences reflect a difference in style and approach on the part of the respective heads. In one case the head has been directly involved in the development of the language class from the outset and has a strong personal commitment to it. The other head, while not neglecting the language class, inherited it on arriving at the school and was never given a clear brief for its working and relationship to the rest of the school. In his eyes it had to take its place along with the other three areas of the school (nursery, infant and junior).

Pupils

While it was clear from the outset that these units would be concerned with infant age children of normal intelligence who had specific language or speech disorders, some difficulty was experienced in formulating a precise admission policy. The main problem lay in isolating communication disorder, as distinct from other factors, as the primary handicapping condition in children of pre-school age. Of the initial batch of 12 or so entrants, it became evident in the case of some that their language problems were merely an aspect of general learning difficulties. Given the concern to feed children eventually into full-time ordinary schooling those working in the service had sought to eliminate misplacements of this kind. With time staff felt they had achieved this; late in our fieldwork the consensus was that the vast majority of prospective candidates were being picked up, that misplacements had been virtually eliminated, and that admission criteria were not too high or unrealistic. It was affirmed that pupils with language problems who were not placed in one or other of the classes were being capably dealt with elsewhere: 'Language disordered children requiring less intensive therapy worked with speech therapists in other departments of the local service.'

Precisely what kind of language difficulties do children who are accepted exhibit? In the main they will have severe difficulties with comprehension and/or expression. Some have an associated phonological disorder. Occasionally a child is admitted who has an exceptionally severe phonological disorder but no serious language disorder. Children with additional physical handicaps are routed elsewhere. Those children with additional learning difficulties are directed to the language class attached to an ESN(M) school. Children with significant hearing loss, or with emotional disorder of which their language is a symptom rather than a cause, are not accepted.

Great emphasis is placed upon the earliest possible referral. This was a particular difficulty in the early days but has since been largely resolved. The existence of the two classes was not always known to would-be referring agencies. In some cases children's language difficulties remained undetected, largely because of insufficient knowledge about language disorder within professional and lay communities. (A particular problem was the rather common attitude that 'things will right themselves of their own accord in time'.) For these and other reasons late referrals were common in the early days. Nowadays, however, children are being identified much earlier – at two or three years of age. This has highlighted the need for further provision at pre-school level. While nursery schooling and speech therapy on a weekly basis can be provided for most pre-school children, those with significant language problems would benefit from more intensive support.

Most children reach the classes by way of the Child Development Centre where they are assessed by the language team. (A minority are picked up within the schools' own nurseries.) The majority of referrals are from speech therapists, educational psychologists or GPs. The assessment undertaken by the language team is multi-disciplinary and involves the following personnel: paediatric neurologist; speech therapist; and educational psychologist. A senior clinical medical officer, also based at the Child Development Centre, examines the children, particularly their hearing and vision. Each child will also be seen by a social worker who completes a social workers' SE form, SE(SW), peculiar to the authority.

Assessments carried out by the language team are typically informal but wide-ranging. Their basis is getting the child to carry out various practical tasks and observing his or her reactions, supplemented by questioning of the child. There is relatively little use of formal testing. The concern is to pick up on the child's "general level of symbolic thinking ... What can he copy or write? How quickly does the child learn, pick up ideas? What sort of social skills – feeding, dressing, washing – does he have? Can this child stand being away from the home for long? What's the nature and level of his play with other children?" The various members of the multi-disciplinary team interact easily and freely: "We tend to all do our own thing and everybody else's thing ... We tend to look at the total child within our own sort of background and discipline" (psychologist) – rather than each professional concentrating on his or her particular specialism and reporting on it later. It is emphasised by the team that assessment must be a continuous activity rather than a once-for-all decision. In this regard, the speech therapist is a crucial liaison agent between the school and the rest of the team.

The team's placement recommendation is forwarded to the Placement Committee. This comprises the following personnel: assistant director of education (special education); senior medical officer (child health); principal educational psychologist; social services representatives and an administrator. None of these will normally have personal knowledge of the children being discussed. They will have received SE forms 2 and 3 and the SE(SW). The Committee normally endorses the recommendations presented to it, and it would be considered exceptional if it reached a contrary decision.

Both of these language classes accept only infant age children. At the end of infant schooling various forward placements are possible: opportunity class; regular class; a further language class; or even special schooling. Thirty-six pupils left the two classes in the six years from April

1974 to July 1980. Thirty-five of these were retained within various local provisions as follows:
- 12 to an ordinary class in their local junior school
- 4 to a top infants class in their local school
- 3 to an ordinary class in their local school but still receiving regular speech therapy
- 2 to an opportunity class in their local school
- 6 to a junior language class attached to an ESN(M) school (one of these no longer needs speech therapy)
- 8 to junior language classes attached to other types of special school (at least two later transferred to an ordinary or opportunity class in their local school).

With regard to following up pupils when they have left, it is the speech therapist's responsibility to maintain a watching brief. Pupils are formally discharged one year after leaving the language class unless there is continuing need of regular or occasional speech therapy. It is considered important to allow sufficient time to ensure progress is satisfactory over a reasonable period of time.

Staffing

Each class has its own teacher in charge. In one case there are two classroom assistants, one of whom is a trained NNEB; in the other there is only one assistant. This difference is a historical one. The head teacher in question was asked if she would be willing to accept a boy with severely disturbed behaviour. She agreed on condition that a full-time assistant was provided for him. When he later transferred to a special school, the head managed to retain the assistant by agreeing to a rise in the number of children in the unit from six to eight.

Both teachers have been through ordinary teacher training; neither has a specialist qualification in language disorder. (Until 1979 no relevant training had been available apart from the dual speech therapy/teaching qualification.) Both had been on the staff of the school prior to this appointment. One had taught at the school for three years. Having left the area for some time she returned, applied for the position and was appointed. As part of her preparation she taught in a school for pupils with severe learning difficulties for one term, as well as visiting various types of special school. She also sat in on speech therapy sessions and visited language units outside the authority. She attended a two-term evening course on language disorder and was pursuing a specialist course of training at the time of her appointment. The second teacher also spent time before her class opened visiting relevant provisions elsewhere, speech therapy clinics and so forth.

As regards the assistants, one is a trained NNEB with an interest in language development. Two of them have been in post since the start. Considerable importance was attached by one head to having a stable staff – particularly since there was a deliberate intention of providing training 'on-the-job'. The nursery nurse had accompanied the teacher in charge and head teacher on a part-time evening course organised by the speech therapy service.

The involvement of outside agencies, in particular the speech therapists from the language team, is a notable feature of this provision. There are two therapists, each with responsibility for one of the classes. Each spends one full day per week in school, providing individual therapy, conducting specialised assessment as necessary and liaising with the teacher in charge over the programming of the individual children. The educational psychologist visits more occasionally, at the minimum termly, or when requested by one of the teachers in charge. His routine visits are directed toward ensuring children are progressing; visits requested by a teacher will be for a more specific purpose, eg helping to treat a particular child who is manifesting disturbed behaviour. In the past links with social services have been very sound, though on most of our visits social workers were on strike and no social worker involvement was possible. It should be noted that the classes suffered from a high turnover rate of staff from these agencies in the early days, with numerous changes of psychologist, speech therapist and social worker. Better continuity has been achieved in recent years.

Accommodation and resources

Both classes are housed in classrooms within the body of the parent school. In one case the location is quite central, just off the hall which is extensively used for assembly, PE, music and movement and so forth. In the other case the classroom is relatively isolated within the school as a whole, though it is close to the nursery and the reception class – with which there is most contact. Playground space is very limited in this school, with no grassed area. In both cases the classrooms are quite spacious, an important factor given the hyperactive nature of some of the children.

Both classes are financed off the special education budget. Thus, necessary items of equipment, classroom consumables and so on are financed separately from the main school. The capitation allowance for pupils in these classes is approximately three times that of a child in the parent school. Both classes are well-resourced and possess adequate stocks of curricular and play materials.

Curriculum

The working philosophy of both classes is one of concentrated individual or small group teaching based upon sound infant school practice, allied to specialised therapy and attention in regard of the specific language disorder. In general terms, basic skills work occupies each morning with creative and play activities in the afternoon. Children's individual programmes reflect their particular problems, which can vary widely. All will have difficulties with specific aspects of language development (eg an immature or abnormal 'speech sound' or phonological system, or an expressive language delay) accompanied in many instances by difficulties with general educational development (eg poor short-term memory, an inability to sequence, poor fine or gross motor skills, extremely limited reading ability). The children keep in contact with the work their age peers are engaged in through the particular programmes followed in the language classes together with opportunities for integration, as detailed below.

A careful balance is maintained between specialist language work and the normal school curriculum. These are the primary responsibility respectively of the speech therapist and the teacher. The former conducts detailed assessment, determines a programme of work and provides individual treatment. The latter follows the normal infant curriculum as much as possible, as well as carrying out practice on speech or language exercises devised by the speech therapist.

The speech therapist's contribution is clearly a critical part of the specialist provision on offer. The following account of their involvement in the curriculum, as it obtained toward the end of our study, has been offered by the therapists in post:

'The two speech therapists... have a broadly similar approach. Variations (eg in the amount of time devoted to group work) are the result of differences in the individual styles of therapists and teachers, and in the particular needs of the children in a given unit at a given time.

'After initial detailed assessment, long-term aims are arrived at and broken down into short-term aims with a time scale of weeks. A programme of specific activities is drawn up which is designed to achieve these aims and is suited to the individual child. Assessment is continuous and both therapy techniques and long-term aims are modified in the light of a child's progress...

'The speech therapist's assessment covers the general areas of language comprehension, expressive language and the intelligibility of speech. Language comprehension is looked at in relation to established developmental norms supplemented by standardised tests of receptive language, in particular the Reynell Developmental Language Scales. The child's receptive and expressive vocabulary is also assessed. A somewhat arbitrary division of expressive language into structure content and use is found useful in assessment and therapy planning. Where detailed assessment of structure is needed the LARSP profile, developed by Crystal and his colleagues, is used. Content and function of language are linked with a child's more general symbolic abilities....

'The intelligibility of a child's speech is also assessed. Difficulties here may be due to poor monitoring by the child or to a delayed or deviant phonological system. Less frequently they may be due to an articulation disorder – ie poorly co-ordinated motor control for speech. Occasionally a child will have a very specific problem, such as hypernasality due to a poor mobility of the soft palate. Where a phonological disorder is the problem, the therapist will analyse the child's deviant 'speech sound' system. On the basis of this analysis, and bearing in mind the normal developmental pattern of speech, the therapist will devise work to help the child develop a normal and intelligible system.

'In both units the therapist and teacher jointly keep a work book for each child in which long and short term aims are recorded, together with the specific activities involved in the daily therapy programme (eg games to help establish the use of verb-plus-object utterances; minimal pair work to establish a particular contrast in the "speech sound" system). As well as weekly discussion of these programmes and of the group work associated with them, both teacher and therapist make notes in the book of how the child copes with the work and of the progress made.'

Monitoring progress

There are both informal and more formal measures taken to appraise pupils' progress. The former are the personalised diaries which the teachers in charge keep, in which are entered particular things of note (eg an unexpected or pronounced improvement, a persistent failure in some aspect of schoolwork). The first part of each entry typically focusses upon the child's personality and emotional or social development; this is the teacher's subjective appraisal. The second part details progress in the area of language and number and is somewhat more objective. These diaries are completed on a fortnightly basis. In cognisance of the amount of time they take, one teacher has two free periods each week partly in order to maintain this diary. They are acknowledged to have most meaning for the teacher herself, who has the necessary detailed knowledge on each child against which these comments and observations must be 'read'. They were described by one head teacher as an "educated opinion" about the child's educational development, as opposed to the more definitive pronouncements expected of an educational psychologist who has formal tests at his disposal. The workbooks jointly maintained by the teacher and speech therapist are a further informal means of monitoring progress.

On a more formalised level, case conferences are held at least annually, at which the circumstances of each pupil in the unit will be comprehensively reviewed by a multi-disciplinary team comprised of: paediatric neurologist; educational psychologist; speech therapist; school medical officer; teacher in charge; and head teacher. In advance of the conference itself the three professional workers most closely involved (teacher, therapist and psychologist) produce a joint report which serves as the basis for discussion. This addresses various aspects of the individual's development: basic details including any changes in home background; physical attributes (eg appearance, vision, hearing); general development (including social independence, relationships with adults and peers); general ability (a general account from the psychologist, plus information on the child's play); educational attainment (reading, writing, spelling, number); and language and speech (including comprehension, expression, language content, vocabulary and phonology). Also included are teaching objectives and specific therapy aims, together with an overall summary for the immediate future. These quite exhaustive reports are supplemented at the conference with tapes designed to illustrate the improvement a child has made or any area of continuing difficulty.

Integration

All pupils attending these language classes experience some integration, but there are considerable variations in the nature and extent of the integration both between classes and within them depending on the progress of individual pupils. In broad outline, the difference between the classes is that in one integration tends to be for individuals whereas in the other the emphasis is on group activities. There are some group activities in the former case of course – music and movement, hymn practice, television, lunch and playtime (though language class children have the playground to themselves for part of each day). PE was taken with a class from main school at one stage, but the clumsiness and poor gross motor control of several of the children impeded the flow of the lesson, and it was decided it would be best for them to do it on their own.

This school has a definite strategy for feeding pupils into ordinary classes. The decision to initiate the process is taken by the teacher in charge, in consultation with the speech therapist and the class teacher involved. It is done carefully and on an individual basis – "They are weaned out gradually from this very protective situation" – and only when the pupil has given clear signs of progress in both basic attainments (reading, writing and number) and general language development. Typically, a pupil will begin by spending part of each afternoon in the ordinary classroom, participating in creative play activities. The amount of time spent there will be gradually increased, though care is taken to ensure that the progress made within the language class is not jeopardised. A pupil can easily be withdrawn should anything untoward occur. Ultimately he or she may become a full-time member of the class, being withdrawn only for perhaps 15–20 minutes of specialised language work each day, before eventually being transferred to the local school.

The emphasis in the other class is, as noted, on more extensive integration for the group as a whole. This developed initially for two reasons: first, the teacher in the language class exchanged with the reception class so that her children would have contact with 'normal' children and also so that each teacher had a break from the children she had primary responsibility for and could have experience of another group; secondly, both classes were timetabled for television and music and movement at the same time and "it seemed sensible to put them together". No attempt is made to integrate as a group into the infant class, mainly because children in the language class are considered too immature. However, four pupils have been individually integrated into this class, and a further two into the reception class. All told, they spend about 25 per cent of their time with classes in main school.

The teachers in charge of both language classes see themselves very much as an integral part of the parent school. In one case this union is formalised – the teacher is a member of the school staff and also is responsible for language development within the school (she advises other teachers on the use of language materials, or where a child is presenting particular problems, and may even refer the child to the speech therapist). In addition, she takes a period of singing with the whole school once a week, and is in charge of a second year infant class one afternoon each week. At the second school, the very good personal relationships that obtain reflect the personality, tact and hard work of this teacher – helped by the small size of the school. Where there has been an exchange of pupils this has been done with the overall benefit to her own pupils in mind. Any advice upon language problems that this teacher offers is done informally and reflects her assimilation into the school.

In general terms, the children in both cases have found wide acceptance within the parent school. However, this has not always been the case. At one of the schools a good many of the children accepted in the early days had emotional and behavioural problems in addition to considerable communication difficulties and low ability. This was rather a shock to both the staff and to parents with children already at the school. It led to a good deal of isolation at first – they were regarded by some main school pupils as rather freakish. This necessitated patient explanation on several occasions from the acting head. The situation was eased with the arrival of further children whose behaviour was less erratic.

Since this time good relations have developed, subject to the limitations imposed by the children having to be bussed to and from school. At one school it was pointed out that friendship patterns closely reflected where the children came from – "It takes a long time for anybody to be accepted, it's a very close-knit community." In the other location, both teachers in the school and the head were adamant that there had been no difficulties in the way of teasing or lack of acceptance. Individual personality was considered the significant factor in winning acceptance – more than, for example, level of intelligibility. The age of the children also helps – infants become accustomed to abnormalities very quickly. Other relevant factors included the high visibility of the language class children in the school, and the degree of involvement in the life of the school by the teacher in charge.

Parental involvement

Involvement with parents is seen by teachers in terms of general contact rather than engaging them in any specific, structured programme of language for their child. Structured involvement was not perceived by either of the language class teachers as necessary or appropriate. "These kids have had intensive teaching here" was one teacher's comment. She pointed to the presence of three adults in her class, which meant that when children were set work they were very closely supervised and could be quite tired by the end of the day. A head teacher, offering support for this view, noted, "I feel it is much more important for that mum to be a mum." There was a general belief that the parents of many of the children would not be very forthcoming if their active involvement was requested. Parents were concerned and interested of course, but the common perception was that they were handing their children over to the experts and did not seek or want a direct involvement for themselves: "A lot really don't want to know what you are doing although they are interested in the results."

Contact between teachers and parents takes place on school premises, either on the occasion of open days, which are held termly, or when a parent takes up the open invitation to visit whenever he or she feels the need. The open day is particularly important in that the small number of children in the classes allows the teacher to spend a reasonable amount of time (up to 30 minutes) with each parent, seeking to get across the importance of proper attitudes toward the use of language, appropriate correction and so forth. From talking to a small number (four) of parents there was every indication of satisfaction with the opportunity for contact afforded by such occasions. One criticism was voiced about the timetabling of parents' visits in one class; while this guaranteed each parent an exclusive session with the teacher it tended to preclude contact with other parents, something that many would have welcomed. The "free for all" arrangement that prevailed in open days in the other class led to a good deal of interaction between parents, and indeed resulted in some lasting friendships.

One particular factor which makes contact with the home more difficult to arrange, and effectively impedes contact between parents, is the distance most of these parents live from school. Teachers seek to get around this by relying on written communication. They emphasised that with regard to disseminating relevant information on a child, or consulting the parent over important issues – for example, transfer on at age seven – then parents were kept fully informed.

Speech therapists had a closer working involvement with families, but it was still much less than they would have liked. Constraints of time and distance (and lack of observation space in the schools) made it difficult to work in a close and structured way with parents. Their more modest aim is 'to visit each child's home at least twice a year and see some of them for weekly or small group intensive therapy during the school holidays'. There is also a home/school book for some children which contains specific weekly work for the parents to do with their children.

Parents spoke in very positive terms about the benefits their children had obtained from attending the language classes. One mother, whose son had been attending for 15 months, remarked upon how he had "picked up smashing" in this time. He was able to talk now, while his reading and writing had "come on a treat". "I don't think he would have come on the same if he hadn't gone there." Another mother, whose son had previously attended an ordinary infant school, noted, "[Before] he couldn't write, he couldn't even count... Since he has gone to this school he's marvellous... Everyone can understand him now. Now I can send him on a message – before I used to give him a note." In a third case parents told of how their son's speech had previously been unintelligible and his behaviour quite uncontrollable at times. Now he was capable of holding a conversation and his behaviour was more consistent. His mother was particularly pleased with his progress at reading while his father fully endorsed the placement: "If I knew any child in a similar situation I would recommend they go there."

Summary

This authority has comprehensive provision at primary level for pupils with speech and language disorders. There are five classes in all, supported by a language team operating from a hospital-based Child Development Centre. This account is focussed on the two classes located in ordinary schools, both for infant age children. These have developed effective ways of working with infants with speech and language disorders and have returned approximately half of their leavers to ordinary full-time education. They share a common approach and offer a broadly similar provision, though there are some significant differences.

The main questions for the future in a provision of this nature have perhaps to do with maintaining the momentum and level of service already achieved. There are a few further considerations, however:
1. Are the monitoring arrangements adequate when pupils are discharged from the language classes? Would a more long-term follow-up indicate, as it has done in some other instances, a need for a more prolonged involvement on the part of the language team?
2. Will it prove necessary to establish provision at secondary stage?
3. None of the classes for pupils over the age of seven is in an ordinary school. Will staff – and parents – be happy for this to continue?
4. Would children benefit if ways could be found of involving their families more actively and systematically in the effort to meet their special needs?
5. Are the classes sufficiently well established to cope with a change of head teacher, or being assigned a lower priority by one of the numerous support agencies?

Part Six
Links between Special Schools and Ordinary Schools

We present here two programmes which are rather different in kind from those discussed so far. Both originate in special schools, not ordinary schools. In each case the school in question has sought new roles for itself and developed innovative ways of working. The relevance to integration is that, in different ways, they enable pupils who might otherwise receive their entire schooling in special schools to remain in or return to ordinary schools. In one case this is achieved by working in a close structured way with class teachers; in the other by providing intensive remediation geared to returning pupils to ordinary school and then returning them, with support, over a phased period of time. Both provide working examples of how special schools can develop their traditional roles, make the accumulated experience and expertise of their staffs more widely available, and contribute in a comprehensive and relevant way to meeting special educational needs.

13
Supporting the ordinary school

This account describes a programme of liaison between a new school for pupils with learning difficulties and local primary schools whereby teachers from the former help to meet children's special educational needs in the latter by advising class teachers and supplying them with structured learning materials.

Background to the liaison with ordinary schools

Greenfields is a new (1977) purpose-built, all-age school for pupils with learning difficulties, located within an expanding township. It has places for 110 pupils, though numbers on roll rose only gradually from the initial intake of 28. Staffing expanded as pupil numbers increased – though it should be noted that from the outset no fewer than five teachers, in addition to the headmaster, and two ancillaries, were employed. This was a reflection of the favourable staffing ratio of 1:8 agreed before the school opened.

When the school opened the authority made it clear – without specifying how – that active links with local schools were to be developed, that 'the school should be organised to cater more flexibly for pupils with learning difficulties in the ordinary schools, rather than any rigid categories [of handicap]'. There was the intention that the school should develop as the area special school serving the needs of the locality. This view corresponded with that of the newly appointed head of Greenfields who was determined that his school should not operate along traditional special school lines. Mindful of the limitations inherent in the customary concepts of remediation, as manifest for example in those peripatetic remedial services whose involvement commences once a pattern of failure is well established with little attempt being made to influence the educational environment, he sought to develop a way of working that went beyond pupils' particular difficulties to the context in which they occurred.

He envisaged the role of the school not just as tackling the educational problems of individual pupils but also as getting to the roots of these problems. While sympathetic to the notion of providing intensive remedial support he felt that this did not go far enough. It was not simply a case of a pupil having a problem or disorder which was contained entirely within the individual. "The whole picture", including the school environment, had to be considered, so that it was not "just a matter of a kid being given a massive dose [of remediation] from us". As a result, it was decided to work with local schools so that the latter would be better able to meet the needs of their pupils with learning difficulties. This would also offer the opportunity to disseminate specialist expertise, influence the educational environment of these schools and contribute to the educational development of a much larger group of pupils than could be considered for special school placement.

Having determined that the involvement should be with schools in the local community, the crucial issue remained: how precisely to structure this more broadly conceived service. A significant step forward was to identify the characteristic features of the developing school. These included the following:

　i) It was a new school and there were no established ways of working.

　ii) There was an entirely new staff, appointed after the head took up office and sharing the broad consensus on major educational issues. It was the head's preference that they should be teachers from the ordinary primary school.

　iii) By definition, all members of staff had a commitment to teaching pupils with learning difficulties, thereby facilitating the development of strategy.

　iv) A favourable staffing ratio of 1 : 8 was agreed by the authority.

　v) Admissions to the school were regulated by the school psychological service to enable staff to engage in activities other than teaching (eg curriculum development).

　vi) Learning resources were being developed, in part because of perceived limitations in existing commercial learning materials, eg their inadequate pacing for slow learners and insufficiently specific objectives. It was felt that these same learning materials

could be utilised in dealing with pupils in ordinary schools who exhibited learning difficulties.
vii) The internal organisation of the school, with members of staff being allocated to specific areas (assessment/nursery, transition, junior, senior) permitted the flexible deployment of staff necessary if a member of the team was to be released for, say, an afternoon in order to work in another school.

Finally, there was the influence of the discussion going on at the time about the possible adoption of the Portage model of service delivery. Portage is an instructional package developed for parents of pre-school handicapped children, whereby specialised resources and specialist advice and guidance are made available to parents via a team of home teachers. The teachers visit the home and help parents to teach specific skills which are closely related to their child's particular needs. After extensive deliberation it was agreed to introduce a modified version of Portage in the immediate neighbourhood, with Greenfields serving as 'home base' for the multi-disciplinary home-teaching team. The distinctive characteristic of Portage, working *with* parents to enable them to teach their children, was also felt to be relevant to working with schools. Indeed it embodied certain advantages over other ways of developing teachers' skills. Its structure lent itself to effecting real change in lesson planning and classroom behaviour, and also served to ensure that developments, once initiated, would be maintained.

What the school liaison should comprise

Regular and extensive debate about the precise nature of the school liaison ensued, involving the head teacher and a member of the school psychological service who was heavily involved in establishing the Portage project. (Later, a member of Greenfields' staff who was chosen to initiate the liaison was also included in these meetings.) They agreed that liaison should consist of feeding in a teacher together with learning materials – developed with Greenfields' own pupils in mind in the firs instance – on a weekly basis. A procedural outline for establishing liaisor was arrived at. This could take two forms:
(a) formal contact with the head teacher of an ordinary school with ; view to providing specialised support for a pupil or pupils brough to the attention of the school psychological service by the schoc concerned;

(b) informal contact between the respective head teachers of the special and primary schools, leading to identification of suitable clients for liaison purposes.

Contact was to be with primary schools in the first instance, preferably infant departments, since this was the level most appropriate for the learning materials developed so far within Greenfields.

The next step, in either instance, would be a preliminary meeting and discussion between the visiting teacher and in (a) the teacher of the referred child, in (b) a class teacher indicated by the head. Weekly visits would then commence. At the close of each weekly session visiting teacher and class teacher would agree on a specific programme of work, backed with resources from the special school, to be followed by the pupil(s) identified. (A condition of participation in the scheme is that a head teacher must agree to the member of staff being freed from teaching duties for part of the time that the visiting teacher is present so that the two can exchange views and plans.) What had been achieved in the intervening week would be jointly appraised by both teachers on the occasion of the next visit. It was considered essential that involvement should be confined to a small number of schools initially, to increase the likelihood of success. Also, additional schools would be introduced gradually and then only to the extent that Greenfields could accommodate the increased demand on both its personnel and resources. Each visiting teacher would develop contact with a maximum of two schools.

The nature of the proposed liaison and the intention behind it were publicised in various ways. Several social evenings were held at Greenfields to which staff of schools within the immediate locale were invited. Typically, there would be a formal presentation (eg from the head teacher or a member of the school psychological service), with learning resources on display and members of Greenfields' staff on hand to answer teachers' queries. (Each member of staff had assumed responsibility for a particular area of the curriculum. Four main areas were covered: *reading* – the school developed its own reading scheme (SNIP) comprising 150 common words introduced in 30 books; *number* – comprising four main areas, (i) early recognition and counting up to 10, (ii) using logiblocks to develop the powers of reasoning, (iii) Cuisenaire rods for number bond practice, simple addition and subtraction, and (iv) Dienes apparatus introducing the concept of 'tens and units'; *fine motor* – covering manipulation, dressing, feeding, using cubes, painting and creative, pencil and crayon work; and *language* – broken into four areas, (i) listening, labelling, discrimination, (ii) listening, learning, understanding, (iii) expressive skills and (iv) creative writing.) Those teachers who expressed an interest were invited back subsequently for an extended and more focussed discussion. Also, regular meetings of head teachers of schools within the community served as an additional forum for outlining plans and canvassing opinion.

Initiating the liaison

The scheme formally got under way as a consequence of the referral of a particular child to the school psychological service. This was a seven-year-old whom we shall call Sheelagh, who was experiencing serious learning difficulties. The psychologist involved had participated in the discussions concerning the format that the proposed school liaison should take. Having seen the girl in question and discussed her circumstances with the class teacher and the head, he made various suggestions aimed at improving the girl's educational programming. Although these were readily taken up by the school, the hoped-for improvement failed to materialise. It was felt that Sheelagh might need to transfer to special school in the long term. For the present, the psychologist, mindful of the planned liaison, notified the head of Greenfields that here was a suitable client, attending a primary school that had a caring and professional attitude to children with learning difficulties and furthermore was likely to be receptive to receiving assistance from outside.

Subsequently, the head of Greenfields and the member of staff who would be involved visited Sheelagh's school. They were welcomed by the head teacher, who was broadly conversant with the planned liaison and accepting of it, though not unquestioningly. Sheelagh's circumstances were debated at length. She was considered to be experiencing marked learning problems and was falling progressively further behind her peers, both in her educational and (as emphasised by the school) social development. It was agreed that the time prior to her projected transfer would be used to introduce her to programmes of work and particular teaching techniques that she would encounter at Greenfields. The visiting teacher's hope was that the proposed transfer would be reconsidered if she was seen to be doing appropriate work within her own school.

We propose to examine Sheelagh's case in some depth. The visiting teacher conducted his own criterion-referenced assessment. Reading was not a particular concern as she had a good sight vocabulary and demonstrated signs of developing a phonic approach to reading.

Comprehension and retention were well below her reading capacity. Presented with simple pictures and asked to arrange them into a sequence she revealed no grasp of order or understanding of sequence. This inability to order events was readily apparent in her quite arbitrary approach to number. She was able to count and recognise numbers beyond the level at which she could perform number operations. She lacked understanding at the concrete level – which made it impossible for her to tackle new assignments without considerable assistance from the class teacher. Even then any newly acquired ability was rarely retained if there was any interruption in its practice or a slight modification to the way work was presented.

Preliminary meetings between Sheelagh's teacher and the visiting teacher revealed differing interpretations of the root of the girl's learning difficulties. The class teacher's view was that Sheelagh's pronounced learning difficulties were such as to require constant one-to-one teaching, which she was unable to provide in a class of over 25 pupils. However, the visiting teacher felt that perhaps much of the difficulty stemmed from inappropriate programming. Referring to the Fletcher Maths scheme which the class were working on, he considered it was beyond Sheelagh's capability and "totally unsuitable" in her case. A direct consequence was that she was forever demanding her teacher's attention. The visiting teacher noted that although "there is a lot that Sheelagh *can* do, the school seems to want her removed because of the distraction she presents". His immediate task was to provide work that Sheelagh could do by herself, thereby reducing the demands she made on her teacher.

The specific programme of work that the two teachers agreed on was organised in such a way that the class teacher would need to spend very little extra time with the girl. Attention was paid to three areas: number (using cuisenaire rods and worksheets); language development and sequencing activities (using taped material plus pictures and worksheets); and logic and relationships (using logi-blocks and worksheets). All the learning materials had been prepared by staff of the special school and were mostly a self-contained package. They were accompanied by clear guides to content and method, thereby enabling a classroom ancillary to provide any individual attention that proved necessary. They were to be used at those periods of the day when the class teacher perceived that Sheelagh's inability to cope with school work caused her to present a significant management problem.

To sum up, the purpose behind this particular intervention was that by, for example, giving Sheelagh work to do involving cuisenaire rods at a time when her classmates were working on Fletcher maths, "you are removing the time when [she] sits there mesmerised because she doesn't understand it". Related to this was the concern to avoid Sheelagh's making undue demands on the class teacher, "because that [excessive demand] would be further evidence that she should be somewhere else... It's creating change in the teacher's attitude to the fact that appropriate work is given to Sheelagh to strengthen [areas of weakness]... It's really convincing the school, the teachers involved, that it is a viable proposition to keep her on..."

Weekly visits made by the teacher from Greenfields, each one of at least two hours' duration, combined with the early success that Sheelagh was able to achieve working on these learning materials – "geared to give her total success" – led to a notable improvement in her social competence, attributable in part perhaps to an improvement in her self-esteem. In the few weeks remaining till the end of term it was unrealistic to expect any fundamental improvement in her level of attainment. However, one critical breakthrough was made: modification of the class teacher's attitude toward Sheelagh and her difficulties through a growing realisation that her special needs *could* be met within the ordinary school.

One consequence of this change in attitude was the decision to postpone transfer to special school for a further term. Accordingly, Sheelagh moved up to a first year junior class where she continued to receive weekly attention from the specialist teacher. At the close of the school year the school's own view was that Sheelagh no longer needed such extensive support from the visiting teacher. Furthermore, any lingering doubts as to whether she should be transferred were finally dispelled.

Sheelagh's case has been presented in some detail to give the reader an understanding of what is entailed in this model of service delivery. Her case is not atypical – as the following brief account of Zoe demonstrates.

The success achieved with Sheelagh led, perhaps not surprisingly, to requests for assistance with other pupils at the school – some nine in all. One of these was Zoe. The visiting teacher again conducted his own assessment. He noted in a diary specially maintained on these pupils that she was 'a quick, bright girl who had inexplicably made no progress in any aspect of her school work other than oral work' since coming to the school two years previously. His report continued: 'The label "specific learning difficulties" would suit her well – no reading, considerable fine motor difficulties, reasonable mental arithmetic but unable to cope with any written maths work.' (This diary is the source of the visiting teacher's accountability to the head of Greenfields, and is the basis for their weekly discussions on individual pupils.) She seemed a nervous child, and her inability to record results or even copy written work was leading to mounting frustration. He considered she had suffered through having been put with an inexperienced teacher who did not know how best to go about meeting her specific needs. An approach along the lines of 'give her the simplest reading book we've got – she may get something from it' was not considered particularly helpful.

The programme developed for Zoe consisted of the special school's own reading scheme (employing synchrofax and language master machine); number (using cuisenaire rods linked to systematic use of this apparatus which, in turn, was related to Zoe's ability to represent number and number combinations pictorially); and fine motor activities (intended to improve her written presentation). Zoe quickly progressed in all aspects of the programme. Most significantly, she experienced her first sustained success in over two years of schooling. The class teacher noted a marked change from what had previously been a restless and inattentive child, and commented (in a report prepared for the school psychological service):

'Her success in her work has completely changed her attitude to school. Because she now enjoys writing and number she will often choose this work in "choosing activity time". Number has progressed well... When playing number games she is quick and shows initiative... Her fine motor skills have improved but at times still tend to be shakey. She will draw and write very small... Her number progress has been far greater than reading.'

Zoe and two other children of the same age (top infants) were now viewed much more positively in the school. However, as the visiting teacher observed, "They've only developed into bright, alert children recently. Before, they were a pain in the neck, either babbling wildly or sitting lethargically." The critical factor was recognised to have been the provision of appropriate learning materials. As another class teacher observed, "They [children] are doing a lot more work than they would be doing if I was on my own... because he [visiting teacher] has broken it [curriculum] down to these simple steps."

The continued development of liaison with mainstream schools

At this point we step back from individual case histories to consider the further structural development of this programme of liaison. A short while after commencing working in Sheelagh's school, the head of Greenfields made an informal approach to a second school within the vicinity. This was an infant school which practised team teaching based upon vertical grouping. The two heads had already liaised over other matters, and an agreement in principle to establish working contact between the respective schools was readily forthcoming. It was left to the visiting teacher to determine the precise nature of this contact.

Differences from the earlier experience quickly became apparent. His early meetings were exclusively with the head teacher, whose perception of what the scheme sought to achieve was somewhat at odds with his own. Despite careful and repeated explanations the view persisted that he was an 'expert' coming into the school to induct certain fairly inexperienced members of staff. The head of Sheelagh's school had readily accepted that the primary emphasis was on assisting a particular pupil who was experiencing problems with learning, whereas this second head saw it primarily as an opportunity to enhance the skills of certain members of staff. Of course, it does both things, but the precise footing on which the working involvement is effected matters greatly. In the eyes of the visiting teacher the second head did not appreciate 'the point that liaison starts with a child, and that through the child the two teachers work together to achieve stated goals'.

There were difficulties, too, in identifying pupils to work with. The head selected a number of pupils from classes taken by particular teachers. Having carried out his customary assessment and after talking with members of staff, the visiting teacher concluded that there were probably other pupils in the school whose need of support was greater. There followed protracted negotiations before eventually a compromise was reached: "We have ended up with kids we want plus the members of staff she [head teacher] was most concerned about" (head teacher, Greenfields).

The six children selected were based with three teachers, two of whom were new to the school. It quickly became apparent that an across-the-curriculum attack on the problems these pupils faced was putting an intolerable burden upon staff who were already under pressure. Further discussion with the teachers themselves resulted in a modified intervention: for the time being the remediation would be restricted to introducing the SNIP reading scheme.

Written accounts from the teachers involved presented some months later testify to the improvement that was brought about:

'In September Henry could not recognise any words... [Now] Henry can make his own SNIP sentences using the vocabulary from the first three books. [He] has come out of his shell. He will communicate with me now...'

'In September Charlie had no reading vocabulary and his attitude to reading was "I can't do it and I don't want to do it"... Charlie had no difficulty in using the cassette recorder or language master... [He] is currently reading SNIP book 4, and learning the vocabulary for Book 5. [Each book in the series introduces five new words.] Since he started using the scheme his writing and letter formation have improved but if he isn't watched closely he is extremely careless... [He] can make sentences of his own using the vocabulary from the first four books...'

As had happened at Sheelagh's school, the success achieved by this intervention led to interest being shown by other members of staff. An additional two teachers began working co-operatively with the visiting teacher to organise reading programmes for four of their pupils. Further discussion focussed on the possibility of extending the intervention of other areas of the curriculum.

The programme of liaison with ordinary primary schools within the community has continued to build upon these beginnings. Another member of the special school staff became involved and took on responsibility for the liaison with Sheelagh's school. The original visiting teacher, freed from this particular responsibility, sought to develop contact with a third school, again where a particular child had been referred to the psychological service for possible special education. Subsequently, a fourth school became involved, and by 1980 no less than 80 pupils were being serviced by four members of Greenfields' staff. By no means did all of these have such pronounced learning difficulties as Sheelagh or Zoe. For a good many it was sufficient that they made use of the specialised learning materials, with any progress made being noted down, so that the visiting teacher could quickly appraise any improvements or continuing difficulties and plan accordingly, spending relatively little time in direct contact with these particular children. It should be noted that by this stage plans had been drawn up to extend this involvement to all 11 primary schools in the community, although it was recognised that any further expansion could not come about without the appointment of additional staff.

Impact of the liaison upon participating schools

Staff involved in the planning and inception of this scheme intend that this collaborative working shall achieve more than the educational improvement of those pupils involved – important though this is. It is envisaged also as a form of in-service training, one that has certain distinctive advantages.

They recognise that the effort to influence educational practice in schools must be made gradually and subtly. It is unrealistic to expect too much for the label of outside 'expert': "We have got to have a passport to get to the teacher – the passport is the [curriculum] materials" (head teacher, Greenfields). There are both short and longer term concerns. In the short term the emphasis is on the individual pupil, ensuring that he or she is provided with appropriate learning tasks and experiences, and helping the class teacher to use her time with the pupil to the best possible advantage. The learning materials that visiting teachers make available are considered the key to eventual success – both for the individual pupil and of the scheme as a whole. Visiting teachers have considerable direct involvement with pupils – initially in an effort to ensure educational progress, but partly for the purposes of monitoring work undertaken during the preceding week and for assessing the suitability of that work for the pupil in question. With time the extent of this direct involvement decreases – though it never disappears altogether – in line with the increasing proficiency displayed by the ordinary teacher and the greater number of children being served. As noted earlier, not all of the children seen have pronounced learning problems.

The long-term concern is to extend the skills and expertise of the ordinary teacher. Throughout, great importance is attached to contact with the class teacher. Discussion between visiting and class teachers serves various functions: it facilitates joint assessment of any progress to date; allows for any difficulties that may have arisen to be aired, and possible strategies for overcoming them planned; and leads to a mutually agreed programme of work for the ensuing week. It is also seen as laying the groundwork for teachers themselves to develop their own learning materials.

But to return to the specific question posed: What is the impact of this liaison on the schools involved? How far is the intention of influencing a pupil's 'total circumstances' realised? Those responsible for the programme's planning and execution were firmly of the opinion that they

were able to exert a substantial effect, even in the short term. This was evident in numerous ways:
  i) Within the first two schools there had been a noticeable shift in attitude among teachers who had participated. Seeing for themselves that pupils of whom they had limited expectations could show dramatic improvement, both in attainment and attitude, while retained within the school, was considered to have had 'a marked psychological impact' upon teachers.
  ii) Not only did teachers view pupils more positively but their ability to deal with them was enhanced. Through regular discussion with the visiting teacher, focussing upon both individual pupils and appropriate learning materials, and through more extensive and more highly specified interaction with teaching colleagues, teachers had begun to develop a working expertise that conventional in-service training courses would be unlikely to achieve.

Consider the following account provided by Sheelagh's junior teacher:

'Seeing the work which Sheelagh is capable of doing has helped me with other slow-learning children, and discussion of their needs has led to the preparation of special worksheets. The discussion which takes place about individual children's needs is always at a deeper and more effective level than general staffroom discussion – being able to observe and discuss others' methods in practice, with children one knows and can observe, reveals ideas for teaching strategies which one might not otherwise either have thought of, or have dared to try out.'

  iii) This child-centred approach to teaching has in certain instances led to a re-appraisal of teaching strategies both at a micro and macro level. Individual teachers have adapted structures and activities found in the specialised resource materials, and have begun producing their own materials intended for all levels of ability within their classes. For instance, they were better able to specify differing goals for different pupils working on the school's own reading schemes. Teaching groups, previously rigidly adhered to, have tended to become more flexible. Thus, the school which Sheelagh attended modified its organisational format, introducing a team-teaching approach for those children who were the subject of the liaison programme.
  iv) Enhanced communication was not confined to class and visiting teachers. Teachers who previously taught in isolation were increasingly finding a natural ease in discussing common problems and sharing resources with their colleagues.

v) In some schools, adjustments to timetabling have been made, whereby individual teachers are freed from teaching duties for some part of the week to engage in curriculum planning, developing learning materials or, should they so desire, providing individualised instruction for pupils experiencing difficulties with some aspect of their learning.
vi) Ancillary workers have been given a more constructive role supervising pupils working on self-contained programmes of work. This, in turn, has allowed class teachers to operate more flexibly.
vii) The expectation of Greenfields' staff that if they could demonstrate success there would be a "ripple effect" has been realised. Initial involvement in all cases was with a given pupil or group of pupils. In every instance, however, other pupils have become involved – either through being referred to the visiting teacher for his or her appraisal, or through being part of a group of pupils that the visiting teacher has gathered around the initial pupil. Furthermore, teachers have of their own accord extended the use of these learning materials to a wider circle of pupils.

Factors making for success

A number of factors can be identified as having a bearing on the success achieved:
i) The authority has supported the venture by maintaining a favourable staffing ratio and providing additional finance.
ii) The public relations exercise carried out in advance helped establish a receptive, relatively fertile climate within which to operate. Considerable interest in the liaison has been apparent from the outset.
iii) Staff from Greenfields won over the heads of the various schools within which they worked, and their commitment and enthusiasm were instrumental in obtaining a positive reception from members of staff.
iv) The form that this particular intervention takes is essentially collaborative – between visiting and class teacher – with an accountability component built in. It matters that visiting teachers have a specific rather than a general purpose – "We are not just offering spurious advice... [We] are trying to get in on what is

causing the problem – alerting the school to utilising resources better" (head teacher, Greenfields).

v) Visiting teachers are all practising teachers and are seen as such. Liaison is just one part of their weekly commitment – each spends a sizeable part of every day with his or her 'own' pupils. "It's better to err towards someone who looks and talks like a teacher.... they have got their feet on the ground about teaching, can empathise with the teacher about the problem... can see through the teacher's problems and, by using our materials, can suggest ways to the teacher of manipulating [the] classroom or organisation" (head teacher, Greenfields).

vi) Learning resources are made available to the ordinary school. No additional effort – at least initially – is expected or demanded of the class teacher. Indeed, quite the contrary. Children who have been presenting practical problems – either because they cannot do work set without a good deal of assistance or because they are disinterested or even mischievous – perhaps as a reaction against schoolwork that is beyond their capability – no longer represent a source of concern to the teachers because they are routed on to self-contained packages of work that *is* within their capability.

vii) In addition, pupils spend time each week with the visiting teacher who, as a visitor to the school, is readily distinguishable from their usual teachers: "They see me as the chap... that brings them the goodies... Life has [suddenly] taken on a more presentable complexion..." (visiting teacher).

The following remarks from one class teacher relate the success achieved to the curriculum materials. Outlining how to date she had simply worked to instructions, she concluded: "I haven't had to sit down and ask myself what would be suitable for these children." Her second comment underlines the fact that what were once problem pupils are now less so, and points to the reason for this transformation: "they are doing a lot more work than they would be doing if I was on my own... because he [visiting teacher] has broken it down to these simple steps". In a nutshell, the availability of relevant curriculum materials, materials that most class teachers would not have had the time – and possibly the expertise – to develop for themselves, is the critical ingredient. Pupils can work much more independently on these finely graded learning materials, thereby reducing the demand on the teacher for overt control.

School liaison and remedial provision

This programme of liaison with ordinary schools has certain similarities with the operations of remedial services. There is a common aim of helping pupils (mostly at primary level) to overcome their learning difficulties while remaining in the ordinary school. This programme is based on a special school, however, and is structured quite differently from conventional remedial services. So it is instructive to look at the differences and note some of the advantages enjoyed by Greenfields. (We are not suggesting that all remedial services are the same, but there are common patterns and certain drawbacks that are the subject of comment by many professionals working in the area.)

1. The liaison programme operates from an increasingly well-stocked resource base – the special school – where the presence of pupils with a wide variety of learning difficulties, together with a team of teachers engaged in both curriculum development and class teaching, ensures the production and organisation of learning materials *across the curriculum*. Remedial services by contrast tend to concentrate on one aspect of the curriculum, viz English, particularly the area of reading; also, they are not usually in a position to engage in curriculum development and tend to rely upon conventional learning resources.
2. The favourable staffing situation allows Greenfields teachers to confine themselves to a maximum of two schools each. This enables them to provide an in-depth service and to continue to provide it for as long as considered necessary. Visits are on average of at least two hours' duration and may be for a half-day. The caseloads of many peripatetic remedial teachers are far too great to permit such levels of support. Some have as many as a hundred pupils on their books and are confined to brief weekly visits at best. Many acknowledge these difficulties they work under and regret their inability to provide more intensive support and to maintain it over a longer period.
3. The priority is to identify children who are beginning to experience problems with their learning as early as possible in their school careers – "It's going down to the infant school and seeking to identify where you think they're failing." Also, the introduction of more appropriate learning experiences within the infant school should prevent some learning difficulties developing in future as they will be dealt with at source.

4. The programme emphasises close contact and active working collaboration with ordinary teachers. Indeed its focus is on the class teacher and developing his or her skills rather than working directly with pupils. This again is problematic for peripatetic remedial teachers. However much they wish their work to be closely integrated with the work in the classroom, their teaching role predominates and there is often too little time for communication and consultation with the class teacher.
5. The liaison programme makes a significant contribution to in-service training. Class teachers are involved systematically in producing and carrying out programmes of work and in teaching – under supervision – pupils with learning difficulties. In this way they acquire specific skills as well as a general competence in dealing with such pupils. In addition, class teachers are invited to Greenfields for particular purposes, eg to experiment with preparing their own learning materials.

Some practical difficulties encountered

One of the main difficulties encountered to date has been conveying what precisely is entailed in the service being offered. The head of Greenfields noted how the behaviour of colleague heads and teachers in schools would sometimes suggest that they had got the gist of the scheme – and yet subsequent events would prove this had not been so. In one case a head teacher persisted in viewing it almost exclusively as a means of training relatively inexperienced members of her staff. The visiting teacher found himself involved with relatively new teachers "who weren't very settled in the school". More important, these teachers "hadn't perceived the kids as very great problems"; they had not been at school long enough to be able to identify pupils who could benefit from this intervention. Even after the scheme had been operating at the school for several months doubts were voiced as to whether the head teacher "has a clear idea that this is an alternative model of delivering special education".

A second related difficulty concerns the need to counteract teachers' expectations about interventions which emanate from sources outside the school. Teachers' expectations will probably be based on their experience of remedial services or the contribution to educational programming that educational psychologists or advisers make. It is hardly surprising perhaps that many will have limited expectations and may even be downright sceptical about the contribution of *any* outside agency. One visiting teacher, speaking of his early experiences in schools, remarked on the virtual disbelief displayed by teachers – "they find it hard [to believe] that we are going to go there and work with [them]". A head teacher, who was influenced by previous experiences with remedial services, remained highly cautious about the intervention even though he was willing for his school to be involved: "A teacher comes out once a week for an hour a week. He listens to these children reading and there really is no feedback. If the proposed intervention is just carried on in the same way as this reading service it is not going to be very much use."

A third area where potential difficulties exist concerns how the visiting teacher chooses to carry out his or her role. Inevitably they will be regarded as the 'expert' when they visit a school for the first time. They are well versed in teaching pupils with learning difficulties; they are the ones who have developed the learning resources that the ordinary teacher is being invited to use; and they are coming into a classroom where there is a pupil whom a teacher has acknowledged that he or she cannot cope with. The safeguard against potential hostility or resistance – taking for granted that the visiting teacher will display tact, patience and understanding throughout this delicate task – is that he or she *works with* the problem pupils in the first instance, and that the *collaborative* nature of the venture is emphasised.

A fourth area of difficulty is that some class teachers' hopes are raised unrealistically. Let us refer back to Sheelagh's case again. Here, success was not immediate. Very early on the class teacher – and others in the school – were considered by the visiting teacher to be "expecting a lot: that if we put her through this material she'd get it instantly". Clearly this was unrealistic. There then followed a period when the hopes and expectations of school staff slumped. During this time, although Sheelagh was showing signs of improvement, her situation was viewed selectively by teachers. Instead of concentrating on the favourable signs they became preoccupied with her former difficulties. A comment in the diary maintained by the visiting teacher illustrates this: 'The teacher's records were completed and well documented although I did feel that there was an over-readiness to point out Sheelagh's difficulties, even if significant improvements quickly followed.'

Another potential source of difficulty was identified by one head teacher of an ordinary school. Calling for close collaboration between the two sets of staff at the outset of the scheme, he observed: "I would want the fullest communication, otherwise there's the danger that we could say, 'let that person [visiting teacher] deal with the child [presenting difficulties]'." In this regard, the firm line taken by the special school at the outset, insisting that the ordinary school retain the pupil even though he or she is making demands which they feel unable to meet, is crucial.

Another aspect of the liaison that in practice proved more difficult to achieve than was perhaps anticipated concerns how Greenfields' staff make their entry into a given school. In the first instance this was not a problem – there was a particular child (Sheelagh) who had been identified as having special educational needs, and an appropriate programme was put into operation. In the second case, however, the contact arose because the head teachers had had other dealings together. There were considerable problems in getting the liaison to work, partly because of an over-concern for involvement on the part of the head and a perceived reluctance to delegate. These difficulties tended to "cut off communication points" between the visiting teacher and the class teachers, and inhibit the liaison programme in ways that would perhaps not have arisen if the approach from Greenfields and the terms of entry to the school had been more specific.

What practical lessons have been learnt?

From their involvement with the initial three schools, staff of Greenfields learnt various lessons. First, they decided that henceforth they would not become involved with a school until that school either directly or indirectly (through the psychological service) had alerted them to a pupil in need: "It is much easier when a school has asked for help." How entry is gained to the individual teacher's classroom is quite critical – "You've got to get teacher's goodwill, got to have some clear inroads into the teacher's classroom." Should a teacher suspect that this has come about because he or she is judged to be lacking certain skills, then inevitably the visiting teacher must expect to face resistance and defensiveness. On the other hand, if the emphasis is on the individual pupils and the problems they raise, visiting teachers are far more likely to be welcomed and the individual teacher is less likely to feel that he or she is failing in some way. The involvement of the psychological service, in a quasi-managerial 'gatekeeper' role, has come to be regarded, in retrospect, as the means of "keying us into a legitimate service".

The second major lesson learnt is implicit in the first: the involvement is only likely to be successful if the teacher in the local school has 'blown the whistle' on a particular pupil and requested some assistance. For this to happen it is felt that the teacher needs to have had reasonable experience within the school rather than being a relative newcomer to its pupils and its ways of operating.

A third lesson is that ideally the team of visiting teachers would like to work with infants in the first instance, extending the service up into junior school where necessary as children move through the educational system. This concern came about initially because the learning materials developed within Greenfields were considered most appropriate for children of infant age. It is less critical now since the resources of the special school have continued to expand, thereby allowing the intervention to be extended to an increasingly wide age (and, implicitly, ability) range. However, it is still considered important to get to children early in their school careers before initial, possibly fairly minor, learning problems have the chance to develop into more substantial 'blocks' to learning.

Fourthly, the crucial importance of regularly maintained records has become ever more apparent. The extent to which class teachers set specific learning tasks varies enormously, reflecting the individual's use of task analysis and degree of familiarity with both the materials in use and the purpose behind the intervention. The value of precise records, constantly updated, is that this enables the visiting teacher to assimilate quickly the events of the preceding week. They may well form the basis for discussion between class and visiting teacher.

A fifth point is that originally it was envisaged that ordinary teachers would fairly quickly assume responsibility for the production of any supplementary learning resources. However, while this involvement is not discouraged, it is now considered better in the early stages that the bulk of the resources should continue to be prepared within the special school. There is a tension here which those involved admit they have yet to resolve satisfactorily. Given a close working relationship between visiting and ordinary teachers, one where the ordinary teacher is anxious to develop his or her own learning resources, then naturally staff of Greenfields are reluctant to be seen to discourage this enthusiasm. However, as more children are taken on from any particular school, there comes a point where the scheme can only be maintained by having more and more in the way of ready-made packages of learning materials in order to minimise the demands on the time of any of the teachers involved.

Finally, the increasing size of the team of visiting teachers – currently four strong – has placed greater emphasis on the need for uniformity of assessment within the expanding number (four at present) of schools being served. To this end the existence of criterion-referenced test materials, developed by the school psychological service, is clearly important.

Summary

This is an example of a special school which in addition to educating approximately 100 pupils at the school is seeking also to meet pupils' special educational needs *within* their own schools. This is achieved by working with teachers and providing them with finely structured learning materials devised by the special school. Teachers from the latter are assigned to this work for part of their timetable. Individual pupils are assessed by the visiting and class teachers, who agree jointly on specific work to be done by the pupils on a weekly basis. There is frequent and systematic follow-up, with the visiting teacher spending up to half a day a week in the school.

As well as providing special education for a considerable number of pupils while retaining them in their own schools, the programme has had important spin-offs for the class teachers, whose teaching skills and sensitivity to special needs have developed. Most of the children included in the programme have made good progress though it is recognised that the programme is not a panacea for all special educational needs. A striking endorsement of its success has been the request from the heads of schools in the township that Greenfields should assume responsibility for meeting the needs of all pupils experiencing learning difficulties at primary level.

The future development of the programme raises numerous questions, particularly in relation to expansion. They include the following:

1. The principal concern to date has been to establish links with primary schools. Contact with the comprehensive school has been confined to the joint production of learning materials and has not extended to significant working with secondary age pupils. To what extent will such working be possible within the existing framework? Can the present structure be adapted sufficiently, or will it prove necessary to develop quite new ways of working?
2. It is the intention to expand the service to cover all primary schools and the single comprehensive school in the community. The point has been reached, however, where there can be no further expan-

sion of the service without additional staff appointments. Financing and curriculum development are other areas where the pressures are beginning to show. Will it be possible to maintain the current momentum and level of service as the enterprise continues to expand? How will the authority respond? Would it, for instance, be helpful to formalise this model of service delivery and institute alternative structures that moved further away from traditional school structures?
3. To date the liaison has not extended beyond schools in the immediate vicinity of Greenfields. If it were judged beneficial to extend it and make the service available elsewhere, how would this be best done? How determine which elements of the programme could be exported, and how set about it?

14
Transferring pupils from special schooling

This special school for young with communication and other disorders seeks to deal with their specific problems and then introduce (or in some cases re-introduce) them gradually to ordinary schools.

Hollybush School

Hollybush is a diagnostic and assessment school serving a large rural authority. It occupies new purpose-built premises opened in 1976. It provides for 30 children with residential accommodation for up to 15. Children are aged between two and six on first admission and can stay for up to three years. The average age of children on admission is just over four years; priority is given to pre-school children, the emphasis being on early diagnosis and remediation. Sixty-six children have been admitted in the first four years of operation. Of these 35 have been moved on to other longer-term placements, approximately half to ordinary classes and half to special classes or special schools.

Given the explicitly diagnostic nature of the school and the fact that the children are so very young, admission criteria cannot be hard-and-fast. A general criterion is evidence of 'serious developmental abnormalities; especially a large discrepancy between mental ability and language development or between expressive and receptive language. Likewise, it is used as a placement for children whose problems do not fit clear patterns, "children who are conundrums, who cannot otherwise be placed". The majority of children do in fact have relatively serious communication disorders, not just for instance articulation difficulties. Some are behaviourally disturbed as well or display extreme hyperactivity. A document from the school notes the range and complexity of the problems it faces – 'severe mental handicap, brain damage, specific language disorder, maladjustment, bizarre behaviour and autistic features... frequently have multiple handicaps'.

Children referred – mainly by medical consultants, educational psychologists and speech therapists – are initially admitted for a three month period. All children put up for entry are appraised by a multi-disciplinary team comprising senior clinical medical officer, senior educational psychologist, head teacher and social worker. All the children will have been seen with their parents before they are formally considered for admission. Each child is discussed again at the end of the initial three month period and thereafter at six monthly intervals.

The school has seven teachers including the head and a full complement of ancillary and care staff. It has the services part-time of a speech therapist and good links with other agencies. The school offers a pleasant environment with excellent facilities. Apart from open-plan work areas, there are an adventure playground, sand pit, water therapy room, observation room (including a remote-controlled camera), lounge for the use of visiting parents and a flat which parents can use as necessary.

Great importance is attached to contact with parents and facilitating visits by them. The school is open from 7.00 am until 11.00 pm and parents, some of whom work on shift systems, are encouraged to come in at whatever hour is convenient to them. When very young children need to be admitted on a residential basis, parents can come and stay and work with their child until they feel that the child is settled and can be left.

Aims and objectives

The school has outlined a threefold function for itself:
'i) Assess the precise nature of the child's problem and advise on future needs.
'ii) Initiate a prescriptive programme and eventually integrate the child into the appropriate long-term school.
'iii) Provide a place for parents to come for help.'

The first step is to clarify the nature of the child's problems and gather detailed information on them. Speech therapy and school psychology reports, and possibly notes on paediatric management, will be available on entry. Staff build on these with detailed observations of their own, initially on the basis of a 'broad general involvement and experience for the child in an open situation with several adults present' and gradually in a more structured way. The school has produced general developmental guidelines to assist in assessment. They cover: acquired skills (feeding, toileting, social skills, etc); related behaviours and responses (to sound, to people, play, etc); reasoning; concentration span; and language (receptive and expressive). These 'guidelines for directed observation' cover the full range of normal developmental expectation and lead to baseline data for each child.

This criterion assessment leads to an initial programme after three months. This is developed on an individual basis for each child, building on the developmental expectations under each of the headings. It is planned to use the College of Speech Therapist's 'Material for language stimulation' for detailed curricular suggestions. Four headings would be used: general experience; auditory perception; other perceptual abilities; and conceptual development. A sufficiently detailed account of a child's present level of development along with a model of development will imply a programme of work – in listening, auditory discrimination, visual and tactile memory, body image and so on. As an appropriate prescriptive programme is developed and put into practice, feedback is obtained by continual observation of the child, daily discussion among the adults and monthly case conferences. It should be noted that special action has sometimes to be taken to deal with emotional or behavioural problems. Thus, behaviour modification programmes have been implemented for a number of children.

When the child is ready for transfer an integration programme is formulated and implemented over a period of time. This is discussed in detail in the following section.

The transfer procedure

The procedure of transferring a child commences with the identification of a suitable candidate. This is essentially the head teacher's judgement in consultation with members of his staff. Factors that indicate readiness for transfer to ordinary school include: improvement in the child's understanding of language; quite good expressive language; the beginnings of concept formation; an indication of the ability to 'make out' in the social sense; and a reasonable level of independence. Given the 'precision teaching' approach followed within the school, staff are able to specify quite precisely a child's level of development in different areas.

Over the past three years a specific procedure for effecting the transfer has been devised. This is followed in all instances though the particulars vary with the individual case. We illustrate the procedure by referring to the transfer of a child whom we shall call Freddy.

Freddy had in fact attended his local school for a time before being excluded, ostensibly on the grounds of his extremely poor behaviour. (Not all children that Hollybush accepts will have commenced statutory schooling but the intention is always to route them to the neighbourhood school. To this end Hollybush seeks to maintain at least minimal contact with every child's local school.) Freddy spent 12 months at Hollybush before it was decided that he might transfer back. The procedure was initiated by an invitation to his parents to discuss his progress and future placement. They agreed with school staff that an approach should be made to the local school and offered to visit the head teacher to discuss this with her. She proved to be extremely wary about having Freddy back, fearing a renewed outbreak of disruptive behaviour. The parents' visit was followed up by a visit from the head of Hollybush, requesting that Freddy be allowed to make a weekly visit to the school.

The head agreed to this, despite her misgivings, and phased visits over a period of time commenced. (These visits were later interrupted by illness.) On the initial visit Freddy was accompanied by his teacher and the deputy head from Hollybush. It was little more than a courtesy call. It was followed up with an invitation to the head and Freddy's prospective class teacher to visit Hollybush and stay to lunch. On the next occasion that Freddy and his teacher visited he spent one and a half hours in his prospective class. At this point the decision on whether to continue the process of transfer was left up to staff of the school. They agreed to this, and on the next occasion Freddy attended for half a day. He was left with his prospective teacher and classmates. By this stage, full transfer was imminent.

Another example of the transfer procedure is provided in the following (written) account from a Hollybush teacher describing the steps she followed with another child, John.

'I visited with John on approximately four occasions. The first two visits were only about one hour's duration and the class teacher was happy for me to stay in the classroom with John and help with story time, etc. During playtime John was put in the charge of a responsible child and observed from inside the school to make sure there were no problems. On the next visit I stayed in the staffroom while John joined his class and on the following occasion I took another class while their teacher was on a course. On this occasion John stayed for school dinner and readily copied what the other children did as regards collecting his food etc. He coped admirably. These visits occurred during the latter half of the summer term and it was felt that John was ready to start school with the new intake in the September. After John had been in school two weeks the school was contacted to check on his progress and later during the term I visited him to see how he was faring.'

A number of points about the procedure deserve underlining. First, Hollybush staff emphasise to their colleagues in the local school that when a child visits he or she is on trial; furthermore, that they (in the local school) have the ultimate say as to whether or not the child shall transfer completely. Their approach to a school is along the lines of, 'We would like you to help us with the further assessment of X. We think he/she might be ready to transfer. Could you give us your opinion in your situation?' In point of fact, any child who does transfer completely is retained on the special school roll for a further half-term and it is made clear that he or she can be accepted back at any point during this time. This seems to be an important reassurance for the ordinary school.

Secondly, great importance is attached to advance preparation. Hollybush staff are adamantly against "just imposing a child on a school and a teacher" and insist on the need to prepare the various parties involved: the child's prospective peers – otherwise he or she may be treated as a curiosity; the parents of the child being transferred; the parents of children already at the local school (one of the potential problems is that parents will worry about their own children imitating poor language patterns); and the teachers of the school.

Thirdly, the transfer is effected in an informal, highly personalised manner: "It can't be done through an official set of procedures ... you need a direct link with the people responsible for treating the child subsequently." Accordingly, one of the main advantages is that ordinary schools are "being invited to help a child ... they are not being imposed on by a system". Fourthly, some information about the child is made available to the ordinary school, though details are deliberately restricted in an effort to encourage schools to reach their own conclusions about the child rather than take on, perhaps unquestioningly, views and attitudes relating to a stage of development that has been superseded.

Once full transfer has been effected there is some limited follow-up. (This is much less than Hollybush staff would wish, and it is an area they would like to develop.) There may be a visit by the child's former teacher after a few weeks of full attendance, and the head of Hollybush telephones his colleague head after a month to check that all is well. Thereafter it is left to the head and/or class teacher in the ordinary school to maintain contact. What liaison there has been has generally taken the form of head teachers speaking to one another on the telephone.

The children seemed to be making good progress and were well placed in their schools. We visited four of the schools and found in each case that head and class teacher were quite happy to have the child. In one school the head noted that they were coping with several other children who had more serious problems than the girl we were enquiring about. A questionnaire sent to the receiving schools by Hollybush corroborated and extended this picture. Fourteen of the replies were from schools where the child was a regular member of an ordinary class. All answered 'Yes' to the question, Does the child 'fit' into your school? They pointed out how well the child had settled down and become an accepted member of the class and school. All were well accepted within their classes – 'at first he was something special but now he is completely accepted', 'the children accept that his work is different from theirs, but do not treat him as different when playing with him'. A few of the children were protected or treated as younger than their age – '[they] tend to do things for him and answer for him'. There were problems of course. Some of the children had unusual behaviour patterns, especially at the outset, and their learning difficulties did not disappear on transfer. In spite of the problems, however, all felt that their school was an appropriate placement for the child in question. They affirmed that, barring unforeseen developments, he or she would stay at the school for the normal term. (In one case an extra year was going to be required.)

Issues

This practice raises many issues bearing on the transfer of pupils from special schools to ordinary schools and on the implications of such transfer for the role of special schools. We discuss a number of these briefly here.

Information made available on a pupil
> 'One of the most difficult aspects of the integration process ... is how you give the [local] school an adequate background understanding of the special problems and needs of the child without making him/her sound so "different" that they feel it won't work.'

This observation from the deputy head of Hollybush pinpoints a dilemma that they face: Should special school staff seek to transmit their own detailed understanding of a child and his problems, or should they leave it to the local school to generate its own understanding of the child? The head of Hollybush seemed to favour the latter, speaking of giving "a censored report", and implicitly saying to teachers, 'we would prefer you to make up your own mind'. He claimed also that most colleague heads when offered the chance of looking at a child's file declined the offer as they preferred to carry out their own assessment and make up their own minds. One head indeed informed us that "I don't take any notice [of the file]" when a pupil is being considered for transfer. Others, however, were unhappy about the amount of information they had received. One head did not receive a file, censored or otherwise, until the child had been in his school for four months, and he believed that he and the class teacher would have benefited from earlier access to it and the information it contained. Two others regretted the absence or written documentation, one remarking on how 'some developmental progress report would have been appreciated'. While some teachers were glad of the information received, others were not particularly interested in finding out about a child's circumstances. A Hollybush teacher who had accompanied a child into his local school commented that 'the head teacher and staff did not inquire greatly as to John's strengths and weaknesses, nor did they seek any advice on handling him or dealing with his still present problems'. A colleague opined that the teachers "don't usually want to [discuss a child] ... they have not really shown much interest in what I have said and certainly haven't asked relevant questions". The absence of questions could of course in some cases reflect teachers' lack of familiarity with this type of child and ignorance of the appropriate questions to ask rather than a lack of interest per se.

The question of the transmission of information needs to be seen in various contexts. To the extent that the placement in ordinary schools is in part to further the assessment of a child and class teachers are being invited to participate in this, it might be felt that they had need of more background information, guidance to structure their observations and so on. On the other hand, much of the information is historical and may refer only to the child's earlier situation, prior to the stage when placement in an ordinary school could have been contemplated. This information could mislead teachers and distort their perception of the child, as well as worrying them unduly about their capacity to deal with the child.

Difficulties facing the ordinary teacher
Many of these children still have problems when they return to ordinary

schooling, and teachers faced various difficulties in consequence. These were pointed out by the teachers themselves and by Hollybush staff. Many teachers found it difficult to provide the necessary degree of individualised attention in the setting of a large class with many competing interests. How to sustain the child's concentration was mentioned in at least five cases. Some teachers expressed a desire for specialist guidance when dealing with children's speech disorders and felt they needed better access to speech therapists. Others sought advice on how to devise appropriate individual programmes of work.

Hollybush staff referred in particular to problems of continuity and differences in teaching approach. While the effort was made to smooth a child's transition by bridging the gap between work done at Hollybush and the programmes of work in the new school, problems did follow from the variety of reading and/or number schemes in use in the different schools. Sometimes there was quite a break in continuity. It was observed of one school that "their approach to the problem hasn't followed on from the sort of approach we've had here [at Hollybush]". Apart from the differences in programmes of work and teaching approaches, some teachers were felt to be lacking in flexibility in their handling of children, and this could be to the detriment of those newly arrived from Hollybush. Another problem was what was perceived as a restricted view of education in some schools, with an undue concentration on the 'basics'.

Over and above these considerations, it was suggested that there were some problems arising out of teachers' expectation of difficulties. This reflected their lack of knowledge about special education and the function of specialist centres such as Hollybush. The thinking seemed to be: 'The child has attended some form of specialist establishment, therefore he is in some way different from the normal and needs a specialised approach which I as an ordinary teacher cannot provide.' The head of Hollybush put it as follows: "Once they've been labelled ... teachers say, 'I don't know anything about this child ... I don't know how to treat him' ... they become special [simply] because you diagnosed a temporary condition." Various members of Hollybush staff engaged in the transfer procedure had noted the "trepidation" with which ordinary teachers first met a child being considered for transfer. They found there was a "great deal of uncertainty on the part of the receiving school" and teachers' anxiety was sometimes such that "they don't behave spontaneously". "Dealing with fears people have" was considered by one Hollybush teacher to be a major element in the process.

This anxiety reaches a peak perhaps in the case of children returning to the school they formerly attended. Take the case of one boy, Adrian, whose transfer was documented by the member of Hollybush staff involved:

'... Adrian had attended the nursery class attached to his local infant school. The school had suggested that Adrian needs a placement at special school due to his incomprehensible speech, a degree of lack of understanding and, in particular, his uncontrollable behaviour. The meeting [with regard to returning the boy] which occurred between the headmistress, the parents and other people involved was obviously fraught and the accounts of what was said varied greatly depending on whose version it was.'

The teacher's account continues:

'The class teacher was fairly cool and distant at first but after a number of weeks admitted that she had been waiting for Adrian to have a tantrum or behave very badly ... she [had been] surprised how good his behaviour was and how well he concentrated ...'

Adrian's class teacher had no prior knowledge about him other than what she had received from the headmistress. It was considered however, that the head – who had been "wary about having [Adrian] back" – had transmitted her fears to the class teacher who acknowledged that "I keep expecting him to do something and he hasn't". This was quite unjustified in the light of his current behaviour. In fact, it was only after he had been a model pupil over an extended period that the teacher came to accept him for what he was *now*. In another instance, a boy whose untoward behaviour had been a cause for concern in the local school, there was again an unwillingness among some teachers to accept that improvement had come about from a period of special schooling: while he seemed quiet, there was always the chance that "his true self might come out again" ...

What role for the specialist educator?

To the extent that teachers' problems were often simply anxieties and uncertainty arising out of lack of experience, the role of the specialist was one of providing basic reassurance. A comment on one teacher who worried about a child who constantly called for attention was: "All she wanted to know was was she doing it alright." Another teacher from Hollybush described how she would always stay on the premises when visiting with a child, "in case I was needed". The need had never arisen, but this teacher still maintained that her presence was justified – "I feel this added a degree of reassurance for the child and the school, alleviating any anxiety." In the extended example of the preceding section, reintroducing Adrian to his old school had to be handled extremely cautiously, with the Hollybush teacher seeking to anticipate every eventuality and to plan accordingly. In a further example, a teacher from Hollybush accompanied by two of her children joined a mixed group of first and second year infants on one day each week. The class was split into three groups and responsibility for them exercised jointly by the class teacher and the member of staff from Hollybush.

The issue of continuity in educational programming arises when a child transfers from a prescriptive programme at Hollybush to a less formally structured approach in an ordinary school. It is clear that focussed discussion and joint planning on the particular programme to be pursued with any transferring child are most important. When a likely candidate for transfer has been identified it becomes the responsibility of the member of staff involved from Hollybush to find out what teaching approach the local school employs and the particular schemes of work that are utilised. For the remaining time that the child is retained within Hollybush, staff seek to adapt the teaching programme as much as possible so that a reasonable level of continuity is assured. There was the intention at one stage to feed both child and individual programme of work into the local school, but this was not implemented.

It could be argued that specialist teachers need to adopt a more explicitly advisory role than obtains at the moment. Some Hollybush teachers believed that a higher level of intervention on their part might be in the children's interests. At the moment, they had little influence on a child's education once the transfer stage was complete, even though some explicit guidance on teaching approach, classroom management and so on would have been useful. This view was reinforced by the questionnaire responses from the schools. Asked if 'a continuing aftercare or advisory service' would have been useful, a majority said that it would, both for the sake of advice to the school and support for the home.

Conflicting views on readiness for transfer
We noted earlier how the decision to commence transferring a child rests almost exclusively in the hands of Hollybush staff. While staff in the receiving schools are consulted and can indeed refuse to accept a placement, the selection of children for transfer is effectively a matter for Hollybush. This is unavoidable since they know the children best and, given the limited involvement of outside agencies such as the school

psychological service, are the only ones with a detailed professional knowledge of them.

The difficulty in this situation lies in the extent to which special school staff are able to appraise a given child's development – and so readiness for transfer – in relation to mainstream norms. Staff were not unaware of this, one for example noting what a salutary experience taking over a class in an ordinary school had been – "showed me how far behind ours are". Teachers in ordinary schools also referred to this. Commenting on the fact that Hollybush staff only saw a child in the typical special school situation, one head observed that behaviour could be controlled more easily there, that it was perhaps a less stress-inducing environment for the pupils, and that in any case abnormal behaviour could be tolerated more easily there than in a class of 30 other pupils with a single teacher in charge. Other teachers pointed out that children who had made considerable progress by Hollybush standards could still be far behind the level of normal children.

There is no easy answer to the dilemma posed here. The initiative for transfer must remain with the special school since the pupils are in its charge and since many ordinary schools need considerable encouragement to accept a child who has spent time in a special school. This means that in some cases – by no means all in this situation, it should be noted – the special school is cast in the role of persuading schools to accept children who are well suited to transfer. On the other hand, the everyday dealings of special school staff are with children with special needs and it is difficult for some to keep mainstream norms in mind, particularly if they have not taught in ordinary schools. The experience of implementing the transfer procedure has effected an improvement in this regard. It is to be hoped that the development of more extended links with schools and closer working contact with classes in them will lead to greater unanimity on children's readiness for transfer.

Bibliography

ANDERSON, E. M. (1973). *The Disabled Schoolchild*. London: Methuen.
COPE, C. and ANDERSON, E.(1977). *Special Units in Ordinary Schools*. Windsor: NFER (for University of London Institute of Education).
DALE, D.M.C. (1972). *Deaf Children at Home and at School*. London: University of London Press.
DALE, D.M.C. (In Press). *Test of Speech Production: consonant articulation*.
DEPARTMENT OF EDUCATION AND SCIENCE *Ministry of Education* (1962). Circular 10/62. London: HMSO.
DEPARTMENT OF EDUCATION AND SCIENCE (1972). *The Education of the Visually Handicapped* (Vernon Report). London: HMSO.
DEPARTMENT OF EDUCATION AND SCIENCE (1973). *Staffing of Special Schools and Classes* (Circular 4/73). London: HMSO.
DEPARTMENT OF EDUCATION AND SCIENCE (1967). *Units for Partially Hearing Children* (Education Survey No. 1). London: HMSO.
FOLLWELL, S. N. (1943). An enquiry into the use of speech in after-school life. Unpublished thesis, University of Manchester.
GULLIFORD, R. (1971). *Special Educational Needs*. London: Routledge & Kegan Paul.
HAMP, N. W. (1976). *Picture Aided Reading Test*. Northampton: Arkle Goodman.
HEGARTY, S. and POCKLINGTON, K. (1981). *Educating pupils with Special Needs in the Ordinary School*. Windsor: NFER-Nelson.
JACKSON, S. (1971). *Get Reading Right*. London: Robert Gibson.
JAMIESON, M., PARLETT, M. and POCKLINGTON, K. (1977). *Towards Integration: a Study of Blind and Partially Sighted Children in Ordinary Schools*.
LANCASTER, A. (1981). ICAA list of educational provision for the speech and language disordered child. London: Invalid Children's Aid Association.

LINDON, R. K. (1963). 'The Pultibec system for the medical assessment of physically handicapped children', *Developmental Medicine and Child Neurology*, **5,** 125-45.

LING, D. and LING, A.H.)1978). *Aural Habilitation: The Foundations of Verbal Learning in Hearing Impaired Children.* Washington DC: Alexander Graham Bell.

NATIONAL COLLEGE OF TEACHERS OF THE DEAF (1976). List of Schools, Units, etc. for Hearing Impaired Children.

NEALE, M.D. (1958). *Neale Analysis of Reading Ability.* London: MacMillan.

SHERIDAN, M. (1975). *Stycar Chart of Developmental Sequences.* Windsor: NFER.

SINCLAIR TAYLOR, A. (1981). A follow-up study of children with specific speech and language disorders. Unpublished BPhil (Ed) dissertation, University of Birmingham.

TANSLEY A. E. (1967). *Reading and Remedial Reading.* London: Routledge & Kegan Paul.

TIZARD, J. (1964). *Community Services for the Mentally Handicapped.* Oxford: University Press.